PRAISE FOR *SHREWD SAMARITAN*

"I cannot think of a better book on how to take small steps toward making our world a little less poor and unequal. I cannot think of many more careful, caring, and entertaining messengers than Bruce Wydick. He is the expert you want to invite into your living room to walk you through the business of saving the world, one sponsorship, classroom, or micro-loan at a time. I would recommend this beautifully written book to any friend, parent, or student of mine."

—CHRIS BLATTMAN, RAMALEE E. PEARSON PROFESSOR OF
GLOBAL CONFLICT STUDIES, UNIVERSITY OF CHICAGO

"Bruce Wydick is one of the world's leading thinkers about the intersection of Christian faith and cutting-edge development economics research."

—JAMES CHOI, PROFESSOR OF FINANCE, YALE UNIVERSITY

"*Shrewd Samaritan* illustrates why Bruce Wydick is one of the leading—and most useful—Christian economists in the world. Synthesizing the latest research, biblical wisdom, and a highly-accessible style, Bruce cuts a clear path through mountains of complexity. Highly recommended for anybody seeking to emulate the head, heart, and hands of Jesus Christ."

—BRIAN FIKKERT, PRESIDENT OF THE CHALMERS CENTER AT
COVENANT COLLEGE AND COAUTHOR OF *WHEN HELPING HURTS*

"High callings merit hard data. Bruce Wydick lays out a vision for service to others that is rigorously inquisitive and empirical—not instead of but because it is deeply grounded in faith."

—PAUL NIEHAUS, ASSOCIATE PROFESSOR OF ECONOMICS AT U.C.
SAN DIEGO AND COFOUNDER AND CHAIRMAN OF GIVEDIRECTLY

"This is a must-buy book for anyone who wants to contribute their treasure, time, and talent to help others. Bruce Wydick combines a deep, faith-based concern for the poor with exceptional skill as an economic researcher to offer insightful, actionable guidance to us all."

—CHRIS BARRETT, ASHLEY PROFESSOR OF APPLIED
ECONOMICS AND MANAGEMENT, CORNELL UNIVERSITY

"Simply superb! Wydick masterfully combines the best current scholarly research with moving stories and lucid writing. This book offers an amazing combination of sophisticated academic scholarship by a distinguished economist with clear, moving writing and concrete, practical application. Wydick even manages to make technical issues intelligible to the average reader. This is superb popularization at its best. A must-read."

—Ron Sider, Professor Emeritus of Theology at Eastern University, Past President of Evangelicals for Social Action, and Author of *Rich Christians in an Age of Hunger*

"If you think global poverty is an intractable problem with no solutions, think again. Bruce Wydick provides clear evidence of how any person can not just give but give effectively. Amid so much poverty in the world and so many organizations clamoring for support, he shows clearly which programs can turn you from a Well-Intentioned Samaritan into an effective, Truly Good Samaritan. Wydick's tireless work in helping organizations evaluate the effectiveness of their programs inspires, and his research on child sponsorship programs has influenced my own family's giving."

—David Evans, Senior Fellow at the Center for Global Development, Washington D.C., Formerly Lead Economist at the World Bank, and Coauthor of the 2018 *World Development Report*

"Born from years of rigorous research and a genuine passion for poverty alleviation, this book is a valuable resource and a compelling read for anyone with a heart to help the poor. Intelligently informed and crafted with warmth, compassion, and humor, let *Shrewd Samaritan* be your guide to investing in effective interventions on behalf of the most vulnerable among us."

—Santiago "Jimmy" Mellado, President and CEO of Compassion International

"This book makes it very evident that Bruce Wydick has a singularly important capacity to unite the best insights of rigorous economic research with a deep commitment to serving the human dignity of all, to the great benefit of both our economics and our moral lives."

—Paolo Carroza, Director of the Kellogg Institute for International Studies, University of Notre Dame

"Bruce Wydick shows us how combining a deep ethical commitment to the promotion of human welfare with rigorous research skills in economics and impact-evaluation methods can help us make wise choices as to how to get effectively involved with this important and potentially highly rewarding project. His own experiences in the field and his professional way of thinking about it will be a source of inspiration for many who want to understand how we got to where we are with global poverty, inequality, and injustice—and how to use time and money to potentially do something meaningful about it."

—ALAIN DE JANVRY, PROFESSOR OF AGRICULTURAL AND
RESOURCE ECONOMICS AT THE GOLDMAN SCHOOL OF PUBLIC
POLICY, UNIVERSITY OF CALIFORNIA AT BERKELEY

"A compelling and insightful book on the underlying causes of poverty and prosperity, the poverty traps that perpetuate inequality, and solutions that recognize and affirm human dignity. Wydick carefully examines the evidence for different approaches and provides both a cogent and compassionate reflection on what works best."

—DIANNE CALVI, CEO OF VILLAGE ENTERPRISE

"Bruce has a unique perspective on the world. His training as an economist and his commitment to following Christ leads him to ask questions that economists, aid workers, and people of faith rarely do, and to use tools and perspectives that ensure the answers he finds are trustworthy and reliable. This book will make you better at loving your neighbor in need whether next door, downtown, or in another country."

—TIM OGDEN, MANAGING DIRECTOR OF THE FINANCIAL
ACCESS INITIATIVE, NEW YORK UNIVERSITY

"Bruce Wydick's *Shrewd Samaritan* combines the gifts of a storyteller with the mind of an economist, showing us how the responsibility to love our neighbors can be motivated by both compassion and prudence. I have not read a better book about how Christians should think about global poverty."

—MATTHEW ROSE, DIRECTOR OF THE BERKELEY INSTITUTE

"People of faith are commanded to care for the 'least of these,' but in a world with scarce resources and a desire to truly help, what works and what doesn't? Bruce Wydick has written a book filling a much-needed space at the intersection of compassion, faith, and credible public policy. It covers such topics as the causes and consequences of poverty, as well as contemporary efforts to escape these traps through microfinance, cash transfer, and more. This is a source of wisdom for those of us desiring to care for our neighbor by addressing their impoverishment."

—Scott Cunningham, Associate Professor
of Economics, Baylor University

"*Shrewd Samaritan* is an invaluable gift to anyone who wants to love their global neighbors well. As an economist with lots of practical experience, Wydick guides us through international complexities and the latest research, while also remaining attentive to the importance of faith and dignity. We learn insightful ways to think, act, and give—all in service of love."

—Kent Annan, Director of Humanitarian and
Disaster Leadership at Wheaton College, Author
of *You Welcomed Me* and *Slow Kingdom Coming*

"This book is for all who have a heart for the needs of others and want to make a real difference. Wydick draws on his extensive experience as a professor of economics 'on the ground' in many poor countries, and his study of child sponsorship, microfinance, and education, to give us new perspective. With wit and winsomeness, he explains how a better understanding of ourselves, those in need, and the economics of poverty will help turn our faithful compassion into effective help."

—Judith Dean, Professor of International
Economics, Brandeis University

"In *Shrewd Samaritan*, Bruce Wydick has written a book that is both enjoyable to read (which is not the case for most writing by economists) and an excellent source of information on what individuals, organizations, and even governments can do to reduce poverty. I highly recommend it to anyone who wants to help the poor, both in their own communities and in poor communities throughout the world."

—Paul Glewwe, Professor of Applied
Economics, University of Minnesota

"I am sometimes overwhelmed with the good and righteous causes that deserve my attention and support. Thank you, Bruce, for showing me and many others how we can pay attention and be productive, but in ways that use our unique gifts, experiences, wiring, and personality. Otherwise, we would be well-intentioned but useless, living in fear that like Oscar Schindler, "I could have done more," or succumbing to the temptation to make the list of burdens longer each day."

—FRED SMITH, FOUNDER, THE GATHERING

"If you've ever wondered about effective ways to help poor people, you must read this book. As a shrewd Samaritan himself, Bruce Wydick combines a compassionate heart with the mind of a rigorous economist. From his heart, he encourages us to love our global neighbors as much as God does. As an economist, he assembles and explains tons of research on types of assistance that really work to help the poor. Read the book, take it to heart, act on it, and you, too, will show love to your neighbors that makes a real difference in their lives (and yours)."

—ROLAND HOKSBERGEN, PROFESSOR EMERITUS
    OF ECONOMICS, CALVIN COLLEGE

"People who care about poverty can feel they face a difficult choice: blindly 'just give' or 'give up.' *Shrewd Samaritan* offers all of us a framework and a motivation to give in a way that truly helps people by addressing the root causes of poverty, injustice, and violence.

—CHAD HAYWARD, EXECUTIVE DIRECTOR, ACCORD NETWORK

"Readers who pick up the book for tips on becoming part of the solution to global poverty will find that the book actually does much more than that: it will elevate their perspective on both the problem and potential solutions, inspire them to act as Shrewd Samaritans, and provide insight into the practice of development economics along the way. The book, itself an expression of his Christian discipleship, succeeds because Bruce is uniquely qualified personally and professionally to provide these perspectives, insights and inspiration."

—TRAVIS LYBBERT, PROFESSOR OF AGRICULTURAL AND RESOURCE
    ECONOMICS, UNIVERSITY OF CALIFORNIA AT DAVIS.

"Dr. Wydick, a long-time scholar and writer about and on behalf of poor people around the world, expertly weaves together a readable, concise summary of the latest work on global poverty. In *Shrewd Samaritan*, he brings together his unique perspective as an economist, a person of faith, and an NGO organizer to combine academics, personal inspiration, and an illuminating look into the practical side of helping others. In this very readable book, he shows we can use our heads to direct our hearts and do the most good possible."

—JEFF MOSENKIS, POLICY AND COMMUNICATIONS
    MANAGER, INNOVATIONS FOR POVERTY ACTION

"Bruce Wydick synthesizes decades of research in economic development to light the way towards effective anti-poverty interventions, challenging us to love our neighbors with all our minds as well as with all of our hearts. It helps that he himself is at the front lines of NGO development work and is the distinguished author of influential studies on program outcomes. This encouraging book deserves to be read by anyone interested in the great task of promoting global human flourishing."

—STEPHEN L. S. SMITH, PROFESSOR OF ECONOMICS AT HOPE
    COLLEGE AND FACULTY PARTNER WITH THE VALUES & CAPITALISM
    PROGRAM AT THE AMERICAN ENTERPRISE INSTITUTE

"*Shrewd Samaritan* deftly weaves together vivid descriptions of life in the poorest regions of the world, stories of the motivations and efforts of benefactors looking to help, and economic studies that cast light on how to realize our shared aspirations for a better world. The result is a readable and compelling argument for greater involvement in helping the global poor."

—MICHAEL KEVANE, ASSOCIATE PROFESSOR OF
    ECONOMICS, SANTA CLARA UNIVERSITY

SHREWD
SAMARITAN

SHREWD SAMARITAN

Faith, Economics, and the Road to
Loving Our Global Neighbor

Bruce Wydick

W PUBLISHING GROUP

AN IMPRINT OF THOMAS NELSON

Published in Nashville, Tennessee, by W Publishing, an imprint of Thomas Nelson.

Thomas Nelson titles may be purchased in bulk for educational, business, fund-raising, or sales promotional use. For information, please e-mail SpecialMarkets@ThomasNelson.com.

Unless otherwise noted, Scripture quotations are taken from the Holy Bible, New International Version®, NIV®. Copyright © 1973, 1978, 1984, 2011 by Biblica, Inc.® Used by permission of Zondervan. All rights reserved worldwide. www.Zondervan.com. The "NIV" and "New International Version" are trademarks registered in the United States Patent and Trademark Office by Biblica, Inc.®

Scripture passages marked CEB are from the Common English Bible. Copyright © 2011 Common English Bible.

Any Internet addresses, phone numbers, or company or product information printed in this book are offered as a resource and are not intended in any way to be or to imply an endorsement by Thomas Nelson, nor does Thomas Nelson vouch for the existence, content, or services of these sites, phone numbers, companies, or products beyond the life of this book.

ISBN 978-0-7852-2153-1 (eBook)

Library of Congress Control Number: 2019901084

ISBN 978-0-7852-2152-4

Printed in the United States of America

19 20 21 22 23   LSC   10 9 8 7 6 5 4 3 2 1

CONTENTS

INTRODUCTION

While I was at a concert in college, I responded to a flyer requesting volunteers to sponsor a child overseas. For years I read the letters from this little girl in El Salvador. Ruth seemed happy to be sponsored, and I was happy to sponsor her. But there was always a nagging voice in the back of my mind that asked, "Does this stuff really work?"

One day, after reflecting again on this question, I decided to find out.

One of the advantages of working as a development economist is that sometimes my job makes me feel a little bit like Indiana Jones—we're both professors, and we both get to travel around the world digging into mysteries. But instead of looking for ancient treasure or cursed statues, I have the privilege of getting into the trenches and exploring whether international poverty programs actually work.

Starting in 2008, and with the support of some immensely helpful graduate students and coauthors, I began a long-term research project to find out if international child-sponsorship programs actually help sponsored kids. We looked for partner organizations to carry out the research, and it turned out Compassion International was the only organization willing to submit to an independent review of their program. That was handy, because Compassion was the program I worked through to sponsor Ruth in El Salvador.

Children sponsored by Compassion receive tuition benefits for schooling, nutritious meals during the week, health insurance, and about eight to ten hours a week in an afterschool program that emphasizes both tutoring and Christian spiritual formation. In discussing the impact evaluation with the organization's monitoring and evaluation director, we stumbled upon a vein of gold for a researcher: as Compassion underwent a major worldwide expansion during the 1980s, they used an arbitrary age-eligibility rule to limit sponsorship eligibility to children twelve and younger. This arbitrary rule allowed us to compare the life outcomes of children in the same family, now all grown up, who were on opposite sides of the age rule when the program rolled into their village. It gave us a valid control group.

We began the study in Uganda, looking at the adult life outcomes in education and employment from those who had been sponsored years before as children. When we ran the econometrics on the first set of data, my jaw nearly dropped off the bottom of my face. The impacts were enormous on educational completion—far larger than in a conditional cash transfer program in Mexico that had been celebrated for years.

I flew back to the Compassion headquarters in Colorado and met then-president Wess Stafford, who greeted me with a warm handshake.

"Your program works," I said.

"I know," he smiled.

Six countries later, the study was published in a top economics journal edited at the University of Chicago, and it received attention from the BBC, *USA Today*, and news media across the country. Now people know—the program works.

It's been my experience that most people have a genuine desire to help the poor—including the poor in their communities and even the poor on the other side of the world. But it's also been my experience that most people do not feel confident about the best ways to help.

That's why I've written *Shrewd Samaritan*.

This book is for people who are wondering how they can have a meaningful and effective relationship with the global poor, the poor overseas, and the poor in our midst. It is about loving and caring for the poor in a way that moves past our best wishes and intentions, toward an engagement that bears fruit among the poor and in our lives as well. It is poverty work that is both heart and mind: kind like the Good Samaritan, but also shrewd in its discernment.

An important theme of this book is that effective poverty work is not simply a matter of becoming a more committed practitioner, missionary, donor, or activist. There are many who couldn't be more committed to the welfare of the poor, but who are ineffective in their work or in their giving. Effective work with the poor begins with understanding the nature and causes of poverty, understanding why different types of interventions have been ineffective and effective, discerning one's role in the larger picture, and then carefully and patiently using this knowledge to partner with others in facilitating change.

If you are an ordinary person living in a rich country with a regular job, a spouse, or kids (or none of the above) but who wants to understand how your life can positively impact someone living in poverty across the globe, this book is written for you. It will break down myths you may have been told about the causes of poverty, and myths about effective responses to it. It will help you to understand why rich countries are rich, the causes of inequality in rich countries like yours, and how to discern what your role in addressing poverty can be. It will give you some practical ways to make a big difference—even if you keep your day job.

If you are a development practitioner working for an NGO, this book is written for you. I will give you new frameworks for thinking about your work, about why some approaches you may take bear fruit and some never seem to. As a development economist, I also want to connect you in an engaging way with what the latest research finds to be effective and ineffective ways to address poverty. Some of this is research I have had the privilege of carrying out myself with colleagues, research that, along with looking at the long-term effects of Compassion International's child sponsorship program, has examined the impact of the TOMS Shoes giving program in El Salvador, how the cleft palate surgeries of Operation Smile affect the lives of teenagers in India, the effects of Nestlé baby formula on infant mortality across the globe, how we can increase the impact of microcredit loans, and the role that hope and aspirations play in development more generally. But more than this, I would like to introduce you more broadly to the fascinating insights of a new generation of poverty researchers that is beginning to make significant inroads into understanding what kinds of approaches are genuinely effective at fighting poverty. One of my goals for this book is simply to help support you as a practitioner in your good work.

If you are a Christian or a person of faith, this book is for you. So am I. But you may be surprised at how much of what I present in this book appears to be "secular" in nature. This is true because good science helps us do good poverty work, like a surgeon who is trying to understand the best ways to repair the human body. And I believe when it comes to fostering human dignity and human flourishing, there is no fully "secular" work. As the Jesuits have convinced me where I teach at the University of San Francisco, in the end fostering human dignity is all God's work—whether we are conscious of that or not. And when we care for the poor, the scriptures say that we care for Christ himself, and this is a rather awesome thought.

If you are a nonreligious person, this book is written for you. Maybe most especially for you. You may be mildly annoyed that I build a foundation on parables told by a first-century carpenter/rabbi. You may be puzzled by my references to spiritual things generally and the Judeo-Christian framework specifically as both a motivation and framework for poverty interventions. But given the mounting new empirical evidence not only from the positive impact on economic development from historical missionary work but also from recent randomized controlled trials and quasi-experimental studies of faith-based interventions, this book may challenge your preconceptions that religion is irrelevant to economic development. Moreover, seeing economic development presented within a framework of human dignity and human flourishing may not only help you to communicate more effectively with your faith-based practitioner colleagues but also challenge the traditional secular approach that measures human development mainly in terms of statistics related to health, education, and income.

If you are committed to the global poor, I encourage you to read on whatever may be your background, to renew your commitment to the good fight of caring about the poor, and to consider the possibility of working more closely with those of us who have found that our Creator's grace for our own brokenness has motivated our own foray into the brokenness of global poverty.

What is most important? That the needs of the needy are met or that we become the kind of people who meet the needs of the needy? There is no better place to be than playing one of the instruments in the symphony of redeeming a broken world. But part of this redemption is what God wants to do not only *through* us but also *in* each of us as he uses us in this work. Christianity differs from many other religions in that it is not primarily about our personal purity or spiritual state of mind. It is not primarily about rules or mountaintop spirituality.

Instead, our human purpose is to more and more deeply understand God's grace for us, and to direct that grace toward our neighbor: the neighbor in our family, the neighbor in our community, and even our global neighbor— especially the neediest among these. The purpose of this book is to help us all move farther and better down that road. And if this is the road on which you would like to travel, this book is written for you.

Part 1

THE ROAD
TO LOVING
OUR GLOBAL
NEIGHBOR

Chapter 1

WHAT IS A SHREWD SAMARITAN?

I want to begin this book by telling you a story about my dentist. Dr. David Yee's modest office is located on the street level below his house, near the corner of 31st Avenue and Clement Street, a few miles from my office at the University of San Francisco. Most people avoid going to the dentist. I never avoid going to the dentist because I get to talk to Dr. Yee. Even during the odd unfortunate visit when oral excavation is required, his calming face, hovering above my open mouth like a smiling moon, has for twenty years offered reassurance during tense episodes of drilling and repair.

After learning during my early visits that I was a development economist, Dr. Yee would ask me if I had been to any "crazy new countries" lately. After sharing a few stories about recent travels and research projects, I would ask him if he had done much traveling. "No, afraid I'm a bit of a homebody," he would say. "The city is plenty for me."

One visit I asked him with my mouth propped open, "Eh-uh auh uh oo-in wah uh oa enk-le in-ins?" which translated from dental-cleaning language is, "Ever thought about doing one of those dental missions?" Being a veteran interpreter of the dialect, he replied that yes, he had considered it but hadn't quite got his courage up. Had I been to any crazy new countries lately? And so the conversation looped for some years.

But as he was ushering me into the dental chair before a routine cleaning in 2011, he turned to me and announced proudly, "I went on a dental mission last month."

"That's great," I responded enthusiastically. "Where?"

"Jamaica."

"How'd it go?"

The dental mission to Jamaica had gone well, just not as anticipated. Dr. Yee had envisioned preparing a vast equipment bag with cleaning instruments: tooth pickers, plaque scrapers, spit suckers, mouthwash, polishers, and bags of brushes and floss.

"You won't be needing all that," the missionary dentist had explained. "All we do here are extractions."

He arrived in Kingston and walked down the steps of the plane onto the tarmac where the missionary dentist greeted him. "Did you bring your forceps?" Yes, they were somewhere in the suitcase. "Excellent. How many extractions can you do in a day?"

Dr. Yee had never pondered this statistic, much less tested its frontiers on his upper-middle-class San Francisco patients. "Maybe eight?" He paused nervously. "How many do I need to do?"

"Yesterday I did 140."

Dr. Yee considered this spectacular figure. It sounded inhumane. He imagined something like an assembly line for tooth extraction with dentists wrenching rotten molars out of cringing patients with blood-splattered dental bibs, tossing them out of the chair, and then yelling to the front of the line: "Next!"

But what he learned in Jamaica was quite the opposite. In a place where infections are rampant and immune systems are weak, infected teeth can be deadly. Without an extraction, the infected tooth creates a puss-filled abscess that can spread to the alveolar bone containing the tooth sockets. If the abscess infects the alveolar bone, one of two things can happen, depending on whether the infection resides in an upper or lower tooth: If an upper tooth is infected, bacteria can spread from the alveolar bone through the maxillary sinus, resulting in a sepsis of the brain. After losses in cognition, speech, and personality, the condition can lead to death within weeks. If the infection is in a lower tooth, it can spread to the jaw where an infection in a rear molar may swell to the point that it blocks airflow through the trachea, resulting in suffocation.

The missionary dentist explained that time spent on cosmetic issues, or even maintaining the lofty standards of Western medical care, carries a high opportunity cost in the world of rural missionary dentistry. In these makeshift rural dental clinics that are set up in churches and community centers, missionary dentists are met with long lines of patients suffering from abscessed teeth waiting for treatment, that is to say, extraction. Dentists have a limited amount of time at each site, and a dentist who pulls 10 teeth a day instead of 110 could leave 100 lives at risk.

As I listened to Dr. Yee share his experiences, I was impressed with the missionary dentist because he sounded like an economist. He understood the cost of allowing our fuzzy feelings to dictate our actions to people in need rather than a concern for their health and well-being.

Even so, this was a radical and rather distressing change in approach for Dr. Yee. He relayed a story from the dental mission in which an abscessed tooth of one young man was so decayed that it crumbled under the grasp of his forceps, leaving pieces of rotten tooth root embedded deep in his gum. It would require hours of additional work to finish the job to his high standard of care. Meanwhile, other patients with abscessed teeth waited anxiously in line, hoping to receive attention before the 5:00 p.m. deadline, by which the dentists had to leave to avoid driving on a perilous road in total darkness. As time moved past the deadline, a young man who looked like he was hiding a golf ball in his cheek approached Dr. Yee in tremendous pain. Would he please extract his tooth? The other dentists shook their heads no. Would he be back tomorrow? Unfortunately, not—they had to treat patients in another village. But they would return next year. He hugged the boy, and they waved goodbye.

In missionary dentistry, slow work carries a high price.

A year later, as I settled down in that same comfortable dental chair, I asked Dr. Yee if he had been to "any more crazy countries" lately. He said that yes, he had: he had done a trip to Haiti, one of the most satisfying experiences of his career, both in terms of his impact on patients and the partnership he felt with the other dentists. A few years later the list had grown to El Salvador and the Dominican Republic, along with a return trip to El Salvador.

As I rose up out of the dental chair, Dr. Yee ushered me toward a corkboard in his office, where he exhibited pictures of some of his patients grouped by the different countries in which he had worked. The dental mission trips had clearly transformed Dr. Yee. From them he had developed a deep compassion for those without access to health care. Moreover, joining his new *heart* for others was a new *head* for others. He had begun to learn the art of triage, operating with the skill of a M.A.S.H. medic, prioritizing patients who were likely to receive the greatest benefit from an extraction and treating them as efficiently as possible. He also began to emphasize prevention during his visits. With paltry access to dental services, training children to brush and floss their teeth would shorten the waiting lines for extractions on the next visit. It wasn't all about being Dr. Dental Superman, rescuing people from infected teeth. When possible, it was about loving others by preventing pain and suffering in the first place.

My dentist, Dr. David Yee, was becoming a Shrewd Samaritan.

Given a Chance

Mike Burnett is the father of my friend Tom Burnett, and he lives in Memphis, Tennessee, after serving as a Northwest Airlines pilot for thirty-five years. Mike, who might be confused with Hudson River pilot Sully Sullenberger if you saw him in his cockpit, became involved with international child sponsorship while he was serving as a pilot in the navy. It began while he was based in the Philippines at the US Navy base at Cubi Point.

"The economy of the whole area revolved around the US Navy base," Mike recalls. "The streets were lined with clubs, bars, prostitutes, everything catering to the navy serviceman. It was a really seedy area."

On days off, the pilots and sailors would hang out in bars near the Olongapo River, where children would float by in rafts, begging for money. Navy men would throw coins to them, and when the coins missed the rafts, the boys would dive for them into the river, a stinking cesspool of human refuse that acted as a sewer for the local area. None of the children were in school, but in Mike's estimation, pretty much all of them should have been. He felt compelled to do something. Moved by an emotional Sally Struthers appeal on TV, he began sponsoring a five-year-old Filipino boy named Dino through Christian Children's Fund, now called ChildFund.

Being an airline pilot offered some significant advantages for visiting sponsored children. During time away from flying Northwest 727s around the country, Mike could fly free to virtually anywhere in the world. And so, over the years, he took advantage of his free flights to return to the Philippines for regular visits with Dino.

Mike remembers the emotions he experienced during his first visit to Dino's house—a corrugated iron shack located next to a dump, where the family and their neighbors would scavenge for castaway items. The families living near the dump lived off wealthier people's garbage. The floor of the house was part of the unimproved dirt street. The family had one large, disheveled bed in which all members slept together. It was a level of poverty Mike had never witnessed before, even during his days at Cubi Point.

Mike looked at Dino on that first visit after his sponsorship began. Unlike the other children, his hair was combed. His face was clean. He was not headed to the dump to scavenge. He wore a new school uniform and a small school backpack that carried a few books, pencils, a pad of paper, and lunch. He looked like a normal schoolkid.

Mike realized that Dino had been given a chance. He wanted other children to have the same chance, so he decided to sponsor more of them. During a flight layover in South Korea, he learned that many of the barmaids who worked outside his hotel were homeless and had no place to sleep. These women would offer to sleep with male hotel guests simply in exchange for a bed and shelter for the night. He was determined that at least one girl would not have to trade her body for shelter. Not long after, a photo of a young girl, Kim Yoon Nee from South Korea, appeared on the Burnette family refrigerator.

Over the next thirty-five years, Mike and his wife, Lynn, sponsored a long series of children—boys and girls from Guatemala, Ecuador, Brazil, Mexico, Kenya, and other countries. He would use vacation time to fly and visit their sponsored children, listening to their situations, talking with their parents, hearing their dreams, encouraging them to stay in school and to never give up no matter what life threw at them.

Mike was unable to visit just one of his sponsored children: Lanina, in Brazil. Mike discovered that Lanina lived so far up the Amazon River in the heart of the rain forest that, even with his flying benefits, it would have cost $10,000 for a short visit, equal to the cost of supporting three more children. He knew he would likely never be able to meet Lanina in person, yet he and Lynn prayed regularly for each sponsored child, for health and protection, for their families, and against the many forces that daily oppose their growth and flourishing.

Despite the changes he sees in his sponsored children, Mike has always felt the biggest impact from being an international child sponsor has been on him.

Mike sends each of the children money for Christmas and their birthdays. He recalls a story from a visit to one of his sponsored children in Guatemala, Juan José, where he asked Juan José what kind of present he bought for himself with his birthday money. The ten-year-old boy replied that he did not use the money to buy a present. He used the money to buy medicine for his sister, who was sick. Contrary to the reverse, Mike had the feeling that God had brought along Juan José to help a middle-aged airline pilot grow into the person he was intended to be.

Not every story was a happy one. Mike recalls Geri-Anne, a Native American girl he sponsored on an Indian reservation in Montana. Her mother had suffered psychological damage from birth that made her unfit for parenting. Geri-Anne's father, never married to her mother, was a fur trapper and was absent from Geri-Anne's life. In contrast to many of the other faraway places he visited, where poverty was at least somewhat mitigated by a measure of happiness and contentment in family life and community, Mike found the reservation to be a cheerless place. Alcoholism and depression were rampant among the tribe; houses and public buildings were unkempt and run down. Domestic abuse of women and children was the norm. Then, one day, a letter appeared from ChildFund stating that Mike would no longer be able to sponsor Geri-Anne. The organization had run an audit on its project at the reservation. The books failed to balance, and they had found money leaking from the pipeline that connects sponsor to child. The project would be closed.

Still, the majority of Mike's efforts were not only well-intentioned, but also effective.

About six years after he had graduated and left the sponsorship program, Dino from the Philippines sent Mike a letter. Dino was visiting the United States with a traveling dance troupe. The troupe would be performing in Los Angeles and New York. Would Mike come to see him? Since New York was closer to Memphis, he chose the New York venue, which was packed with Filipino Americans enjoying a night of home culture. Mike recalls being the only white guy in attendance, but this made it easier for Dino to pick him out of the crowd. They embraced and cried, and Mike told Dino how proud he was of him and what he was making of his life.

I asked Mike what he thought made the biggest impact from the relationships he had with his internationally sponsored children. He told me it depended on the child, and he was keen on understanding the unique needs of each one.

Dino, always at risk for dropping out of school and succumbing to the toxic allures of scavenging, constantly needed to be reminded about the importance of staying in school. Mike wrote Dino every few months, and in every letter Mike reiterated that he expected Dino to finish high school. It was something he needed to repeat to Dino again and again, simply because Dino needed to hear it again and again. He was under constant pressure to leave school to contribute to the immediate needs of his family.

During his visits and in his letters, Mike has tried to kindle aspirations for his sponsored children and encourage them to reach high to realize these aspirations. This soft but inspiring voice is one that impoverished children do not hear with the frequency of affluent children. It is a hallmark of some child sponsorship programs that may be responsible for much of their success, something we will discuss later in this book.

Mike has found that some children already have ideas and dreams for their lives. They just need a helping hand with school fees and other needs for which they lack resources and the knowledge that somebody out there loves them and is rooting for them to succeed. With many of the girls that he sponsored, however, showing that he and his wife cared about their lives helped them amplify their aspirations. For other children, he would simply emphasize how much he and his family cherished them and wanted their good.

One gets the feeling that Mike is someone who studies children and their needs with a focus that others bring to a study of literature or economics or computer chip engineering. He is an example of someone who has taken stock of his abilities and opportunities, and how they have matched with his desire to help others. One by one, Mike has changed the lives of children around the world, and all the best research indicates that the children whose lives he has changed are likely to go on to change their own children's lives.

Mike Burnett is a Shrewd Samaritan.

A Tale of Two Tales

What is a Shrewd Samaritan? The answer to this question is the purpose of this book. To begin we will consider one of the world's most renowned short stories, a parable told by Jesus of Nazareth in the first century to address the age-old question of one human being's responsibility toward another. And it goes like this:

On one occasion an expert in the law stood up to test Jesus. "Teacher," he asked, "what must I do to inherit eternal life?"

"What is written in the Law?" he replied. "How do you read it?"

He answered, "'Love the Lord your God with all your heart and with all your soul and with all your strength and with all your mind'; and, 'Love your neighbor as yourself.'"

"You have answered correctly," Jesus replied. "Do this and you will live."

But he wanted to justify himself, so he asked Jesus, "And who is my neighbor?"

In reply Jesus said: "A man was going down from Jerusalem to Jericho, when he was attacked by robbers. They stripped him of his clothes, beat him and went away, leaving him half dead. A priest happened to be going down the same road, and when he saw the man, he passed by on the other side. So too, a Levite, when he came to the place and saw him, passed by on the other side. But a Samaritan, as he traveled, came where the man was; and when he saw him, he took pity on him. He went to him and bandaged his wounds, pouring on oil and wine. Then he put the man on his own donkey, brought him to an inn and took care of him. The next day he took out two denarii and gave them to the innkeeper. 'Look after him,' he said, 'and when I return, I will reimburse you for any extra expense you may have.'

"Which of these three do you think was a neighbor to the man who fell into the hands of robbers?"

The expert in the law replied, "The one who had mercy on him."

Jesus told him, "Go and do likewise." (Luke 10:25–37)

Christians and non-Christians alike, everybody loves the parable of the Good Samaritan. It has robbers, violence, a good guy, a couple of religious bad guys (always good for juicing up a story), and its message about loving our neighbor is beloved by people of all colors and creeds. A good deal of our ethics in Western society originates from this parable.

But a few chapters later, Jesus tells us another parable—one that is less known, not as popular, and a little *strange*:

There was a rich man whose manager was accused of wasting his possessions. So he called him in and asked him, "What is this I hear about you? Give an account of your management, because you cannot be manager any longer."

The manager said to himself, "What shall I do now? My master is taking away my job. I'm not strong enough to dig, and I'm ashamed to beg—I know what I'll do so that, when I lose my job here, people will welcome me into their houses."

So he called in each one of his master's debtors. He asked the first, "How much do you owe my master?"

"Nine hundred gallons of olive oil," he replied.

The manager told him, "Take your bill, sit down quickly, and make it four hundred and fifty."

Then he asked the second, "And how much do you owe?"

"A thousand bushels of wheat," he replied.

He told him, "Take your bill and make it eight hundred."

The master commended the dishonest manager because he had acted shrewdly. For the people of this world are more shrewd in dealing with their own kind than are the people of the light. I tell you, use worldly wealth to gain friends for yourselves, so that when it is gone, you will be welcomed into eternal dwellings. (Luke 16:1–9)

If there were a popularity contest among all the characters in the parables of Jesus, the Good Samaritan would probably win. Nobody is against the Good Samaritan because being against the Good Samaritan is like being against Mother Teresa or Oskar Schindler or the firefighters who ran into the World Trade Center.

In that same popularity contest, the Shrewd Manager would probably finish last. The Shrewd Manager, accused of fraud, seems to do little to redeem his character by giving discounts to his master's debtors. He appears to be a lazy, deceitful, double-crossing little quisling, not to mention a very bad employee. Yet in this alluringly freakish parable, as with the Good Samaritan, Jesus holds up the Shrewd Manager as some kind of example worth emulating. Why?

This book is about learning to live the message of the Good Samaritan in the context of the globalized world of the twenty-first century. That said, the Shrewd Manager also has something to contribute to this discussion. The problem with the parable of the Good Samaritan isn't understanding the parable. It's living out the lofty standards it defines for loving our neighbor as ourselves. In contrast, the problem with the parable of the Shrewd Manager is understanding what in the world this parable means and what we're supposed to learn from it. Specifically, what does the Shrewd Manager understand that Jesus thinks his disciples don't understand?

The Shrewd Manager, despite possible character flaws, understands at least one important thing: money is temporal, but people and relationships are not. Since you are the intermediating steward of any money or resource in your possession, you are to shrewdly mobilize your worldly wealth to serve people.[1]

The original Greek word for "worldly wealth" used in the text is *mamónas*, translated in the old King James as "mammon." That term refers not just to money but to possessions and one's resources generally. The word *manager* in ancient Greek is *oikonómon*, from where we get the word *economics*. So in the Greek, the manager is literally the rich patron's hired "Econo-Man."

Jesus uses the example of the Shrewd Manager to gently chastise the disciples as "people of the light" who are naïve in their understanding of how to use worldly wealth. In a rhetorical device that Jesus often uses in other parables, he makes a point by illustrating a humorous extreme. It's as if Jesus is saying: "Check out how the shrewd *oikonómon* (Econo-Man) manipulates the *mamónas* (mammon) in his ledger to build an employment network for himself after he is sacked—so shrewdly that his boss even *praises* him for it. And if he can pull that off, how much more wisely, beautifully, and creatively could you use your *mamónas* to love and care for the people around *you*?"

The early disciples were not alone in their naïveté about worldly resources like time, talent, and money. Unfortunately, we still don't get it today. There are too many kind, twenty-first-century people with good intentions, whose impact on those living in poverty is hampered by their inability to 1) understand the root of problems; 2) harness the resources available to them to solve the (right) problems; 3) understand the cause-and-effect relationships related to poverty; and 4) distinguish between "warm glow" feelings of being a benefactor and creating tangible impacts for an intended beneficiary.

If we want to genuinely help people living in poverty rather than just feel good about believing we have helped, we are not merely to be *Good* Samaritans. We must be *Shrewd* Samaritans. We must be people with not only big hearts but also minds like the Econo-Man, who are not naïve in their use of worldly resources. This means learning to love our global neighbor wisely, one might say even "shrewdly," by harnessing the resources at our disposal—our time, talents, opportunities, and money—on behalf of those who are victims of injustice, disease, violence, and poverty. The Samaritan and the Econo-Man together represent a kind of yin-yang tension between heart and mind that is crucial for those who seek to be agents of positive change.

In later chapters I will share insights from the latest research in development and behavioral economics, as well as from experience in the field, about ways we can address global poverty that are transformative not only for the poor but also for ourselves. But first I want to share another story, a story about a woman named Melinda.

Immeasurable Impact

Melinda French was born in 1964 to Joseph and Elaine French of Dallas, her father an aerospace engineer and her mother dedicated to the well-being of Melinda, her older sister, and her two younger brothers. The French family was very middle-class; Melinda earned money as a teenager mowing lawns, cleaning people's ovens, and doing other odd jobs for neighbors. One day in 1980, her father brought home an early Apple III, which she would use to do the accounting for the French family business, a small network of rental properties. And so, along with other academic subjects, Melinda became fascinated by computers.

Melinda completed bachelor's degrees in economics and computer science, then an MBA from Duke University, then accepted a job at Microsoft, where she became a software developer for well-known products such as Publisher and Encarta. She was captivated not just by programming but also by the larger picture of business—the myriad aspects of creating successful consumer products. Then, in 1987 while working at Microsoft, she met someone who would dramatically change the course of her life, the CEO and president of the company, and her future husband, Bill Gates.

Bill and Melinda Gates married in 1994, and early on they decided that the purpose of their marriage would not lie in amassing greater and greater amounts of wealth for themselves and their heirs. They began to devote the same intensity and focus that they had given to software development to investigate solutions to the most critical problems faced by the global poor. They read. They networked in development and philanthropy communities. They attended and spoke at global poverty and development conferences. In 1994 they launched the William H. Gates Foundation, which in 2000 merged with the Gates Learning Foundation to become the Bill & Melinda Gates Foundation.

In an interview with *Christianity Today*, Melinda Gates discussed the origin of the Gates Foundation: it was during a walk on the beach during a trip to Zanzibar, an island off the eastern coast of Africa. In Zanzibar they had been studying a marriage questionnaire through the Catholic Church to help them discover the purpose of their relationship. It was then they felt a strong prompting to give away their wealth for the benefit of the global poor.

She shared the role that her Catholic faith has played in both creating and shaping the objectives of the foundation: "I went to a Catholic school from kindergarten to 12th grade and attended church with my family every Sunday during that time. The New Testament speaks to me. Jesus was always reaching out to the poor, always trying to get people to not see the poor as different from other people. That was ingrained early for me. . . . For me, faith is about faith in action. With this deep-seated belief, Bill and I believe that all lives have equal value. We try to live that out in what we do as a foundation."[2]

After creating the foundation, Melinda's life took on a new mission: how to give away a $40 billion fortune to reduce global poverty and suffering in the most effective way.

The decision of Bill and Melinda Gates to transform their immense wealth into a giant global poverty fund attracted followers, and at least one very important one. In 2006, instead of creating his own foundation for distributing his immense wealth to charitable causes, Warren Buffett pledged to donate 80 percent of his wealth to the Gates Foundation. This decision was strongly influenced by Melinda's presence in the organization. In an interview with *Fortune* magazine, Buffet commented about his close friends Bill and Melinda, "He's smart as hell, obviously. . . . But in terms of seeing the whole picture, she's smarter."[3]

The combined assets of the Gates-Buffet fortunes are breathtaking by any standard. The total assets of the foundation today are approximately $51 billion, and by 2018, the Bill & Melinda Gates Foundation had already given away $46 billion, greater than the entire amount given away by the Rockefeller Foundation through the course of its one-hundred-plus year history.[4] It is on pace to disperse perhaps $100 billion to causes related to eradicating global poverty.

But perhaps even more impressive than the mass of wealth held by the foundation is its commitment to *effective* intervention. Even relative to other well-known foundations, it has painstakingly selected interventions for its funding that offer the greatest impact per dollar on human lives. For this reason, a considerable share of the foundation's resources is allocated toward global health in areas such as the prevention of preventable illnesses including tuberculosis, pneumonia, HIV, and especially a class of neglected tropical diseases such as river blindness, guinea worm disease, helminth infection, sleeping sickness, and *lymphatic filariasis* that are widespread in places like South Asia and sub-Saharan Africa.

The record of the Gates Foundation in helping eradicate *lymphatic filariasis* alone is impressive. There are 120 million people in the world who suffer from that illness, which is commonly known as elephantiasis. This is a horrible mosquito-borne disease that causes grotesquely swollen body parts that turn victims into social and economic outcasts, the equivalent of twenty-first-century lepers.

Bringing together a global alliance of pharmaceutical companies, governments, the World Bank, and global health organizations, the foundation has funded five billion treatments for the disease. Because the disease is often located in remote regions, the foundation has supported intensive software development of precision mapping to locate small concentrations of sufferers from *lymphatic filariasis* with an eye toward complete eradication by the year 2020.

The Bill & Melinda Gates Foundation has also strongly supported research that tries to uncover the most effective ways to help the poor. The foundation has provided significant funding to institutes such as the Jameel Poverty Action Lab at MIT, Innovations for Poverty Action, and the Center for Effective Global Action at UC Berkeley, at which I am a research affiliate. Funding for these organizations underwrites efforts to study the relative effectiveness of different poverty interventions through the use of randomized controlled trials.

The Bill & Melinda Gates Foundation has already had an immeasurable impact in reducing suffering around the world from poverty and disease through funding poverty interventions that we know to work. Through its funding for research, it will arguably have an even greater impact through more effective interventions in the future. Melinda Gates has played an integral role in shaping the conscience of an immense global transfer of wealth that will continue to affect hundreds of millions of lives around the world.

By every standard, Melinda Gates is a Shrewd Samaritan.

Heart and Head

Shrewd Samaritans love not only with their hearts but also with their heads. They are continually learning how to love their neighbor *better*. They are motivated by feelings of compassion and a yearning for justice, but their *actions* are guided by careful reflection that is centered on the well-being of the other. They make mistakes in their attempts to care for people, whether in their own communities or far beyond, but they humbly and continually learn from these mistakes.

Shrewd Samaritans understand that their individual calling is not to solve all of the world's problems. Instead, they understand specific roles in which they are called to thoughtful, committed engagement in domains within their unique sphere of influence. These roles and domains may be intensely personal, including caring for a needy family member, children, parent, or the disabled woman down the street.

Others may feel called outside their family or close community: a marketing manager senses a calling to serve low-income micro-entrepreneurs in sub-Saharan Africa. In responding to this, she extends herself into a domain that is congruent with her expertise and sphere of influence but outside her normal community setting. Another person may choose to financially support organizations that improve education, health, or income-generating capacity for a group of people in a similarly faraway corner of the globe. Others may become engaged with domestic poverty, addressing the needs of kids in inner-city schools, the jobless, and the homeless. Still others may be called to love their neighbor through work at the systemic domain, perhaps at a government policy level.

All of these are valid and important, and those who have found a calling to love their family members and neighbors within their natural community setting are to be lauded.

Yet in this book, my purpose is to develop a road to more effectively loving our global neighbor. Because in an age of globalization, what we can call our neighborhood or our potential sphere of influence has expanded—dramatically. Through the globalization of media, we are aware of needs to which our ancestors could never be cognizant, much less respond to in any meaningful way. Through the combination of the Internet and mobile technology, we are able to transfer resources around the globe while relaxing on a park bench. Increasingly, it will become our global neighbor who takes us out of our comfort zone and challenges us with the needs of a broken world.

Chapter 2

THE SIX *i*'s

On the day before his death, Martin Luther King Jr. delivered his famous "I've Been to the Mountaintop" speech. In it, he described the road to Jericho taken by the Good Samaritan:

> The Jericho road is a dangerous road. I remember when Mrs. King and I were first in Jerusalem. We rented a car and drove from Jerusalem down to Jericho. And as soon as we got on that road, I said to my wife, "I can see why Jesus used this as the setting for his parable." It's a winding, meandering road. It's really conducive for ambushing. You start out in Jerusalem, which is about 1,200 miles—or rather 1,200 feet—above sea level. And by the time you get down to Jericho, fifteen or twenty minutes later, you're about 2,200 feet below sea level.
>
> That's a dangerous road. In the days of Jesus it came to be known as the "Bloody Pass." And you know, it's possible that the priest and the Levite looked over that man on the ground and wondered if the robbers were still around. Or it's possible that they felt that the man on the ground was merely faking. And he was acting like he had been robbed and hurt, in order to seize them over there, lure them there for quick and easy seizure. And so the first question that the priest asked—the first question that the Levite asked was, "If I stop to help this man, what will happen to me?"
>
> But then the Good Samaritan came by. And he reversed the question: "If I do not stop to help this man, what will happen to him?"[1]

Many are so familiar with the parable of the Good Samaritan that we don't realize the revolutionary leap the teaching embodied for its listeners. There are enough radical ideas in this parable to make some of my Berkeley neighbors turn green with envy.

First of all, in the parable Jesus pushed the concept of "neighbor" about as far as possible with his first-century Jewish audience. In Jesus's day, the concept of "neighbor" was generally limited to one's local network of extended family and friends. The outer-neighbor limit extended to fellow Jews at its very edges. Samaritans were not considered to be either neighbors or neighborly because—to put it simply—the Jews disliked them.

Part of this was a result of history: Samaritans originated from Assyrians who in 722 BC settled in the Jewish homeland after exiling the Jewish people out of it for a couple centuries. By the first century AD they had adopted many Jewish religious beliefs and customs, but not enough to convince the Jews that they were Jewish. They were a living symbol of past Jewish vulnerability and weakness. A common slur against Samaritans at the time of Jesus decreed that, "He that eats the bread of Samaritans is like he that eats the flesh of swine." (Doubtful that an insult from a Jew could get much lower than that.) So great had the hate for Samaritans grown in Jesus's day, that even two of his most historically beloved disciples, James and John, became so infuriated at Samaria after some locals had proved less than welcoming to their group that they asked to call down fire on them. Jesus discouraged this idea.

To paint a picture of a heretical Samaritan in a heroic light was revolutionary enough in its own right, but the parable goes beyond even this. By asking Jesus, "Who is my neighbor?" the expert in the law subtly tries to limit the sphere of his own responsibility. He tries to create tight boundaries around "neighbor" that Jesus wouldn't dare violate. He wants Jesus to justify the expert's own antipathy, or at best indifference, to those outside the Jewish fold, a group that in his mind would probably include Roman occupiers, Greeks, other "unclean" foreigners, lepers, and anyone else unworthy of neighborly attention.

In response, Jesus radically expands the notion of "neighbor" in the narrative by first discrediting the superficial religiosity of a Jewish Levite and a priest, subsequently installing a hated Samaritan as his protagonist/hero, and then expanding the scope of "neighbor" to the anonymous person with whom he shares no blood, kin, or social ties.

Relative to the status quo, it is a very upsetting parable.

In order to begin traveling down the road to loving our global neighbor, we need to understand where we are right now. We need that "You are here" spot on the map. Throughout my career, I've noticed that people tend to move through six stages on the road toward loving their global neighbor.

I refer to these stages as the six *i*'s.

Ignorance

To put it rather bluntly, the first stage is simply one of *ignorance*, in which we are mostly unaware of the happenings and needs outside our own little hamlets.

Growing up as an upper-middle-class boy in Davis, California, I was ignorant about issues like global poverty. Foremost on my mind was how I could save up enough money to buy a pet king snake, something that also preoccupied my mother but for a very different reason. When I was in the third grade, I did not know that almost half the world could neither read nor write. When I was in the fourth grade, I did not know about the famine sweeping Bangladesh that year. In the fifth grade, I did not know about the genocide under Pol Pot. I was ignorant of these things. I did not know.

I did not know then, but I am aware of facts about the world like this now. Of course, there are some things that happen in our world that are so terrible that they must be kept from children. However, some adults continue to remain in a perpetual state of ignorance about the conditions that govern the lives of most people in the world. Historically, even adults were kept in ignorance about the rest of the world because barriers to information were high.

Today people living in rich countries have fewer excuses. It is difficult to imagine how a person living in a rich country in the age of cable television, Facebook, Twitter, Instagram, and smartphones could remain in a state of ignorance about the lives of people in poor countries. But life happens, and as the life-stages roll by, we become absorbed with finding the perfect skateboard, the perfect hair, the perfect college, the perfect life partner. Then we long for children, then worry about whether our children are normal (or sufficiently above normal), reflect on whether we have become self-actualized in our career, dream about buying a bigger house (for the benefit of the children, of course), contemplate whether we have made the right friends and social connections, fuss about our creaky backs and declining health, long for the freedom retirement brings, then worry about the purposelessness we feel once we get there. At every stage of life we can find an adequate excuse to fail to engage outside our self-contained, self-absorbed little worlds.

Sometimes we choose ignorance. Although this may seem strange, it is a phenomenon now understood by psychologists and behavioral economists called "strategic ignorance." One could argue that knowing and understanding more could never hurt, but suppose that I could freely obtain information that causes me to feel bad, like getting a test to find out whether I have a terminal disease. The thought of knowing I have the disease might make me feel even worse than the actual consequences from it, so I choose ignorance. I'd rather enjoy life, oblivious to my impending doom, and just keel over one day without the anticipatory anxiety. Or certain kinds of information would make me feel, perhaps out of obligation or guilt, that I must do something I frankly would rather not do, or even that I know that I won't do. In such cases, perhaps I might choose to remain blissfully ignorant.

Recall the priest and the Levite in the parable, who might have liked to believe, who might have even actually convinced themselves, that the man lying on the other side of the road was "resting." Some theologians say the priest and the Levite passed to the other side of the road in order to remain ritually clean from the blood of a dead man, but I don't think so. As a behavioral economist, I think the priest and the Levite passed to the other side of the road to engage in strategic ignorance. If the Levite stopped to check whether the man needed their help, it might have called him to do something that would have messed up his day. Some people don't know because—consciously or unconsciously—they choose not to know.

Indifference

I believe it was in the seventh grade when I learned that there were starving people in the world. I remember when I heard about this in church, and I remember wondering briefly what it would feel like to starve. But I didn't reflect on it long. I was too worried about whether my friend Mike was going to buy one of those new skateboards with the polyurethane wheels, because then I would have to buy one too, or feel left out, especially if Kevin, the new kid on our block, got one. Then Mike would skate around on his polyurethane wheels with Kevin, and I would be left behind on my lame skateboard with metal wheels, flying off the front of it every time I hit a tiny pebble on the sidewalk.

I wasn't living in ignorance anymore, but I was living in *indifference*, the second *i*. People in rich countries who are not ignorant about the plight of human beings in most of the world but care very little about such matters live in indifference to their global neighbor. Perhaps we nominally care about them, but in the great thought hierarchy that governs our brains, thoughts of global neighbors take a low precedence to thoughts about what we will wear that day, how to attract desirable members of the opposite sex, how to deal with an ill-tempered boss, or how to get ahead in life (in whatever special way that applies to us). In the end, that precedence amounts to practical indifference, which is, of course, not an allowable option for Christians.

While Western culture has been historically influenced by Christianity, today it is ruled by an unyielding quest for higher forms of entertainment. Virtually all of us can attest that a large fraction of any increase in our income goes to entertaining ourselves more thoroughly. As our income goes up, we purchase more expensive vacations, more expensive cars, or more expensive concert tickets closer to the stage. There are incalculable other ways we devote ourselves to episodes of short-term satisfaction and diversion. If we were to be honest, most of us care far more about whether our favorite sports team won or lost, or about the plight of our favorite Netflix character, than we do about the well-being of our global neighbors. Everyone from devout churchgoers to humanistic secular liberals claim to love their neighbor, but do we? Really?

Economics teaches a disturbing concept called "revealed preference." Unlike some other softer and more forgiving breeds of social scientists, economists do not care about what kind of person you profess to be, about what you say you like and don't like, or about what you say you might do or would do in a particular situation. Economists only care about the choices you make—what you actually *do*. Some social scientists spend hours and hours interviewing people to understand their beliefs about different things. We don't do that; we infer beliefs from actions. It is what you do that reveals your preferences, not your detailed and flattering description of your preferences. "Love your neighbor as yourself." Are you altruistic? How much of your annual income do you give to the poor? One percent? Less? Economists view revealed preference as a window into the human soul. It alone, not our thoughtful articulations or good intentions, tells us about our concern for others.

When I speak at public conferences about poverty and giving, I often begin by asking the audience to participate in a short exercise. I ask them to create two columns on a piece of paper. In the left column, I ask them to list three significant consumer items that they purchased for themselves in the last year, like a new smartphone, a bicycle, camping equipment, and so forth. In the right column, I have them list three significant charitable contributions they have made during the same period, with an eye toward the welfare of the needy. Clearly the choice of these contributions is important; the lives of other people may be critically affected by them. Then I ask them to raise their hand if they had put a serious effort into investigating the quality of these big consumer purchases. In every instance, at least 90 percent of the hands in the room are raised. I then ask the same question about their charitable donations: how many people made an effort into investigating the impact the donations have made to these charities? Typically less than 10 percent of the people in the room raise their hands.

The results from my informal experiment reflect what recent research has shown about charitable giving in the United States: unlike the meticulous attention they pay to choosing the best smartphone or flat-screen TV, only about 3 percent of American donors even *claim* to have researched the impacts of the charities to which they donate.[2]

Idealism

As people's relationship to the global poor move out of ignorance and indifference, it enters a stage of *idealism*, our third *i*. The universities that I am most familiar with, Berkeley and the University of San Francisco, are places that are pretty engaged in global affairs, and many of the undergraduate and graduate students I interact with every day are not ignorant about global poverty.

Neither are they indifferent toward it. But like many college students today, they are very idealistic in their approach to global issues.

People in the idealistic phase tend to divide the world into three camps:

1. the global poor;
2. rich, ignorant, and indifferent people who do not care about the poor; and
3. people like themselves who are rich, but are *not* ignorant and indifferent, and are therefore willing to support the necessary resource allocation to straightforward solutions that will fix the world's problems.

It is a worldview that attracts a wide following. Serious problems are easily reduced to vague forms of oppression identified within "the system." Answers to the great global problems are simple, and the main solution is to get the identified oppressor to stop oppressing. Any learning that occurs often involves becoming *aware* of problems, rather than deeply *understanding* them. Development studies are relegated to a consciousness-raising exercise. Indifference is addressed through some type of social action, protesting sweatshops, boycotting certain products, and generally disassociating with and demonizing the identified oppressor and other enemies of social justice. Engaging in a serious investigation about either the causes of poverty or the relative effectiveness of different types of interventions or policies receives only cursory attention by the idealist, whose feelings of guilt can only be assuaged by *doing something* despite a paucity of evidence for a causal connection between action and goal. In the end, it is the *feelings* of the idealist that rule the day—the awesome and terrible responsibility of how to deal with so much guilt.

The problem with idealism is that it all too often leads to ineffective action. Our feelings are important, but they are not enough to make a difference in the lives of the poor. To truly care for our global neighbor, we need to move beyond feelings to effective action. Many people stuck in the idealism phase sincerely believe that the world would be a significantly better place if only we would all consume gallons and gallons of fair-trade coffee. The fair-trade movement was initiated by a group of well-meaning individuals with the best of intentions. The only problem is that, like other movements initiated by people stuck in the idealist phase, on average, fair-trade coffee doesn't really work—if *work* is defined as "getting impoverished coffee growers a consistently better deal for their coffee" (a topic we will discuss in a later chapter).

To put it simply, many idealists have an "attribution problem," a difficulty with untangling causes and effects. Too often these become muddled together in the mind of the idealist, whose thinking is shaped through an unorganized clutter of anecdotes. For example, sweatshops—factories in the developing world where people work for low wages—are often misunderstood as a *cause* rather than an *effect* of poverty. The clear implication is that we could reduce global poverty by banning sweatshops. But a more careful analysis finds that sweatshops appear to characterize a rather nasty intermittent phase of economic development that nearly all rich countries have passed through. Failing to understand the simple dynamics of cause-and-effect in global poverty has resulted in countless failed policies and poverty interventions that have cost many livelihoods and lives.

Idealism also does not establish the boundaries necessary for sustainability. A very idealistic friend of mine once invited a homeless man to live with him. Unfortunately, he did this without drawing up a clear set of boundaries, expectations, and responsibilities that might have allowed this idea, hatched in his generous heart, to become a sustainable solution. As a result, the man living in his house crossed boundaries that made the arrangement unsustainable: borrowing money without repayment, eating my friend's food, leaving the house a mess, and so on. The arrangement couldn't work in the long run. It would have been better for him to establish a relationship with the man that was sustainable, and that may or may not have involved his moving into my friend's house.

In the few instances in which I have invited homeless people to stay in my home, one of the first things I have done is lay down a set of privileges, rules, and expectations for their stay that includes the duration of the arrangement. (Feel free to help yourself to *this* food, but not *that*; you must lock the door at night; you may sleep here; you may stay for one month, and so forth.) Boundaries and communicated expectations defy nearly every inclination of the idealist. They are awkward and sometimes even embarrassing to articulate. But they provide the framework within which benevolent interventions can flourish rather than wither. Idealism discourages boundaries; an absence of boundaries produces burnout.

The Good Samaritan understood boundaries. Notice that he sets some parameters around his care for the injured man. He does not have a messianic complex. He does not dabble in codependent behavior. He does not feel worthless unless he lets the injured man dominate the course of the rest of his life. The Samaritan goes far out of his way to help him, but eventually he has his own business to which he must attend. As a consequence, he substitutes some of his money for more of his time—paying an advance to the innkeeper to take care of the injured man—and then he is on his way. Especially when it comes to interventions at a personal level, healthy boundaries allow one to develop a lifestyle of caring for others. It allows caring for others to be sustainable, and thus more likely to be effective.

Even large foundations create boundaries. Realizing that they cannot solve the world's every problem, foundations generally limit their scope within a sphere of concern. Even the Bill & Melinda Gates Foundation, with its tens of billions to spend on global poverty alleviation, restricts its giving primarily to health interventions, while funding some work in agricultural development and financial services access for the poor. Rather than embarking on a mission to "save the world," those who create boundaries—whether they be individuals, churches, nongovernment organizations (NGOs), or foundations—develop competencies in core areas that foster their effectiveness along with making their work sustainable.

Investigation

The process of developing meaningful and effective interventions is largely about learning, about *investigation*, the fourth *i*. There is a certain humility that accompanies a willingness to learn—a humility that belies the idealist, who already has ordained a neat set of pre-prescribed solutions to the most complex global problems. Developing effective interventions usually requires patience, careful study and diagnosis of a problem, thoughtful intervention, and subsequent evaluation of the intervention.

One might make an analogy with the creation of a healthy family. If I want to love one of my daughters well, I need to study her likes and dislikes, the things that make her happy and the things that make her frustrated. Suppose I want to buy her a birthday gift. I need to pay attention to how she has responded to my attempts at birthday gifts in the past and to things she might need, and, of course, I need to communicate with her by asking what she might like for her birthday. I don't buy my daughter a new leaf blower for her birthday even though I, myself, cannot imagine anyone could be happy without a top-quality leaf blower. Loving people well means carefully studying them and understanding their needs, even as they differ from our own.

Obviously, this takes different forms in different contexts. It looks different in the context of a personal relationship than it does in planning a nationwide health intervention, but the principles are similar. Very fortunately for my family, I do not run randomized controlled trials with birthday presents. But I do run randomized controlled trials to assess the effectiveness of poverty interventions in developing countries. When we investigate, we learn about what is helpful and unhelpful, what works and doesn't work, which interventions are effective and which are a waste of money and time.

Informal learning and scientific investigation are the same thing, just at different levels of scale and formality. They are both centered around understanding through observation. Unlike the idealist, an investigator must be "slow to speak, and quick to listen."[3] Informal learning and scientific investigation both involve understanding causal relationships. The ability to identify causal relationships is a basic building block for effective poverty and development work, and probably for life generally.

In development work, we generally focus on the causal effect of a particular type of intervention on an outcome of interest. We might want to know how the adoption of clean-burning stoves affects respiratory disease from indoor air pollution, especially for mothers who spend all day cooking over a smoky fire. We might want to know how providing free shoes to children affects their health and well-being, or how providing clean water reduces diarrhea, the leading killer of children under a year old. We first may want to investigate whether these interventions work at all, then in what context, and then understand how their cost-effectiveness compares with the alternatives. For example, given a limited budget, which has a bigger impact on learning outcomes: providing textbooks to students or decreasing class sizes? (And if you'd like some actual answers to these questions, keep reading. I'll address them and others in the chapters to come.)

Honest investigation leads us to a place where we can be reasonably confident that we are caring for people effectively. It can also be scary for practitioners. I have worked with poverty-focused NGOs that have been tentative about letting researchers carry out scientific impact studies of their programs. Most of these NGOs decided to take the plunge. Others ultimately did not, for the reality was that there was simply too much to lose if the study indicated their work to be less effective than their donors believed.

Based on this experience, my word to donors is to withhold donations to any nonprofit unable to offer credible, third-party evidence that it is helping the people it claims to help. This is a low bar, yet it is a bar that many development NGOs have not cleared. And if a nonprofit is unable to demonstrate that it is benefiting its alleged beneficiaries, it's not clear that it has earned the right to continue to accept people's donations simply to keep the machine running.

When I talk to NGO leaders about the benefits of investigating the impacts of their work, I often use the analogy of driving a car. Understanding the various impacts of the different types of work within an organization is like cleaning a windshield that has been caked with mud. A clean windshield allows the driver to understand how to direct the vehicle. Once an organization has a reasonable gauge of how well and among what populations its programs work, it allows the director far greater vision and control. In practice this allows NGOs to allocate resources toward more effective programs or more effective approaches while shutting down ineffective ones. It facilitates targeting among segments of the population where programs are realizing their biggest impacts. It also allows for honest fund-raising. Fund-raising through promoting carefully selected success stories to the public is not honest fund-raising. But an NGO dedicated to scientifically rigorous investigation of its work can truthfully report the average impacts of its work across program beneficiaries rather than fill its web pages with inspiring but misleading anecdotes that represent outliers in its impact.

One example of how honest investigation has led to greater impact is in the research work that has been done on holistic poverty interventions. Many development NGOs—especially faith-based ones, such as World Vision, Covenant World Relief, Food for the Hungry, and Heifer International—had informally touted the advantages of a holistic approach at conferences and gatherings, but there was little evidence to back up the claim that it was an effective approach. Then a single, comprehensive study provided such evidence.

The Bangladesh Rural Advancement Committee (BRAC), the largest development NGO in the world, offers a "poverty graduation program" that employs a secular holistic intervention targeted at the ultra-poor. As part of BRAC's program, it offers beneficiaries a productive asset (typically in the form of a farm animal they choose from a list), training in the use of the selected asset, access to a savings account, basic health-care training and services, weekly cash grants, and weekly life-skills coaching, especially in the areas of developing self-efficacy and aspirations. The theory behind a holistic approach suggests that an intervention in any one of these areas may be sufficient to lift a household out of poverty, but there is reason to believe that all of these types of interventions may be complementary to one another; each makes the others more productive.

The theory is compelling, but a group of researchers made up of some of the top development economists decided to check. They did this by randomizing the rollout of BRAC's poverty graduation program in six different countries: Ethiopia, Ghana, Honduras, India, Pakistan, and Peru. The results, published in the journal *Science*, showed large and significant impacts on multiple measures of poverty graduation in every country. Researchers and practitioners alike were stunned by the magnitude of the results, which will be discussed in more detail later along with those of faith-based programs. But by all accounts, rigorous investigation has demonstrated that the holistic livelihood approach can be an extremely effective intervention among the ultra-poor. Development organizations can now scale up similar programs with confidence.

Introspection

There is a step on the way to impact that may follow or coincide with investigation. It involves a reflection not just on external needs and effective means for addressing needs, but also on the internal resources, giftedness, ability, energy, and talent one has for engaging poverty and those in need. It is the process of aligning effective interventions with the resources at one's disposal. An economist might talk in terms of the demands of global poverty and about our resources to address those needs as the supply. Impact comes in part through appropriately matching supply with demand. And while I will focus more on personal calling, the idea applies at the organizational level as well. Whether at the individual or organizational level, this involves a step of *introspection*, the fifth *i*. What is the correct role we should play in the larger effort of caring for our global neighbor?

In a later chapter, I will discuss a number of different roles in global poverty and development work: Investigator, Giver, Advocate, Creator, Director, and Practitioner. When we match our giftedness and calling with an appropriate intervention to meet a specific need, not only do we tend to thrive, but our efforts tend to be fruitful as well.

As an economist, my main role has always been as an Investigator, but about fifteen years ago some college friends and I became small-time Creators and Practitioners when we founded Mayan Partners, a small NGO that works in a single village in the highlands of western Guatemala. In this village of 2,300 indigenous Quiché-speaking people, Mayan Partners fully sponsors a village middle school and a community library, partially funds a preschool, carries out public health work, and facilitates artisan microenterprise. Mayan Partners represents the confluence of a need that was presented to us by local village leadership, an understanding of the impact of good rural schools in Guatemala, and a sense of our own desire and calling to be more involved in direct practitioner work. Our professional roles loosely correspond to our roles in the NGO: Ron, the pastor (with the higher-quality relational skills), chairs the board; Peter, the accountant, keeps track of donations; Jim, the businessman, budgets money for the field; nurse Brooke leads the medical work on visits; Robb, the programmer, does the lube and oil changes on the website; Spanish-speaking Kent and I try to keep in touch with what's going on in Guatemala. I will share some things we have learned in our work through Mayan Partners throughout the book. For each of us it is not our primary vocation, only something we love and are committed to together.

A more scaled-up example of someone matching talent and global need is my friend and fellow research affiliate with the Center for Effective Global Action, UC San Diego economist Paul Niehaus. Paul is naturally an Investigator, but he is also a social entrepreneur and a Creator who founded the nonprofit GiveDirectly in 2009 with his graduate school classmates from Harvard and MIT.

I first met Paul when he visited the University of San Francisco shortly after GiveDirectly started, where he explained to a group of faculty and students how he and his friends with an aptitude for mobile technology had considered how digital payment systems could move cash into the hands of the global poor. He explained the system they developed with GiveDirectly, which seamlessly zaps electronic cash from donors over the web into the mobile-phone-based savings accounts of East Africans. The organization has minimal overhead, meaning that 94 percent of donations go to recipients, who typically receive about US $1,000 in three tranches of cash over the course of a year.

GiveDirectly has been listed as one of GiveWell's top charities nearly since its foundation. The organization itself keeps to the boundaries of its original calling and the giftedness of its founders. It does not build schools. It does not distribute deworming medicine or perform surgeries. It does one thing—send cash to the poor with no strings attached—and it does it well. Indeed, most of GiveWell's top ten most effective charities are not those that try to do everything but instead have found a discernable niche that matches the gifts, interests, and abilities of their founders—from Helen Keller International to Evidence Action's Deworm the World Initiative—and have focused on high-impact interventions that intersect their ability and global need.

It is inspiring to see high-tech guys find ways to use their talents to engage global poverty, but also others whose gifts lie in the areas of compassion, administration, advocacy, and other areas outside high-tech. In part 4 we will explore more of the details of how to match giftedness with the needs of the global poor.

Impact

As we move past ignorance, indifference, and idealism to an intersection between global need, effective interventions, and capabilities, we begin to move away from feel-good clichés and toward *impact*, the sixth *i*.

Who is it that has engaged both local and global poverty in meaningful and effective ways? It is potentially both organizations and individuals. It is the development NGO who understands the needs in the context it works, assesses its own capabilities, and implements a program that has been rigorously shown to be both effective and relatively cost-effective. But it is also the suburban soccer mom who leads a parenting class for low-income, single moms in her church basement on Saturday mornings. It is the lawyer who goes before his city council to articulate the advantages of a "housing first" approach to homelessness in his town. It is the retired grandmother who volunteers at a preschool near her house to read books to at-risk three-year-olds, and who patiently helps them develop core socio-emotional skills (in other words, how to play nice with people). It is the high-end paid programmer who zaps $1,000 each month to an impoverished family in Kenya from his cell phone during his commute on the metro along with a silent prayer for their welfare. It is the Mike Burnetts of the world, who sponsor children in impoverished countries, allowing them better education, improved health, and growth into leadership roles in their communities. It is the surgeon who flies to remote areas to carry out reparative surgeries, helping to restore dignity to the lives of children born with physical deformities such as cleft palate, clubfoot, and cataracts. We will discuss the scientific basis for these and other proven interventions in more detail later, but behind each of these responses to poverty lies rigorous evidence for impact.

Part of being able to have an impact on poverty is understanding the nature of poverty, both global and domestic. A basic grasp of the causes of economic poverty and prosperity helps to adopt flexible responses to the world around us because we understand better how the system works to produce these outcomes. We should avoid merely following a recipe; we should understand why it works. This comes from an understanding of what causes people, communities, and nations to economically prosper and to fall behind. This challenging question is the subject of the next section of the book.

Part 2

UNDERSTANDING POVERTY

Chapter 3

WHAT CAUSES POVERTY?

Why are rich countries rich and poor countries poor? And why do some groups of people prosper in one country while others lag behind? A first step to becoming a Shrewd Samaritan is understanding the roots of poverty and prosperity. It is not enough to know that people are poor. It is not enough to be motivated to respond. Without a clear understanding of what causes poverty, it is difficult to do something meaningful and effective about it.

These next few chapters will help lay the foundation for an understanding of the causes and nature of poverty, both global and domestic. What I want to offer you in this particular chapter is a summary of the best that we as economists collectively have to offer on the complex topic of the causes of poverty at the macro level—why some countries have grown to be rich even as others have lagged behind. The next chapter will consider the causes of inequality and poverty within rich countries. The chapter following that will explain different kinds of poverty traps and how learning to distinguish between them allows us to do more effective work. Subsequent to this we will explore the kinds of interventions we have found to be most effective at freeing people from poverty.

But before we have dessert, we have to eat our vegetables.

As an academic economist, I am fascinated by all of the intricacies and details of this research. However, I understand that you, the reader, are not nearly as likely to be as fascinated by the intricacies and details. So to give you some foundational understanding in this area, I want to present an overview of what is considered today to be the best research on the origins of global poverty and wealth, and give you some references in footnotes if you wish to follow up on these intricacies and details.

A Short History of Poverty and Wealth

The first thing to understand about poverty is that it is historically *normal*. Prosperity is abnormal; poverty is normal. The level of material prosperity that we as middle-class people living in industrialized countries enjoy lies in the 99th percentile of the average experience within human history. Indeed, most of human history since the dawn of civilization can be thought of as a giant poverty trap, the kind of human existence described by seventeenth-century philosopher Thomas Hobbes as "nasty, brutish, and short."[1]

During the Stone Age and even into the Bronze age, life expectancy at birth was about twenty-six years.[2] Life expectancy in ancient Egypt, the pinnacle of civilization several millennia BC, was nineteen years, reaching the early thirties for those who escaped death in infancy.[3] Literacy in ancient Egypt was probably limited to no more than about 1 percent of the population, and mostly to a class of scribes.[4] And keep in mind, from about 3000 BC until at least two thousand years later, few had it better than the Egyptians.

We think of Roman civilization as more modern than the societies that existed before it, but in ancient Rome, life expectancy at birth remained only twenty-five to thirty years, with a probability of survival past age ten at only 50 percent.[5] Education was sparse in the Roman Empire in the centuries that surrounded the birth of Christ, mainly restricted to wealthy families employing tutors (who were often slaves) for their children. Literacy was limited to 1 to 2 percent of the population.[6] Even in Roman-occupied Israel, learning was more traditionally oral than written, and only about 3 percent of the population of Israel was functionally literate.[7]

The cleanest statistic economists use to measure economic prosperity, both today and in the past, is per capita income, the average income per person, often called per capita GDP (Gross Domestic Product). In ancient Rome and its wealthier provinces, per capita income was only about $620, which is similar to the poorest developing countries today.[8] In Western Europe, scholars estimate that per capita income was lower than at the peak of the Roman empire for centuries after its decline, around $427 in the year 1000, rising to $771 by 1500, $997 by 1700, and $1,243 by the early 1800s.[9] But by the year 1800, life expectancy in Western Europe was still only about forty years and literacy was still very low in Europe—highest in the Netherlands and Italy at around 15 to 18 percent, but only about 5 percent in Great Britain.[10]

Economic growth in most of the world was low for a long, long time. How long this was is hard for us to fathom. Scholars estimate that per capita income in the year AD 1 was about $450 in China and India, growing to only $545 in China and $600 in India by 1900.[11] Literacy remained extremely low across the centuries in these countries, especially for women. Even by 1900, literacy among women in India was less than 1 percent.[12] Per capita income and literacy rates were slightly higher in the Latin American countries, but as in India and China, life expectancy in the large Latin American countries like Brazil and Mexico had still not moved past age thirty by 1900. Similarly, in 1900 life expectancy in the large African countries such as Kenya, Nigeria, and Congo was around thirty years,[13] and per capita income remained around $400 to $500 by 1900 with literacy at only a few percent of the population.[14] The greater point here is that for millennia, there was barely any progress in the indicators we commonly use today to measure human welfare.

Back in the year AD 1 it would have been hard to predict which countries would have become the richest two thousand years later. The largest economy in the world at the time was India, followed by China, and then the European countries.[15] Technological breakthroughs of many different kinds had been made in China and India and also in relatively advanced civilizations in Mesopotamia, Egypt, and Mexico. Yet these countries remained mired in poverty for centuries along with the rest of the world. Many economic historians refer to this protracted economic stagnation as a "Malthusian Trap," named after early economist Thomas Malthus, in which any advancements in productivity or technology simply brought about population increases that in turn lowered wages and created food shortages.[16] Malthus's pessimism bestowed on economics the unfortunate title "the dismal science."

But beginning somewhere around the fifteenth century, Europe began a virtuous cycle resulting in decade after decade of exponential economic growth. Europe showed nascent signs of economic growth during that time, but it was during the Industrial Revolution of the eighteenth and nineteenth centuries that the economies of Europe, especially Western Europe, truly forged ahead. Only in the later stages of the Industrial Revolution did life expectancy begin to dramatically increase in countries such as Great Britain, growing to about forty years in 1850, to fifty years around 1900, sixty years by 1930, seventy years by 1950, and eighty years today.[17] By 1950, per capita income in Great Britain had reached $4,578. Today it is about $42,000. This is extremely high by historical standards, yet it is surpassed by many countries in Europe, including Ireland, which now boasts a figure of $63,000, significantly higher than its former colonial master. Across the entire European Union, per capita income today is about $40,000.[18] Europe has come a long way.

Likewise has the United States. The American economy lagged behind that of Western Europe, and the United Kingdom in particular, but in the mid-to-late nineteenth century it began to catch up quickly. In 1800 the average life expectancy in the United States was thirty-nine years and income per capita was $1,343. Today, life expectancy is seventy-nine years and per capita income in the United States is $57,325.[19]

Good News and Bad News

Now that you're more familiar with the bigger picture of economic development across civilizations and time, what about in recent decades? How are countries developing today?

Global economic development over the past few decades in the developing world has been a case of good news and bad news. Much of the good news has been centered in Asia, where the economic growth of India and China, two massive countries with 1.3 and 1.4 billion people, respectively, have realized astounding levels of economic growth over the last few decades. Especially in China, integration with global markets has lifted hundreds of millions of people out of poverty. In India there are now several hundred million people leading lives that could be considered "middle-class" by Western standards.

A number of countries in Latin America have also realized significant progress in recent decades, including Chile, Costa Rica, and the Dominican Republic. Some, such as Guatemala, El Salvador, and Honduras, have been caught in spirals of violence and corruption that have caused poverty to persist. Other Latin American countries, such as Argentina, Brazil, and Venezuela, have been plagued by political instability and industrial-scale macroeconomic mismanagement (especially the latter), causing them to fall far short of their potential.

An important piece of the good news is that in the last twenty years some of the highest growth rates in the world have occurred in sub-Saharan Africa in countries like Botswana, Rwanda, Tanzania, Cameroon, Ethiopia, Mozambique, and Ghana. In other African countries such as Sudan, South Sudan, Central African Republic, Burundi, and Somalia, war and civil discord continue to prevent the emergence of conditions in which the seeds of economic prosperity can take root.

This mixture of good news and bad news in global economic development has created greater levels of inequality than have ever existed in the global economy. One might be tempted to say that this creation of inequality is a symptom of progress, and that progress is always likely to be uneven. But the unevenness that is taking place in economic growth is both unprecedented and staggering: Two hundred years ago, the ratio of per capita income between the richest countries and the poorest countries was about 3 to 1. Today it is about 100 to 1. The problem with inequality is that the poor not only suffer the practical consequences of low income, but they also suffer from a sense of discouragement and deprivation through a comparison with people in wealthy countries. It is one feeling to be poor if everyone is poor; it is another feeling to be extremely *relatively* poor compared to others.

Another batch of good news is that, based on the most recent poverty statistics compiled by the World Bank, the percentage of people living in extreme poverty (considered as less than $1.90 a day per person) has fallen by roughly half in the last twenty years to 10.1 percent of the world population, or 767 million people.[20] Although a long way from "catching up," the fact that nearly one billion people have graduated from extreme poverty in the last decades is an astounding fact of the modern era. The real challenge that lies ahead is that eradicating poverty among the still large number of remaining poor is a particularly challenging task. Roughly 80 percent of the people living in extreme poverty today reside in the remote rural areas of the world, not well served by transportation infrastructure, clean water, sanitation, and communication networks.[21] Most of the remainder live in squalor around huge cities rife with violence and other social ills. About half live in sub-Saharan Africa and another third live in South Asia. Many of these are people who remain mired in poverty in the rural areas of East Asia, Central Asia, and Latin America, like the indigenous village in which our NGO works in the western highlands of Guatemala.

Three Schools of Thought

What causes broadly based economic prosperity is one of the most profound questions in academic social science. But it isn't just an academic question. At some point, it becomes a practical question. We have to understand how economic prosperity and other measures of well-being emerged in the past to help inform effective programs and policies today. So what does the most credible research today have to say about this question?

A simple answer that would provide an elixir for poverty would obviate the need for this book. But there are several explanations for the origins of economic prosperity that have emerged as the most plausible in recent years: 1) the view that *geography* is the major determinant of economic prosperity; 2) that *culture* plays the leading role; and 3) that *institutions*, which create the rules of the game for economic life, are what is most important. What I will try to do here is provide an overview of each of these as they inform our understanding of what we are working with as we engage global poverty.

Geography

The geography hypothesis is one of the most intuitively appealing. Countries become rich, the argument goes, because they are blessed with abundant natural resources, happen to be geographically well located for trade and commerce, and enjoy climate advantages. Prominent among those advocating for the geography hypothesis is the well-known economist Jeffrey Sachs. With his collaborators, Sachs has built an argument based on early observations of Adam Smith in *The Wealth of Nations*, who saw increases in the division of labor as the primary cause of economic prosperity. And the division of labor, Smith noted originally, is increased through overseas trade.

Because shipping cargo by land costs approximately seven times as much as shipment by sea, landlocked countries encounter a disadvantage in international trade.[22] Sachs and his coauthors point out that there are thirty-five landlocked countries in the world with a population over one million. Essentially all of these landlocked countries are poor countries with the exception of six located in Europe. Per capita income among these twenty-nine non-European landlocked countries is less than one-third than it is in the countries outside Europe that have access to an ocean.[23]

Geography appears to have affected economic development outcomes in other ways. For example, it does not seem to be advantageous, economically speaking, to be a hot country. Among the 150 countries with a population greater than one million, per capita income in the seventy-two tropical countries is nearly one-third lower than that in the remaining seventy-eight non-tropical countries. Cold climates kill bacteria and viruses quickly, and they are inhospitable to mosquitos and other insects that transport diseases. Those living in tropical climates face a much higher disease burden, with yellow fever, dengue, malaria, and other diseases far more widespread in the tropics than in temperate climates. The same cold winters that kill disease also foster the habit of saving from the harvest for unproductive winters, which is not as essential in tropical climates.

Hotter temperatures also appear to foster aggression and civil conflict. A fascinating piece of research published in the journal *Science* by researchers at Berkeley studied different forms of human conflict, including common crime, political instability, and even the institutional collapse of civilizations. They found that all across the planet each of these forms of conflict increased at higher temperatures, and intra-group violence was found to be highly sensitive to changes in temperature.[24]

Heat also saps people's energy for work. Other important work strongly correlates increases in temperature, even within the same country over time, to lower levels of economic growth.[25] Clearly these studies have important implications not only for understanding the challenges of economic development in hot countries, but also for determining the implications of global warming and climate change on the global poor.

Geography may have also shaped the historical evolution of today's rich countries in complex ways. UCLA geographer Jared Diamond points to the origins of global economic inequality as a result of ancient geographical patterns of agricultural production. Relative to other parts of the world, Diamond argues that the landmass and climate of Eurasia fostered an early transition from simple nomadic hunter-gatherer communities to an agrarian society.[26] European climate and geography favored the cultivation of grains and the domestication of farm animals. This led to their adoption and incorporation into agrarian production much sooner than in other areas of the world. Food surpluses allowed some of the population to move into craftsmanship, leading to the refinement of steel in toolmaking. This greater division of labor fostered trade; trade brought about the emergence of cities.

The close proximity between peoples and their domesticated animals around these cities resulted in the transmission of diseases such as influenza, smallpox, and measles within the Eurasian population. But what didn't kill the Eurasian population made them stronger, or at least biologically more resistant to disease.[27] The development of steel weapons and the fact that people on other continents were less resistant to European diseases than Europeans were to theirs, by the fifteenth century, created the elements of power for Europeans over other peoples. Hence, Diamond's explanation for early European economic development and subsequent world domination forms the title of his famous book: *Guns, Germs, and Steel.*

Culture

The geographical explanation for the differences in economic development is compelling, but it is challenged by others who suggest that culture plays the leading role in the creation of prosperity. Geography, say the critics, cannot explain the vast differences in economic outcomes between Nicaragua and Costa Rica, between the former East and West Germanies, between North and South Korea, and between Haiti and the Dominican Republic. Nor can it explain the historical prosperity of Chinese, East Indian, Japanese, and Jewish minority communities around the globe, even in countries such as the Philippines, Brazil, Indonesia, Fiji, and South Africa, where the majority population remains mired in poverty.

Alexis de Tocqueville and Max Weber were among the first to study the interaction between culture and economic prosperity. In *Democracy in America*, de Tocqueville studied the American appetite for democracy and work in the mid-nineteenth century, reflecting that, "In democratic peoples [in America], where there is no hereditary wealth, everyone works to live. . . . Work . . . is held in honor; the prejudice is not against it but for it."[28]

Similarly, de Tocqueville observed the influence of American culture regarding ownership of property: "In no other country in the world is the love of property keener or more alert than in the United States, and nowhere else does the majority display less inclination toward doctrines which in any way threaten the way property is owned."[29]

Sixty years later, in *The Protestant Ethic and the Spirit of Capitalism*, Max Weber traced the rapid pace of economic development in Western Europe to a culture rooted in the Puritan, Pietist, and Calvinist strains of Protestantism. It was particularly in these traditions that Christianity manifested itself in a culture celebrating the goodness of work. In the Protestant ethic, work was viewed as part of service to the human community, similar to an expression of worship outside the church. Slackers were viewed disapprovingly, manifesting an outward sign of inward spiritual decay.

The late Harvard economic historian David Landes argues that property rights also originated from Judeo-Christianity, not only in the fairly direct eighth commandment ("Do not steal"), but throughout the Hebrew scriptures.[30] The idea that private property should be protected endured in Europe through the Middle Ages, according to Landes, where European kings and even the church itself could not generally flout the respect for individual property rights. It was revived during the Reformation as a bedrock for legal systems enacted as democratic reforms took hold later across Western Europe and Great Britain.

Why are property rights so important? Most economists agree that property rights are a key ingredient to economic prosperity. If governments are not able to guarantee the right of individuals to receive a return from their assets, or even to maintain ownership of the assets themselves, productive investment may not be worth the effort. So, for example, people trying to promote microenterprise development in a country in which property rights are insecure face an uphill battle. Enterprises are likely to stall out at a very small size, something I have seen continuously over decades of economic development work in Guatemala. Property rights create the underpinnings for entrepreneurial initiative and success.

Along with the Protestant work ethic and the respect for property rights, Landes points to an emphasis in Judeo-Christianity of human dominion over nature. Whereas more pantheistic belief systems saw the divine in animals and plants or in a world at the capricious whim of spirit forces, in Judeo-Christianity human agency and choices matter. Furthermore, in contrast with other belief systems that see time as cyclical, Judeo-Christianity views time as linear. There was a beginning (Genesis 1), and there will be an end (Revelation 22). Despite the fall of humanity in Genesis, Landes notes how in Judeo-Christianity there is a sense of progress to a better state, though not without setbacks, and even these can be redeemed through reflection, repentance, and the will to make future choices better.

So culture may explain part of why the economic take-off occurred in Western Europe rather than in other relatively advanced civilizations. The two leading rival candidates by the year AD 1000 were arguably the Islamic cultures of the Middle East and China. While certain aspects of Islamic culture had advanced beyond Europe during the heart of the Middle Ages, especially in the area of science, it did not seem to strongly encourage the *application* of scientific discoveries that might have spurred economic growth.[31] China was also characterized by a high level of technology and invention, including the development of the wheelbarrow, the compass, paper, printing, gunpowder, and porcelain, that was at least on par with Europe for centuries if not, in many respects, ahead. However, efforts at individual creativity were too frequently punished by society and its rulers rather than rewarded. As the famous Chinese proverb reads, "The shot hits the bird that pokes out its head." Lack of reward for creative innovation and the absence of individual rights for ideas and property in China kept invention from initiating a broader prosperity.[32]

An understanding of this history is critical to understanding underdevelopment today. Some of these very same differences—in people's historical view of their agency and possibility, their incentive to explore and innovate, and their relationship with property—explain economic modern differences across countries as well. Chinese economic development took off as soon as individual initiative began to be rewarded under the reforms of Deng Xiaoping in the late 1970s. This has long been true in North America, where we feel entitled to most of what we are given and virtually all of what we earn, providing ample incentive for innovation and work.

In many cultures today, the relationship between what one produces and what one is entitled to is not as strong. In poor countries, sharing and reciprocity are embedded in the culture in a way that seems foreign to us. If the business of a relative or close friend prospers, others in the social network are likely to feel entitled to share in the bounty.[33]

Behavioral economist Pamela Jakiela carried out a fascinating experiment in which subjects in both Kenya and the United States were given a sum of money and then had to decide how much to give an anonymous person in an adjacent room.[34] Some were given a bucket containing different varieties of dried beans and were paid according to how many grams of beans they were able to sort in ten minutes. Others just got the money for free. These were assigned to be the "givers," but others were assigned to be "takers," deciding how much to take from one of the subjects who had been given or earned the money.

On average people were more stingy giving away income they had earned, the Americans far more so than the Kenyans. But the biggest contrast was in the shares that people demanded from the income of others. When the partner had earned his income, the Americans demanded a lower share from their partner than if the partner had received their income as a gift, whereas the share that Kenyans demanded actually *increased* slightly when the partner had earned the income. In short, the Kenyan subjects gave away more income, and they claimed more income from others, regardless of whether they had "earned it" or not.

Jakiela's experiment has key implications for understanding economic development. Sharing income with peers can be a virtue as well as a survival mechanism. However, knowing that you will be expected to share whatever you earn with others may dampen your aspirations. If aunts and uncles, nephews and cousins all have a claim on your income, then it may not be worth it to invest in that new business expansion or even in your own education. The link between one's ability to capture returns from investment and making that investment in the first place is a strong one, and in this regard culture matters substantially. If we do not understand cultural differences in places we try to "do" development, we will constantly face an uphill battle.

Institutions

A third school of thought views neither *geography* nor *culture* as the seedbed of prosperity, but rather the quality of *institutions* in a society. Think of institutions as "the rules of the game," where each society creates its own rules. Institutions consist of informal social taboos, customs, traditions, and codes of conduct, as well as formal legal rights and laws.[35] In societies where the rules of the game create incentives for innovation and investment, poverty quickly gives way to prosperity. Where the rules of the game create incentives for corruption and taking what others have earned, poverty persists. It's almost that simple.

Daron Acemoglu of MIT and James Robinson of the University of Chicago have become the leading advocates of the institutional view, articulated most popularly in their book *Why Nations Fail*. Their short answer to this question is "bad institutions." In an early chapter of the book provocatively titled "Theories That Don't Work," the authors specifically challenge Sachs's geographical and Landes's cultural explanations for poverty and prosperity. Their challenge chiefly comes through identifying a series of "natural experiments" in which a single people sharing a common geography and culture that by happenstance came to be divided by a political boundary that imposed substantially different "rules of the game" between the two groups. The examples they appeal to include Nogales, divided into two cities, one in Arizona and one lying in the state of Sonora across the US-Mexican border, and North and South Korea, divided by a ceasefire at the 38th parallel after the Korean War. They write:

> While "culture" is very different between the South and North [Korea] today, it played no role in causing the diverging economic fortunes of these two half nations. The Korean peninsula has a long period of common history. Before the Korean War and the division at the 38th parallel, it had an unprecedented homogeneity in terms of language, ethnicity, and culture. Just as in Nogales, what matters is the border. To the north is a different regime, imposing different institutions, creating different incentives. Any difference in culture between south and north of the border cutting through the two parts of Nogales or the two parts of Korea is thus not a cause of the differences in prosperity, but rather a consequence.[36]

Moreover, Acemoglu and Robinson argue the idea that the tropics cannot easily support development is belied by the relative successes of countries such as Singapore, Malaysia, Costa Rica, the Dominican Republic, Botswana, and Rwanda. Furthermore, since culture tends to evolve slowly and geography does not evolve at all, they cannot explain the emergence of England as the leader of the Industrial Revolution only subsequent to a set of institutional reforms in 1688 during the Glorious Revolution, nor the sudden emergence of China as a world economic power only after the institutional reforms of Deng Xiaoping.

Acemoglu and Robinson argue that the set of institutions that exist in the countries of the world can be categorized into two groups: *inclusive* institutions and *extractive* institutions. While the former favor the creation of widespread prosperity, the latter promote the enrichment of the few at the impoverishment of the many. Their answer to the question "Why do nations fail?" is that the rules of the game established within many nations are designed for economic extraction by a narrow elite rather than economic inclusion. But how did some countries develop inclusive institutions, leaving others to develop extractive ones?

There is a great mistruth that is propagated in various social science departments on university campuses, claiming that colonization in and of itself is responsible for most of the inequality that exists between countries today. But there are plenty of former colonies that became wealthy countries (e.g., Australia, Canada, Hong Kong, the United States, Singapore), plenty of non-colonizers that are relatively wealthy (e.g., Italy, Japan, Norway, Slovenia, South Korea) and examples of non-colonized countries that are still relatively poor (Bhutan, Ethiopia, Liberia, Nepal). What Acemoglu and Robinson have found is that it's not *whether* you were colonized that matters, but *how* you were colonized.

The authors argue that as European colonizers began exploring new regions in Africa, Asia, and the Americas, many looked to establish new European settlements. In places where European colonizers were able to settle, they created *inclusive* institutions that emphasized property rights and established "rules of the game" that incentivized investment and commerce. These countries generally prospered and comprise most of the roster of high-income countries today.

But settlement by Europeans in some places was impossible due to high rates of mortality from tropical diseases. In these areas, European colonizers established *extractive* institutions that benefited both themselves and a local elite. These institutions were created not to ensure a set of rules for establishing a level playing field for broad participation in the economy, but rather for extraction and shipment of precious minerals and other natural resources and for trade in basic agricultural products. The historical establishment of these extractive institutions in these former colonies, they argue, forms the basis for institutions that are unable to foster a broad-based economic prosperity apart from the extraction of resources.

What's the Answer?

Which of these seemingly competing narratives about the origins of economic prosperity is true: is it geography, culture, or institutions? It is likely that each of these has played a leading role in different eras. In other cases, they have probably worked together. In early human history, geography and climate almost certainly helped establish certain modes of agricultural production that became favorable to trade and the development of cities. It is also likely that the Western Judeo-Christian worldview helped foster certain cultural values around work and property rights, creating an impetus for the development of institutions in Europe. As these became transplanted in other areas of the world, they fostered a broad-based prosperity in many of these regions as well.

Understanding the origins of poverty and prosperity helps us to be Shrewd Samaritans in a number of ways. Realizing that geography likely played an early role in development helps many of us in wealthy countries to realize that our ability to prosper has originated from forces outside our control. Grasping the relationship between culture and economic outcomes helps us to work more effectively as development practitioners within a given cultural context. Appreciating how the "rules of the game" influence people's economic incentives can help us work to shape them in ways that can foster broadly based economic prosperity. More generally, understanding the causes of the wealth of nations lays the foundation for effective global action.

Chapter 4

INEQUALITY AND POVERTY IN RICH COUNTRIES

When we first read the parable of the Shrewd Manager, it is easy to write off the Econo-Man as a conniving fraudster. Why would Jesus hold up the example of someone who offers discounts to his master's creditors in order to court their favor?

Some theologians suggest an alternative interpretation of the parable. This is an interpretation shared by many scholars, and if it is the right one, it gives a deeper insight into the character of the manager in light of that day's economic customs.[1] In first-century Israel, it was common for managers like the Econo-Man to work on commission. They were allowed to keep, as payment for their accounting services, some fraction of the debts owed to their employers as a way of motivating them to drum up business. Those listening to the parable may have thus understood that the deals cut by the manager were taken out of his own commission. This helps resolve the puzzle surrounding why his master praises his shrewdness in cutting the deals with his debtors: it was coming out of the Econo-Man's own paycheck.

Yet another angle adds to the intrigue of the actions of the manager. First-century Israel was characterized by stark economic inequality, where a few powerful people, who were often outsiders, controlled vast amounts of land and resources and hired managers to supervise business dealings while they were away. This stark inequality was an everyday part of the lives of listeners, and they probably understood the debtors to be impoverished, as most were themselves. The parable of the Shrewd Manager is followed by the parable of Lazarus and the Rich Man, the latter of whom is receiving his eschatological reward for earthly maltreatment of the poor. This suggests a unity in the sixteenth chapter of Luke's gospel, the Rich Man representing the negative example, and the Shrewd Manager the positive one. It may be that Jesus points to the manager not only for his shrewdness but also for the abandonment of his loftier position to enter into solidarity with those of more modest means.

If these scholars are correct, there may be more to the Econo-Man than first meets the eye.

Inequality in My Backyard

Each day I travel to work in San Francisco, I am reminded how decades of economic growth and technological development have not equally benefited all. To know San Francisco today, to live here, to work here, is to bear witness to a growing inequality, a divergence in economic fortunes. Savage inequalities plague the city where I work and where I was raised as a young boy. As a toddler I learned to walk on the jazz-filled sidewalks of the Fillmore, a street I now cross each day coming to work at the oldest university in the city, where I teach economics. San Francisco has grown and prospered since my childhood in ways that have brought great material benefits to many but have also left many behind.

I ascend from the underground BART station at Civic Center to catch the municipal bus to the university. The glowing new offices of Twitter stand tall and proud on the edge of the Tenderloin, the poorest neighborhood in San Francisco. As I wait for my bus, I watch a young programmer step over the soiled, jean-clad legs of the homeless man lying on the sidewalk. The act of stepping over another human being doesn't seem to distress him. He has become accustomed to stepping over homeless people now and then on his way to work.

Today in the greatest of ironies, San Francisco is filled with the ravaged victims of its unbridled economic prosperity. How we can understand the economic inequality and poverty that persists in cities like San Francisco, and in rich countries more generally, is the subject of this chapter. The poor in our country are part of the global poor, and it is vital to investigate the factors creating domestic poverty if we are to move beyond idealism and ineffectiveness to create interventions that have impact.

Our Focus of Concern

How do we think about our relative responsibility toward our local neighbor compared with our global neighbor? Many ethicists would argue that we have a greater responsibility toward those proximate to ourselves, including our families, people close to us with whom we have relational commitments, and those in our local communities. Yet for most of us living in relatively rich countries, the needs and the impact that one can make are almost certainly greater overseas.

Without placing explicit weights on "responsibility" versus "need," it is hard to make judgments on global needs versus relational proximity. If you are looking for a simplistic, hard-and-fast rule about whether your calling is to invest your money and time in addressing global poverty or local poverty, or even in caring for someone within your own family, you will not find it here. All of these can be worthy responses to need, but they should be the product of reflection on all the opportunities available to us and our thoughtful response.

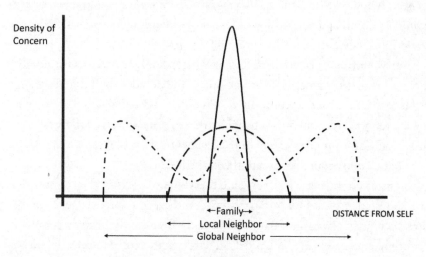

Figure 1

Figure 1 shows the focus of concern of three different people as measured by distance from self. The solid line represents a person whose focus of concern is high over the domain of the family. For example, this may be a mother focused on the needs of young children. The simple dashed line represents a person whose strongest domain of concern is over the family, but whose concern also extends strongly to the needs of her local neighbors. Lastly, the dot-dashed line represents a person whose focus of concern, while substantial for family, is strongly weighted toward the concerns of her global neighbor relative to her local neighbor.

The shape of one's focus of concern depends heavily on the resources at one's disposal, one's life stage, and one's awareness of global and domestic needs. In this chapter we focus on the latter.

Increasing Poverty in the United States

The World Bank has a special number it uses to measure how many extremely poor people there are in the world. Traditionally, that special number has been those living on less than US$1 per person per day, but in 2005 the global poor received a cost-of-living adjustment, which raised the special number to $1.25. In 2015 the special number was raised again, so that now it is $1.90. Of course, the number is somewhat arbitrary; there is, of course, no essential difference between living on $1.89 and $1.90 per day. There is no cap and gown or rendering of "Pomp and Circumstance" when the poor graduate crosses over the World Bank's extreme-poverty threshold.

But a cutoff must be established somewhere, if only to measure the number of people who cross a defined income line as the decades roll by. This change in the people on either side of the special number allows for a kind of extreme-poverty report card. And by this benchmark, most of the world's countries have made significant progress of late in reducing extreme poverty.

That is, most countries except the United States.

Signs of increasing US poverty are everywhere. Areas of the country that have slid further back into poverty have recently seen the reemergence of diseases such as hookworm, a parasite normally found only in poor countries, seemingly eradicated in the United States decades ago.[2] Hookworm thrives in places where people openly defecate, and cases have reappeared in areas of rural Alabama where residents have become so poor they can't afford indoor sanitation.

Figure 2 uses World Bank data to show the percentage of people living under the $1.90 per person per day threshold for the years 1985, 1995, 2005, and 2015 in the three largest countries where data is available in Asia, Latin America, sub-Saharan Africa, Europe, and the United States.[3] The percentages for the three areas in the developing world are given on the higher scale on the *left* axis, and for Europe and the United States on the lower scale on the *right* axis. Clearly the fraction of people living in extreme poverty is higher in all areas of the developing world than in Europe and the United States, but the reduction in extreme poverty in the developing world over the last three decades is remarkable. In Western Europe it increased slightly during the short episode of heartburn West Germany experienced after digesting East Germany, but then it quickly reverted back to near zero. The United States, however, is the exception in this generally encouraging downward trend in extreme poverty. The number of Americans living on less than $1.90 a day has steadily increased over the decades as inequality in our country has become increasingly extreme.

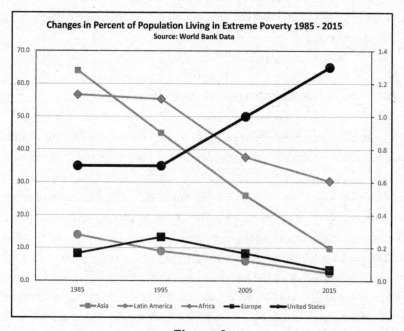

Figure 2

For decades, American poverty has been high, particularly among young families of color with children, and this remains true today. Whites make up 77 percent of the population, but they are only 43 percent of those living under the government poverty line. African Americans are 13 percent of the US population, but they comprise 21 percent of those under the poverty line; Latinos are 18 percent of the US population, but they make up 27 percent of those under the poverty line.[4] This being said, whites continue to make up a plurality of the poor in our country, and recent trends have found that increased poverty among whites is one of the major contributors to the upsurge of domestic poverty. A recent Brookings Institution report found that one of the greatest increases in US poverty was in suburban areas, traditionally a bastion of the white upper-middle class.[5]

There is a debate over the exact number of Americans who live in extreme poverty. Accounting for purchasing-power parity, a way of equalizing the cost of living across countries (where in poor countries things are often cheaper), World Bank data estimates the US fraction at 1.3 percent of the population, which would put the raw number at 4.2 million people. Depending on the definition one uses for extreme poverty, it is possible for researchers to obtain estimates that lie anywhere between zero and twelve million Americans living in extreme poverty.[6]

The Myth of the Guilty Migrant

Although the exact numbers are disputed and subject to different qualifications, few economists dispute two basic facts: 1) poverty in the United States is stubbornly not going away, and 2) inequality in the United States is increasing.

There are some basic factors that have always created unequal outcomes. With some of these most of us are relatively comfortable, such as differences in people's motivation, willingness to work hard, innate talent, creativity, and intelligence. In a free society, these differences will always yield some degree of inequality in outcomes. Most of us are less comfortable with other factors that create inequality, such as differences in family and neighborhood environments, differences in the networks to which some have access, inherited wealth and the lack of it. Other sources of inequality are caused by fundamental societal injustices: racism, gender discrimination, chasm-sized gaps in school quality, and other ways people are disadvantaged.

Today there are also some explanations for the growing degree of inequality that are largely myths. One of these is that, on the whole, immigrants steal jobs from American workers. It is important to dispel this myth because it has been used to justify policies that stifle immigration into the US and the mistreatment of immigrant families. This and the myth that immigrants cause increases in crime have existed since the wave of new European immigration in the early twentieth century, and they have been debunked by numerous careful academic studies.[7] The most convincing among these is a recent study examining the economic effects on native-born Americans of ending the 1942 Bracero program, which allowed nearly 500,000 Mexican workers to enter the United States for low-wage work, mainly in agriculture. Believing that the Bracero program reduced domestic employment and wages, President Johnson canceled it in 1964. But researchers found that removing these half-million Mexican workers from the US labor force had essentially no effect on US employment or wages.[8] The reason is that while migrants do compete with some other low-wage workers for jobs, they also add an equal or greater number of jobs to the economy in less noticeable ways, by increasing demand at local businesses. Some immigrant groups also have disproportionately high rates of entrepreneurship, creating jobs for others.[9] Areas of economic despair are usually those with population outflow, like Detroit and Cleveland, not areas with an inflow of opportunity-seeking immigrants.

So if it's not all about immigration, what are the causes of inequality in rich countries? Several factors have represented entrenched sources of inequality in rich countries since the beginning of the Industrial Revolution, but inequality in rich countries has worsened in recent years through a confluence of subtle but powerful economic forces. They are subtle in the sense that they are somewhat more difficult to identify, and also often become both conflated and confused with one another and with the more commonly understood sources of inequality. I will call the most important of these forces the "ascendency of the geeks," the "global megaphone," the "silver spoon," the "family premium," and the "identity trap." Of course, these phenomena have nerdish economic names as well, like "skill-biased technological change," but I like my terms better.

Ascendency of the Geeks

Modern inequality in rich countries is driven by a race between technology and education.[10] This is the insight of Harvard economists Claudia Goldin and Lawrence Katz, who describe the evolution of inequality in the United States in the following way: For the last 150 years, the United States and other developed countries have experienced unprecedented developments in new technology, changing the demand for different types of skills. In the past, job-related tasks often required physical human strength, men moving physical objects, and upon promotion, the supervision of other men moving physical objects.[11] But as employers adopted new technologies, more tasks required a match between the new technology and the higher level of education needed to understand it in order to make the technology productive.

Goldin and Katz argue that from the late nineteenth century through the 1970s, the United States became prosperous because it was better than any other country at educating its workforce. High school graduation rates increased from 2 percent in 1870 to 77 percent in 1970, and the growth in education and skills in our country outpaced the rate of technological advancement. Even from 1960 to 1970, the number of students completing bachelor's degrees more than doubled, and the number completing master's degrees more than tripled.[12] But since 1980, they argue, the growth rate in education has failed to keep up with the demand for people with technical skills. So in the race between education and technology, technology has been winning in recent decades, creating greater inequality in the United States. At the same time, the demand for manual labor of all kinds has flagged. This has caused the gap between those with and without a college degree, known as the "college premium," to grow increasingly wider.

It is usually unfair to deal in stereotypes, but for the sake of illustration, I will in this paragraph. From the 1950s to the 1970s, the big brawny jocks on the American high school football team who got C's in math still did reasonably well after graduation. They joined unions, worked the swing shift, raised families, joined bowling leagues, and lived a middle-class life. Those from a different high-school clique, the geeks, went to college and bought slightly bigger houses, but they lived in the same neighborhood as the jocks. Today, the gap between the geeks and the jocks is much wider. Those without the training to interface with technology run a significantly higher risk of being below the poverty line, face an increasing inability to form stable families, and comprise the majority of the homeless. It's a different ballgame now for the jocks.

How does an understanding of this race between technology and education in rich countries help us become Shrewd Samaritans? With the Ascendancy of the Geeks, what Shrewd Samaritans must do in the inner city is create, in so many words, Geek Factories. These are interventions that educationally turbo-charge underprivileged children to keep up in the education-technology race. If you want to do something practical to help the domestic poor win this race, volunteering with a local school to tutor one or more children at risk of losing this race between education and technology is a great place to start.

The Global Megaphone

The 2016 election was won based on the narrative that globalization, in the form of free trade and immigration, bore most of the responsibility for job losses in midwestern states, and thus for America's growing inequality. While the overwhelming consensus is that technological change can be handed the credit for most of these developments, globalization has also had substantial impacts on domestic poverty and inequality.

The great twentieth-century economist Paul Samuelson won the Nobel Prize in 1970 for helping us understand how increasingly free trade between nations would affect different groups in the economy. In one of Samuelson's elegant mathematical proofs, he demonstrated that wages and the cost of capital across countries would tend to converge under free trade. What this implies for a high-wage nation like the United States is that the forces of globalization are likely to exert long-term downward pressure on *unskilled* wages.

True to Samuelson's theory, import competition has hit unskilled and semi-skilled workers hard in our country. Particularly in the northern Midwest in states like Indiana, Ohio, and Michigan, the consequences of this economic decline have taken a terrible toll on the welfare of middle-aged American white men. In research that attracted national attention, Princeton's Anne Case and Angus Deaton showed that even as mortality continued to fall among other ethnic groups such as blacks and Latinos, mortality rates surged among white middle-aged males from 1998 through 2013 through marked increases in drug overdoses, suicides, and alcohol-related deaths.[13] The Case and Deaton study revealed much of the growing economic desperation in parts of the United States that have been hit by import competition. In contrast, coastal states, which tend to be more abundant in technology and high-tech labor, have tended to prosper from these same global forces.

What is more, media technology in the form of satellite television, internet-based programming, and other mediums that create a global market for exceptional creativity and talent have created a class of economic superstars.[14] Consider the market for entertainment in the Middle Ages, where jesters and bards roamed the countryside, performing for small groups in villages. Even England's top jester in the year AD 1200 probably didn't earn very much, just the coins tossed from an appreciative crowd. But with the advent of studio recording, the phonograph, and the radio, top talent began to earn more substantial rewards as technology expanded the market for their talent. More recently, the internet and other forms of mass communication have exponentially increased the returns to this top talent. Stephen Curry's NBA basketball contract at $33.7 million per year is driven in large part by his marketability in China and other far-reaching parts of the globe.[15] Technology has allowed not only the funniest comedians and the best singers to market their talent on a global scale, but also the best app programmers, driving up wages for these top 1 percent earners.

This is the impact of the *global megaphone*, which produces economic superstars based on the ability for technology to broadcast and sell their talent across the globe. In contrast, many others work in industries that are unaffected by the global megaphone. Based on the nature and the direct physicality of their work, the local barber, firefighter, schoolteacher, and physician do not get to shout into the global megaphone.

How does the growing wealth of those who benefit from globalization and the global megaphone contribute to the poverty of others? The wealth accrued by the global winners increases the prices of scarce goods (like housing), which then makes them less affordable for others.

This is the phenomenon we experience in the San Francisco Bay Area and in many other coastal US cities. The tech worker I watch walking down the street to his office at Twitter will stay late tonight at his work. Since being lured to San Francisco after finishing his computer science degree somewhere else in the country, he has found a great match for his skills in San Francisco. Twitter provides him free lunch and dinner—all the Twitter food he wants to eat. The free grub keeps him at work longer into the evening. The longer he stays at work to eat Twitter's free food, the more of his software code Twitter uses to penetrate its enormous global market. But the free dinner is cheap compared to the salary it is willing to pay him based on the global revenue he brings to the firm. This salary allows him to outbid other potential renters for an apartment, so that the average one-bedroom apartment in San Francisco now has risen to the equal monthly salary of a public-school teacher.[16]

Understanding these forces of globalization helps us to understand the causes of homelessness. As the public-school teacher is pushed down to the lowest-cost housing available, the lowest on the housing rung get bumped off the ladder and onto the street. For this reason, economists will argue that there is simply no substitute for addressing homelessness than allowing developers to build small-unit affordable housing in these markets. This is a policy that is often politically unpopular with the already-housed, but it is the only way to absorb the global economic forces that dominate these regions.

The Silver Spoon

The French economist Thomas Piketty's book *Capital in the Twenty-First Century* is considered by many to be one of the most important works written by an economist in decades.[17] Revolutionary books in economics do not generally become so for their ideas alone, but for the time in history in which their ideas come to light. John Maynard Keynes's magnum opus, *The General Theory of Employment, Interest, and Money*, was a game changer partly because it was written in 1936, in the depths of the Depression, when people had become fed up with Adam Smith's *Invisible Hand* and instead wanted a hand from the government. Piketty's book has become famous because it is a book about understanding economic inequality in an economically unequal time.

Many Americans may be quick to discount Piketty because he talks about Karl Marx and because he is French. But perhaps one thing that attracts many mainstream economists to Piketty is that, like most mainstream economists, he is no great fan of Marx while at the same time addressing some of the same problems that Marx addressed in his day. Foremost among these is the role that *capital* plays in the creation of inequality.

What are the reasons for this great divergence? Piketty acknowledges technological change and the forces of globalization as important components to growing inequality. His central thesis, however, is that capitalism inherently creates diverging levels of income and wealth within the population. This central feature is that over the course of economic history, the rate of return on investment, r, is virtually always higher than the overall rate of economic growth, g. This inequality, $r > g$, summarizes Piketty's fundamental idea, like Einstein's $E = MC^2$.

What Piketty's little inequality implies is that owners of capital will see their incomes continually growing at a greater rate than the rest of the economy as a whole, so the rich will accumulate income at a greater rate than the poor. This, claims Piketty, means that growing inequality is an immutable characteristic of a free-market economy. He points to evidence from the US, where wealth inequality has grown so dramatically today that the top 1 percent of wealth holders now own 40 percent of the nation's wealth, the highest percentage in decades.[18]

To counteract this inevitable increase in inequality, Piketty argues for high tax rates for rich people, not only on their income but also on their wealth. Admittedly, more experts are engaged by Piketty's analysis of the problem than are enamored of his policy prescriptions. But if Piketty's celebrated work teaches Shrewd Samaritans anything, it is that we not only need to help the poor develop skills to engage the global economy; we need to help them develop the financial literacy to become capital owners, a subject we will explore in subsequent chapters.

The Family Premium

There are also non-economic factors that exert a great influence on the inequality of outcomes in rich countries. I am often stunned at the degree to which social scientists at top research universities, perhaps economists in particular, overlook the importance of the family. What I notice today is that—in their research—social scientists explore a host of different social and economic forces for explaining the outcomes of children. But when it comes to who their own kids are playing with, hanging out with, or dating, all of a sudden they become concerned about the importance of his or her family.

Not long ago the archbishop of San Francisco had me give a talk at a board retreat he was overseeing for Catholic Charities. The topic was the relationship between poverty in our country and the functionality of the American family. In short, there is a high correlation between the functional, two-parent family and positive economic outcomes. The statistic that stood out the most for me in preparing the talk was a simple but dramatic statistic from a 2014 study that the researchers call the "family premium." What they found was that those adults today in the labor force who (a) are married; and (b) were raised in a two-parent family, earn an income that is $42,000 higher than their unmarried peers who were raised in single-parent families.[19] Clearly the statistic deserves a lot of unpacking because it is obviously not purely a causal relationship, but rather the result of a tangled web of correlations, some of which are likely to be causal, but all of which are important. However, the sheer magnitude of the statistic (a difference of more than two-thirds of US per capita income) raises one's eyebrows.

The first correlation behind this $42,000 difference is that kids from single-parent families face grave disadvantages. Relative to children from two-parent families, they have higher rates of school expulsion, high school dropout, delinquency, cigarette smoking, alcohol use, weapon-related violence, sexual intercourse, and suicide.[20] These correlations are undisputed by researchers and are almost certainly causal to a degree. The authors estimate a $5,600 "two-parent" wage premium to those who grew up in two-parent families.

The second correlation is simply that married men earn more than unmarried men; they estimate this "marriage premium" for men to be about $15,900 more. (For married and single women, salaries are about the same.) It may be that married men are more serious about their careers or more aggressive in asking for raises, perhaps because they have more mouths to feed and bodies to clothe. It is also possible that women are simply more likely to marry hardworking men—it is hard to say. However, these two effects appear to reinforce each other, such that when one falls into both of these categories the premium for men and women combined rises to $42,000.

What is disturbing about the magnitude of this statistic is that family breakdown is likely a major channel for intergenerational poverty persistence in this country. And the ominous sign today is that the breakdown of the traditional family among the working class and the poor is almost certainly contributing to the alarming increase in inequality in our country.

While marriage rates were nearly identical among the poor and the rich just a generation ago, marriage has now become correlated with affluence. Marriage today in the United States is sadly becoming a symbol of social status. While it is just as common as ever among educated and well-off Americans (although occurring at a later age and preceded by cohabitation), marriage is becoming increasingly rare among the poor and working class, where itinerant relationships and serial cohabitation are now the growing norm. Children raised in the relative instability of these environments face grave disadvantages compared to their upper-middle-class peers raised in traditional family structures. That instability is then heaped on to their economic disadvantages.

Because of this relationship in our country between family functionality and inequality, Shrewd Samaritans understand that effective intervention often begins with the family. Perhaps the reason it does not receive more attention is that this kind of (often informal) intervention tends to prevent social problems from happening rather than addressing them after they start. Many of the larger macroeconomic forces are out of the control of local nonprofits and ministries, but one of the most effective things people can do at the local level is to help foster healthy families, which become greenhouses for raising successful, well-adjusted, successful children. Moreover, the soft skills, boundaries, and healthy ways of relating that children learn in a stable, loving family are as or more important than the hard skills they learn in school. And unlike many contexts in developing countries, there exist a plethora of economic opportunities in our country for people with a solid education, the skills to match a modern labor market, and the ability to work well with others. It is difficult to overestimate the importance for the role of local churches, parachurch groups, and nonprofits in the support of families in challenging times, in programming that supports love and stability within families, and in the care and nurture of their children.

The Identity Trap

Relative to the global poor, there is a discernable lack of charity in our country toward the domestic poor: *Why can't they simply make use of the opportunities that surround them?* The arguments typically shoot back and forth across political fault lines. Conservatives cite dysfunctional behaviors that keep the domestic poor mired in poverty. Liberals appeal to historical injustices and are quick to point out structural faults in a system they believe to be rigged to benefit the rich. The truth is that poverty is always the product of an array of factors working together, and one tends to perceive those factors as more clearly aligned with (and therefore, justifying) one's own worldview.

The truth is that each of these perspectives—the liberal view emphasizing historical injustices and the conservative view emphasizing character, culture, and choices—form part of a larger set of causal factors. Historical experiences of African, Asian, European, Latino, and Native American people and their reactions to these experiences have helped establish cultural norms within American subcultures. Some of these cultural norms are more and less helpful to securing the education, training, and subsequent employment that secure a place in the American middle class.

Historical and cultural factors work together in creating differences in educational outcomes across ethnic groups. Nobody disputes the basic facts: Test scores, rates of high school completion, and university graduation are lower for African and Latino Americans than European Americans, which are in turn lower than those of Asian Americans.[21] Moreover, a study by the Brookings Institution measuring time and effort spent doing homework paralleled the aforementioned average outcomes for each ethnic and racial group for educational outcomes.[22] What is responsible for this persistent gap? For thorny questions like these, it is easy to come up with pat answers that align with one's view of things, pat answers that are almost always incomplete or misleading.

Personal choices and behaviors, such as time spent studying, are also caused by other phenomena, rather than being simply causal in themselves. In other words, we have to take one step back to understand what might be the factors that could cause black and Latino students to put less effort into their schoolwork on average than Asians and whites. For example, low schooling effort may also be driven by historically low-quality schools or labor market discrimination that diminishes the rewards to schooling. Over time this may create a belief that "effort put into school doesn't pay for people like me."

Beliefs, which may be substantially affected by historical experiences, drive behavior. As behavioral responses become strongly nested within an identifiable group, poverty in rich countries becomes ghettoized, concentrated by geography and race. Geographic poverty becomes reinforced by limited access to the social and economic networks that facilitate economic prosperity for the mainstream majority. These networks not only tend to reinforce expectations of achievement ("So, Amber, where are *you* going to go to college?"), they also create the kinds of personal connections that facilitate success ("Mrs. White, I know an *excellent* SAT tutor for your daughter, Amber"). Domestic poverty is perpetuated by difficulties the poor face in venturing outside local networks.

In the final step in the chain, behaviors—both healthy and unhealthy—tend to manifest themselves as *identities*. Identities tend to cement a person's perception of who they are and of what they are capable. They create prescriptions for attitudes, behaviors, and choices. Behavioral economists have made important inroads into understanding how identity formation has played itself out among subgroups of the domestic poor.

Roland Fryer, an African American economist and winner of some of the profession's top research awards, has studied this dynamic, most famously in an article entitled "An Economic Analysis of 'Acting White.'"[23] His insight is that peer effects may create strong incentives for white students with borderline grades who are influenced to study hard in order to conform to the expectations of their peers based on what it means to be white. But a group of black students of similar ability may be influenced by peers not to study to avoid "acting white." For example, identity as an African American male in the inner city often prescribes a different set of behaviors (indifference to school, not backing down from conflict, a hard demeanor, and so on) that may be helpful for survival in a rough neighborhood but are unhelpful for moving *out* of that neighborhood. In this way, identities of "white," "black," or any other category can powerfully shape behavior and perpetuate economic prosperity or poverty within a given group, or something in between.

The relationship between historical injustice, culture, identity, and prescriptions for individual behavior presents an extreme set of challenges to the domestic poor. In many ways those living in domestic poverty may wish to integrate with the mainstream to take advantage of economic opportunities around them. But they become stuck in a vicious historical, behavioral, and economic cycle.

Effective Responses to Domestic Poverty and Inequality

Breaking the vicious historical, behavioral, and economic cycle of domestic poverty poses a formidable challenge. Aside from the cycle itself, there are political issues where, even in a functional democracy, impoverished subgroups often lack the political clout for obtaining the resources necessary to construct the economic ladder needed to climb out of the hole. But the more difficult problems are more difficult because they are less tangible. They involve a process of healing societal relationships between groups, trust formation, and social, psychological, and spiritual change within society as a whole. It involves individuals within dominant groups owning past injustices, consciously building bridges, and creating opportunities for their domestic neighbors from disadvantaged groups. Among the poor it often necessitates a careful and respectful process of identity reformation, not to necessarily encourage people of color to "act white" but to cement new and creative identities that prescribe behaviors that foster their own flourishing.

Because in rich countries capital and technology are widespread, the best interventions try to match education and skills to existing economic opportunities. This immediately leads to the question of how to improve schools for poor kids, especially in the inner city, one of the most controversial and heavily researched topics over the last half century, which will constitute my focus here. Does simply increasing school funding work? Traditionally there has been skepticism that simply increasing funding to schools would have much of an impact. This was the conclusion of a 1966 report led by Chicago sociologist James Coleman, which found that differences between schools accounted for a small fraction of student achievement.[24] If cultural and behavioral issues are primarily responsible for school failure in impoverished areas, then increasing school funding might simply be throwing money down the drain.

But while reasonably advanced for his time, Coleman wasn't able to identify a causal relationship between school spending and school performance. Of course, it would be unethical to literally randomize the level of funding between public schools. But new research has been able to exploit the near-randomness from the whimsical nature of government school-funding formulas to identify impacts from changes in schooling expenditures.

A recent study using variation in Michigan's school-funding formula finds that a 10 percent increase in per-pupil spending leads to a 5 percent increase in high school graduation, a 7 percent increase in likelihood that a student attends college, and an 11 percent increase in the probability of college graduation.[25] Another recent study finds that a 10 percent increase in per-pupil spending leads to about a third of a year in added years of completed education, 7 percent higher wages, and a significant reduction in adult poverty.[26] The evidence today seems to be fairly convincing—increasing school spending does improve educational outcomes. While there are other approaches that can improve upon simply spending more on education, the best evidence shows it is not just throwing money down the drain.

Two other approaches to improve schooling outcomes for US children have been school "voucher" programs and charter schools. Voucher provision offers what has become one of the most controversial approaches to improving school quality. By providing publicly funded grants for children to enroll in private schools, it allows children in the inner city to potentially bypass the public school system entirely. I have always been sympathetic to voucher programs, especially for inner-city children, because it would seem to allow choices that would otherwise be unavailable to them, along with putting competitive pressure on public schools to get their houses in order.

But the best and most recent studies show ambiguous results from school voucher programs.[27] On the positive side, several studies find strong and significant effects of vouchers among low-income African American students; however, these effects are not universal.[28] And while the competition induced by voucher programs does appear to improve public schools, the majority of studies find that the effect of receiving a school voucher on learning and schooling outcomes is uncomfortably close to zero. Moreover, the evidence shows that voucher programs lead to "sorting," where private schools skim the best students and teachers, leaving the unskimmed to the public schools. Taken together, the evidence on vouchers is mixed at best.

The positive impacts of charter schools are more firmly established. Charter schools receive funding from local school districts but are granted autonomy to experiment with innovative educational approaches. Among these, the largest and most celebrated in the United States is the KIPP (Knowledge Is Power Program) charter school network. About 96 percent of students in KIPP schools are African American or Latino, and 87 percent receive government assistance.[29] The KIPP schools are credited with innovating a "No Excuses" approach that emphasizes selective teacher hiring, strict discipline, development of positive behavior, intensive tutoring, and the relentless drive to equip all students with at least grade-level math and reading skills. The school day is long, typically from 7:30 a.m. to 5 p.m. on weekdays and 8:30 to 1:30 on two Saturdays a month. KIPP uses a holistic approach to develop children through building character traits such as zest, grit, optimism, self-control, gratitude, social intelligence, and curiosity.[30]

KIPP understands the power of identity. It reformulates the identity of students from that of disadvantaged minorities to students identifying themselves as scholars. Their model and the No Excuses approach has been adopted by numerous other charter schools.

How can we tell that schools like KIPP actually work? When charter schools have more applicants than spaces available, enrollments are allocated by lottery. These lotteries provide moments of celebration and heartbreak for anxious parents, as portrayed in the 2010 documentary *Waiting for Superman*. But the randomized nature of lotteries also provides a quasi-experimental feast for social scientists who wish to study their impacts.

Studies on KIPP and KIPP-related schools find substantial positive impacts on attendance,[31] nightly homework,[32] and more generally on time spent in school and school-related activities.[33] This added time devoted to school and the intensity of that time, including many hours spent in intensive individual tutoring sessions, pays off dramatically in scholastic test scores. A recent series of studies in the Boston-based charter schools carried out by MIT economist Joshua Angrist and his colleagues finds impacts on English-language test scores of about 8 percentile points *each year* at a KIPP school compared to the non-KIPP control group. (This means, for example, that a child beginning at the 50th percentile in test scores moves to the 58th percentile after one year and to the 66th percentile after two years.) Positive impacts on standardized math test scores are even higher, a median impact of about 14 percentile points on non-KIPP students each year.[34] Roland Fryer and his coauthors find slightly smaller impacts in studies of No Excuses charter schools in New York City and Washington, DC.[35]

By any standard, the impacts of KIPP are enormous. To put them in perspective, they are more than four times as large as effects typically found from other types of educational interventions, such as class-size reductions, teacher or student incentives, or more teacher resources.[36] They suggest that for African American students, three years at a KIPP high school in Massachusetts would eliminate the typical black-white achievement gap.[37]

What is responsible for such breathtaking results? Researchers unequivocally attribute KIPP's impact to its No Excuses approach.[38] What they find is that charter schools across the country that do not subscribe to No Excuses show mostly insignificant effects. Nor do the effects from No Excuses seem to be limited to "charter" schools; when the No Excuses approach was implemented in nine low-performing public schools in Houston, students showed similar gains. Thus, what some might consider an "old-school" approach to education—school uniforms, strict discipline, an emphasis on character development—is wedded with intensive individual tutoring, individual care, and the "new-school" recognition of the intrinsic value of each child. Such approaches seem to reflect what are considered to be characteristics of positive parenting: a nurturing relationship with high behavioral standards, discipline, and positive expectations.

Moreover, there seems to be a discernable pattern between the impacts of the KIPP schools and other successful global poverty interventions that simultaneously target root issues involving the whole person—such as identity and behavioral psychology—alongside teaching hard skills. That combination tends to be effective. These types of interventions go beyond addressing the needs of the poor in a single (necessary but insufficient) dimension, but simultaneously target social, psychological, economic, and sometimes spiritual concerns (e.g., self-reflection, humility, confession, forgiveness) in the pursuit of genuine human transformation.

The success of holistic approaches underscores the role of identity transformation and addressing poverty by addressing the needs of the whole person. In this respect, the measured impacts speak for themselves.

Chapter 5

POVERTY TRAPS

Part of the radical nature of the parable of the Good Samaritan was that acts of kindness were common among fellow Jews and others of the time, but they were generally practiced in the context of reciprocity. The logic behind reciprocal relationships goes something like this: "I will help you (neighbor) when you are sick/incapacitated/beaten up because, knowing you are part of my network, you will help me the next time I get sick/incapacitated/beaten up."

The lawyer seems to ask Jesus "Who is my neighbor?" not in the hope of *expanding* his concept of neighbor but to help him put boundaries around it. This would have lightened the neighbor-loving load for him, not only because it would limit his sphere of human obligation but also because such "acts of kindness" within one's network return like a boomerang: what goes around comes around.

Game theorists, researchers (like me) who use math to model social interaction, have understood for decades how positive patterns of behavior can emerge out of these mutual-assistance games. People are rational (in a self-interested sense) in helping others if they are able to expect the good deed to be reciprocated in the future when they themselves are in need. Indeed, this is the very basis of why the Econo-Man scratches the backs of his master's debtors—so that he can expect them to scratch his own back later.

Classic research in cultural anthropology has shown these kinds of reciprocal acts foster the survival of a group.[1] As such, the kind acts embedded in these reciprocal aid games are not pure forms of altruism. Jesus, for example, appears to understand this and discounts the kind of "altruistic" acts that occur in the context of reciprocating assistance: "If you love those who love you, what credit is that to you? Even sinners love those who love them. And if you do good to those who are good to you, what credit is that to you? Even sinners do that" (Luke 6:32–33).

Kindness toward people within our network is great—but it is often in our self-interest, and it should not be confused with kindness toward people outside it. The kindness the Samaritan showed toward the anonymous needy person, without capacity to reciprocate, redrew the lines for human commitment to neighbor.[2] Jesus makes it clear that he isn't nearly as impressed with love toward friends as he is with love for 1) enemies and 2) people who will have no opportunity to reciprocate.

Moreover, in the answer Jesus gives to the lawyer, he turns the question around from, "Who is my neighbor?" to, "Which of these three *was* a neighbor?" And in doing so, he reverses the emphasis to the subject and the verb rather than defining the boundaries of the object. When the Samaritan rescues the anonymous traveler, bandages his wounds, and pays for his hotel and recuperation, he expects no reciprocity. It is an act of pure altruism.

Traps Are Bad

I recently read a story in the *New York Times* about a man who was trapped inside an automatic teller machine. You may be wondering how a person could possibly become trapped inside an ATM. The man had been servicing the ATMs in a bank closed for remodeling while they remained functional to patrons outside the bank.[3] After working his way into the tiny space used to service the ATMs inside the bank, the door closed behind him, locking him into what bankers call the "ATM vault." Even more unfortunately, the man had left his cell phone outside. Hours passed while the thick walls of the vault muted his increasingly desperate pleas for assistance.

Then the man stumbled upon a creative idea. He began to slip notes through the receipt slot to ATM users reading, "Please help! I'm stuck in here, and I don't have my phone," but patrons were unmoved, apparently believing that they were the victims of some kind of *Candid Camera* stunt. Finally, a woman who received one of the notes after a cash deposit spotted a police officer. The helpful officer approached, and after carefully inclining his ear to the ATM and hearing the muffled cries for help behind the machine, he initiated the rescue of the embarrassed service technician.

We have probably all felt trapped at different times in our lives, metaphorically, emotionally, maybe even physically. But what actually defines a trap? People are trapped when they find themselves in an undesirable state that denies them the means to escape it. In the parable of the Good Samaritan, consider the trap of the beat-up man along the road. The very nature of his injured state prevented him from mobilizing to a place where he could recover from his injured state. The one thing he couldn't do, get somewhere safe to recover, was the one thing he needed most to do.

Similarly, being stuck in the vault denied the ATM technician access to the one thing—his phone—that would have quickly led to his rescue. A man trapped in a deep hole can't get to a ladder, the very thing that would allow him to escape the hole. A codependent person trapped in a bad relationship lacks the emotional resources needed to function independently, while the relationship itself erodes those same emotional resources. And as we will see, there are numerous reasons why being in a state of poverty may deny a person the very means to escape poverty. Poverty traps operate by the same principle as other traps.

After human society broke through the Malthusian Trap—in which any economic progress was checked by the increasing number of mouths to feed— many economists began to view prosperity as something inevitable for all humankind. This became a theory known as "economic convergence." Poor nations would catch up with rich ones.[4] And according to economist Simon Kuznets, after a period of increasing inequality during the early phases of economic take-off, even the poor people in rich countries would begin to catch up with rich people in rich countries.[5] Poverty was simply the beginning stage of a long but inexorable process toward economic development and widely shared prosperity. Convergence theory was both elegant and appealing because it had its root in an elemental economic concept, "diminishing returns," which governs just about every other economic relationship we understand. Since the first bits of capital in the hands of the capital starved are the most productive, capital should be most productive where it is most scarce—i.e., among poor people. Because it was among the poor where capital would realize the greatest return, capital would naturally flow in that direction, and greater capital accumulation among the poor would create a world of shared prosperity. There was even some empirical evidence to support aspects of the theory.[6]

However, as data from the last century has made clear, "No Country Left Behind" does not well describe the history of global economic growth.

Instead of economic convergence, what exists in the world today can be better described by pockets of virtuous cycles of prosperity and others of vicious cycles of poverty. Thus, one of the key questions in economics is why some are left behind and others are not. The answer that development economists have today is the existence of poverty traps. Like the guy stuck in the ATM, some people are kept in poverty because certain characteristics of poverty keep them from possessing the tools they need to escape it.

Put most simply, people are poor because they lack sufficient income-generating resources. These resources include physical capital, which makes labor more productive, especially when it comes in the form of new technology. It also includes *human capital*: economist jargon for education, training, and the accumulation of practical skills, which amplify people's productivity as they interact with capital and technology. For many in poverty, the nature of their situation actually prevents the very accumulation of the capital, technology, and skills that would help them to escape poverty.

Not all of the poor, and not all poor countries, are stuck in poverty traps. In the decade after the Korean War in 1953, the people of South Korea were desperately poor. Per capita income was about US$100, poorer than any country in the world today. But slowly at first, and then more rapidly, economic growth began to take place in key industries during the 1960s. South Korea began to invest in the education of its workforce; they became very productive and attracted more capital investment. By 1985, South Korea had reached a per capita income of about US$2,500. By 1995, the country had become an export powerhouse with per capita income growing to US$12,300 and to US$18,600 in 2005. Today per capita income in South Korea is about US$30,000, and South Korea's economy is bigger than Spain's.[7] South Korea has one of the highest rates of university completion in the world among twenty-five- to thirty-four-year-olds, 47 percent, significantly higher than the 36 percent figure in the United States, and so is doing better today in the race between education and technology.[8]

Statistics on child sponsorship show the amazing development of South Korea. Less than a decade after the end of the Korean war, Compassion International began its child sponsorship program in South Korea, where at its peak in 1967 it was sponsoring 16,700 impoverished children. By 1993 economic progress had taken root in the country so that there was no longer any need for the program; by that time the number of sponsored children had slowly declined to zero. But then something wonderful began to happen. The change in South Korea wasn't only economic; it was a spiritual transformation as well, and in short time South Koreans began to sponsor children from other countries. The number started slowly then quickly multiplied until today South Koreans sponsor more than 120,000 children through Compassion alone.[9] Apart from the United States, South Korea has now become the organization's largest supporting country in the world.

The escape from poverty by countries such as South Korea over the course of virtually a single generation is the exception rather than the norm. In most cases even identifying the causes of a poverty trap in a particular country is a substantial accomplishment. But how to distinguish between different kinds of poverty traps is critical to effective poverty interventions. Giving a cash transfer to the man stuck inside the ATM would have been a useless irony. Giving the man a ham sandwich would have been nice, in a temporary sort of way, but would not have solved his larger problem. A cell phone, on the other hand, would have been a trap breaker. Likewise, consider the trap faced by the beaten man in the parable. The Samaritan could have intervened in a number of ways that would have been only moderately effective, such as offering the beaten-up man some fresh water, or totally ineffective, such as handing him some coins. (A cell phone conceivably could have been helpful, if for only being two thousand years too early.) The Samaritan's intervention: transportation, taking him on his donkey to the inn where he could be cared for, and then paying for his care was the effective intervention.

In the same way, development economists have identified and classified a wide array of different types of poverty traps. Each of these traps suggests a correspondingly appropriate intervention in context. However, many people with the best of intentions working among the poor have indiscriminately implemented one-size-fits-all approaches to poverty alleviation, interventions that are ineffective because they overlooked the critical investigative step of diagnosis and targeting. Failure to identify and diagnose traps correctly results in chronic ineffectiveness. Distinguishing and identifying poverty traps is critical to poverty interventions just as diagnosis is critical to the successful work of a physician. Antibiotics are effective against bacterial infections, but they are ineffective against cancer; chemotherapy is the opposite.

It is helpful to make some distinctions among these different kinds of poverty traps. One distinction that we can make is between *individual* and *collective* traps. With individual traps, people or families lack a particular resource like food, technology, or credit that they need to advance from the trap. The example of the man stuck in the ATM is an individual trap. With collective traps, people make decisions that keep them poor because others around them are making the same decision, and thus nobody has an incentive to do things differently. Kids join gangs because all the other kids on the block are in a gang. Everyone would be better off if nobody was in a gang, but given that everyone else is in a gang, it seems better to join. So individual versus collective traps is the first important distinction.

The second distinction that can be made is between poverty traps that relate to *external constraints* and those that relate to *internal constraints*. When external constraints are in play, the poor are held back by such things as lack of access to schools, health care, infrastructure, employment opportunities, and credit. All of these we can think of as being "external" to the individual or family unit. They involve tangible material issues. What economists and other social scientists call "internal constraints" relate to how the psychology, spiritual worldview, perceptions of causality, and local customs influence behavior. These may be just as important, but they involve internal issues, ways that people think about and perceive the world.

Classification of Development Traps

Trap: Constraint:	Individual	Collective
External	Type I Nutrition, Savings, Credit, Technology	Type II Schooling, Investment, Health, Environment
Internal	Type III Hope, Aspirations, Self-Confidence	Type IV Spiritual Beliefs, Role Modeling, Customs

Figure 3

Category I Development Traps

Figure 3 classifies development traps into four categories based on whether they are *individual* or *collective* in nature, and whether they relate to *internal* or *external* constraints. As a result, we can clarify our thinking about poverty traps by whether they are external/individual, external/collective, internal/individual, or internal/collective.

Category I development traps are those that involve external economic constraints and cause individuals or individual families to be caught in a poverty trap that is more or less independent of the decisions and status of others in the community.

The Nutrition Trap

A tragic but widespread phenomenon within impoverished regions of the developing world is the Nutrition Trap, probably better phrased as the *malnutrition* trap. It is characterized by a vicious cycle of poverty stemming from low vitamin and caloric intake. It plays out something like the following: Impoverished rural households in Uganda are often only able to afford one meal per day, usually consisting of plantains and cassava. The lack of both quantity and quality of nutrition means that members of the family working their agricultural plot are unable to exert the energy and labor effort needed to produce a full yield on their crops. The low yield results in an income that is insufficient to provide enough food for the family during the next planting season. This leads to reduced productivity on the next crop, which again yields too little income to provide adequate nutrition to the family.

Lack of adequate nutrition governs a cycle that keeps the family chronically poor.

The Savings Trap

A basic economic relationship is that household income can be allocated in two ways, to consumption and to savings. Consumption includes not just purchases of food (which is literally consumed) but also purchases of things that are not literally consumed, like clothing, utilities, transportation, and so forth. Consumption is critical because it allows households to sustain themselves. But the downside to consumption is that it doesn't allow the household to move forward economically. This is the role for savings, which become channeled into investment in the household's future.

When many of us think of investment, the first thing that comes to mind are stocks, bonds, and 401(k) plans. But rural families in poor countries tend to invest their savings in herds, inventory for small household enterprises, small purchases of agricultural land, and in the education of their children, whose adult earnings serve as a retirement plan for their parents. However, we can think of virtually anything that involves a sacrifice of present consumption in favor of higher consumption in the future as a type of investment.

In the area where our NGO Mayan Partners works in western Guatemala, the income needed to provide for basic consumption needs for a normal-sized family is about 50 *quetzales* (the Guatemalan currency) per day, about US$7.00. However, the day-labor wage is also about 50 *quetzales* per day. As a result, simply to achieve subsistence, a family must devote virtually all of its income to meeting present consumption needs, and savings equals zero. This creates a poverty trap. Zero savings equals zero investment, and zero hope for a better economic state in the future. If only income were 10 *quetzales* higher, the family could save that extra 10 *quetzales* and earn some kind of future return on it, or perhaps invest that extra bit of income in more or better education for their children. But because income is so close to subsistence consumption, that hope for investing in a brighter future dims.

The Credit Trap

The Credit Trap is related to the Savings Trap, and if the Credit Trap did not exist, the Savings Trap might not create a trap in the first place. The Credit Trap stems from a very specific flaw in free markets that was discovered by 2001 Economics Nobel Prize winners Joseph Stiglitz and George Akerlof. This flaw they discovered relates to how the market for credit differs from normal markets like, say, bananas. In the case of bananas, a buyer can check to see if a banana is too green, too ripe, or too beat up with bruises from its voyage on the banana boat. If the buyer pays for the banana in cash, both the buyer and seller have full information about what they are exchanging in the banana transaction.

But the market for credit is different. Although the borrower knows whether he intends to repay the loan, the lender doesn't know this for sure, and there is "asymmetric information" in the transaction. This causes two problems for the poor: First, in credit transactions, lenders often have to engage in a costly screening process, a cost that is only justified for big loans, not the small loans desired by low-income borrowers. Second, the lender may insist that the borrower put up collateral against the loan. Collateral involves assets, and by definition, assets are something that the poor do not have much of.

As a result, absent some kind of purposeful intervention, such as microfinance targeted at the poor, low-income borrowers are excluded from formal credit markets. In the credit trap, the poor are unable to borrow their way out of poverty, even if they have productive investments. And the people who end up with access to credit are those who least need it.

The dismal implications of the Credit Trap are that the lack of credit inhibits convergence between the poor and the rich, resulting in increasing inequality. Moreover, enormous inefficiencies may exist in which productive investments by the poor don't occur, simply because they lack the ability to collateralize loans. And if there's anything economists won't put up with, it's inefficiency.

The Technology Trap

Movement out of poverty is facilitated by technology adoption. Technology makes people more productive. High-yield seeds, new fertilizers, and innovative cropping techniques dramatically increase the yields of small farmers. The power of mobile computing has dramatically increased the productivity of urban businesses owners. But technology only improves productivity if people *adopt* the technology, and herein lies the Technology Trap.

The poor tend to be more averse to the adoption of new technologies than the rich. Lower education levels and greater aversion to risk make the adoption of new technology a scarier prospect. Systems that support the use of new technology are typically less widespread among the poor. Moreover, the scale required for new technologies to be implemented is prohibitive for the poor, who, for example, farm on much smaller plots of land than the rich. For example, a corn farmer in the United States will use equipment like the John Deere 1725 CCS Stack-Fold Planter with the MaxEmerge 1.6-bushel hopper, insecticide applicator, and the newly improved pneumatic downforce system.[10]

A corn farmer in Guatemala drops a kernel of corn into a hole and covers the seed with dirt using his foot.

For all of these reasons, the poor may hesitate to adopt new technologies, even technologies that are far more productive than the old technology. The Technology Trap occurs as poverty causes the poor to stay with old, unproductive technologies, and the old, unproductive technologies cause the poor to stay in poverty.

The Sickness/Insurance/Housing Merry-Go-Round Trap

The Sickness/Insurance/Housing Merry-Go-Round Trap is one that affects the poor in places like the United States, especially in urban areas, and especially when someone is separated from a personal support network. I first learned of the trap when taking my freshman economics class on a field trip to St. Anthony's, a dining hall for the homeless in the Tenderloin, the poorest neighborhood in San Francisco. A winsome lay leader named Fitz explained the trap to us with a story that involved a recent graduate of our university (which held the students' attention nicely).

Fresh and graduated, the student was looking for work in the city. But he got sick, and his student health insurance had expired. This forced him to pay medical bills instead of his apartment rent. So he lost his apartment, and after a time of trying to recover on people's living room couches, he wandered the streets of the city, sick, homeless, and without a job. He even pawned his USF class ring in order to buy food and medicine. He couldn't get a job because he was sick. He couldn't get well because he didn't have health insurance or housing. And he couldn't get housing or health insurance because he couldn't get a job. My students agreed with Fitz that if a poverty trap can happen to a USF grad, it can happen to anyone. (Apparently he was even a business major.)

The critical intervention that broke the cycle was housing. Having a place to stay allowed him to get well, and then get a job. The job came with all kinds of benefits, like health insurance and worker's compensation, so if he got sick again he didn't have to fall off the deep end. That virtually anyone in a wealthy country like the United States can fall into such a trap is a blight on our system. Many homeless are perfectly capable of leading productive lives, but they have found themselves in the sickness/health-insurance/housing merry-go-round trap.

Category II Development Traps

Category II development traps are similar to Category I traps in that they involve external economic constraints, but are dissimilar in that they are collective traps, where the decisions of one person affect others and vice versa. Collective traps need to be addressed collectively. Addressing them at an individual level will often be ineffective and frustrating.

The Education Trap

For many decades, the response to low education in poor countries was simply to build more schools. This approach addressed the supply side of the schooling issue, but it failed to address the demand side. After all, why should one bother to spend twelve or more years in school if there are no jobs requiring higher levels of schooling? Because educated people are those who employ other educated people, lack of employment opportunities for those with more education is related to the number of *other* more educated people in the economy. As a result, there is a tendency for households to match the education of their children to roughly the level of education around them. In this way, a less-educated population tends to foster low levels of education in the next generation. In industrialized countries, there is a great demand for education because everyone realizes its value where ample opportunities exist for people with specialized skills (that are created by other people with specialized skills).

The Education Trap, in which households match the low educational choices of others in the economy, is referred to by economists as a *coordination failure*. If only everyone could coordinate on higher levels of education for their children, all could be better off. Governments try to do this through minimum schooling requirements for children, but in many places in the world these laws are violated so extensively that they become hard to enforce, and children routinely leave school before the minimum age.

What is required in such a context are not small attempts at fostering education for a handful of individuals who then have to migrate to other places to find work. More effective is a collective Big Push for education that is sustained over a generation or more—for example, as was undertaken in South Korea. Then economic incentives take over for parents to educate children, and truancy laws become virtually unnecessary.

The Investment Trap

Consider two regions in India, Bangalore and rural northeastern Uttar Pradesh. The former is a booming high-tech metropolis flush with modern capital investment, and the latter is one of the most populous but poorest regions in India. Why is one rich and the other poor? If we fully understood the answer to this question, development economists would be out of a job. But part of the answer lies in the "coordination failure" idea, similar to the one for education. Bangalore, the Silicon Valley of India, attracts investment because so much investment already exists there. All of the economic dynamism and opportunity fostered by previous investment makes the return to new investment higher. In rural Uttar Pradesh, a lack of investment discourages new investment, creating the collective trap.

Something about this may seem strange, particularly if you have had some exposure to economics. We are taught in basic economics classes that resources are more valuable where they are scarce, like water in a desert. But if this were so, Uttar Pradesh should attract more investment than Bangalore, making poverty naturally go away there. This is the basic idea that underlies theories of economic convergence, yet over the few decades we have learned that the world doesn't always work the way that neoclassical economics tells us it should. There is a counteracting force, which economists call *complementarities*, in which existing investment makes additional capital investment incrementally *more* productive rather than less productive. Complementarities exist in all kinds of investment, including investment in education and skills, where those with the highest levels of skills tend to want to match with other high-skilled people. They make places like Silicon Valley and Bangalore a magnet for investment and people with high-tech skills, but leave places like Uttar Pradesh behind.

How can understanding complementarities help us be more effective with the poor? Like the Big Push needed in education, there may need to be a Big Push in other types of investment as well. Just as it is better to invest in the education of all children in a single community, many kinds of investments may be needed simultaneously for a community to economically thrive. This may include investments in small enterprises, one or more large enterprises, water, electricity, transportation infrastructure, internet access, and so forth. If any of these is lacking, the payoff to the others may be low.

The problem is that this level of coordinated investment is expensive, and except in special cases (which unfortunately economists do not yet fully understand) the market is unlikely to create this happy scenario on its own. But it does help us to better understand critical issues in development practice. For example, support for microenterprises such as cash grants and microfinance is likely to have a bigger impact in places where the economy is generally better and where other investment is active too. Where the general economy is in the economic doldrums, interventions like microfinance are doomed to have low impacts. Understanding the implications of complementarities and coordination failures can be frustrating because it may be difficult to realize impacts from small and limited interventions in regions that economic forces have deemed unattractive. And these places are often home to the poorest of the poor.

The Environmental Trap

Poverty and the environment share a delicate relationship. In many places of the world, the poor are especially dependent on the environment for their sustenance, relying on its sustainable use for their well-being. The problem, brought to light by 2009 Nobel Laureate in economics Elinor Ostrom, is the "tragedy of the commons" in which society has a collective interest in a regulated, sustainable use of common pool resources like water, fisheries, and forests, but individuals have an incentive to take from them what they will. With the tragedy of the commons, the individual incentive to over-exploit common pool resources leads to collective irrationality in which all suffer through communal abuse of the environment.

Ostrom's insight is that, in the absence of a strong central state that can set boundaries on the exploitation of the environment, local communities need to create their own collective environmental institutions. If they are effective, these local institutions can create a system of carrots and sticks that reward sustainable users of the environment and punish violators.[11]

The problem is that in poor communities, the resources and organizational capability to create such institutions are limited. Without local institutional oversight over key environmental resources, and especially when population pressure is high, common pool resources can easily become overexploited: Fisheries become depleted, water resources dry up, deforestation robs villagers of access to wood and fuel. In this way, poverty is perpetuated and even accentuated by the degradation of the environment. But the poorer the community becomes through this degradation, the less able it is to possess the necessary resources to create the very institutions that would lead to sustainable use of the commons.

In the Environmental Trap, what is required is the difficult work of bringing together those with a collective interest in a clean and sustainable relationship with the environment in villages and city neighborhoods. This first requires some level of consciousness-raising about the problem (deforestation, land pollution, overuse of water, and so on), and then harnessing this communal interest to create the necessary institutions to regulate use of the commons.

The village in which our NGO Mayan Partners works in Guatemala is facing just such a problem today with communal water usage. The local water committee had established previous rules regulating water usage between homes and local coffee producers, but increasing population pressure has created a need for new rules. At stake is not only the health of families and children from a possible lack of clean water but also the viability of the village's principal cash crop, coffee. We realize that outsiders alone are unlikely to be able to create the institutions to address the Environmental Trap. This is nearly always best left to local leaders, and we hope that the local village leaders will have the wisdom and courage to do so.

Category III Development Traps

While external economic constraints such as lack of education, credit, and infrastructure can lie at the root of poverty traps, internal economic constraints may be just as important. Category III development traps involve internal constraints related to low aspirations, diminished self-confidence, and a sense of general hopelessness. While poverty can cause hopelessness, hopelessness can also perpetuate poverty and a vicious circle centered around internal constraints. A good deal of my own current research lies in trying to understand the dynamics of Category III traps.

The Aspirations Trap

Aspirations play a key motivating role in all of our lives. Nearly everybody who has succeeded at anything has been driven to some extent by aspirations. Most stories we hear from adults who managed to escape lives of childhood poverty began with some important type of aspiration. Many economists today believe aspirations to be a driving force behind upward economic mobility and movement out of poverty. External constraints can create obstacles, but if a human being is internally driven to accomplish something, she often figures out a way to deal with the obstacles. It is never wise to underestimate the human will.

But aspirations can be squelched. Debraj Ray, well-known development economist at New York University, talks about the "Aspirations Gap," the difference between what one aspires to do or be and what one observes as possible from the people in a peer group. If this gap is too small, little effort is exerted toward bridging the gap. If the gap is too big, then it is too frustrating to try. The Aspirations Trap happens when the Aspirations Gap is either too big or too small, but more often the latter. The Aspirations Trap causes the son of a peasant farmer to aspire to be a peasant farmer when he might have aspired to be a policeman, the daughter of a single mother to be a nurse when she might have aspired to be a doctor. A dearth of aspirations creates internal constraints that limit upward economic and social mobility, even when opportunities may exist. In this way, low aspirations become self-fulfilling prophecies.

The Self-Confidence Trap

Related to the Aspirations Trap is the Self-Confidence Trap. I may aspire to be a doctor, lawyer, or banker but have no confidence in my ability to get there. And if I don't believe I'm capable of moving from point A to my aspiration at point B, then perhaps trying isn't worth the effort. Economists, anthropologists, and psychologists often refer to this problem as a "narrow locus of control" or "low self-efficacy," but more generally it simply relates to a person's perception of her own capabilities and her ability to shape the events around her life. Aspirations are about dreams; self-confidence is about perceived capability.

The Self-Confidence Trap may stem from being part of a discriminated class in society, from being a person of color, from being female, or from simply being poor. It can begin at an early age in which real and tangible constraints, such as poor nutrition, poor health, or parents burdened with the constraints of poverty, prevent a child from excelling in school. The child falls behind, receives repeatedly negative feedback from schoolwork, and from that point on develops a low perception of his capacity to learn. If he believes himself incapable of learning, the child then begins to wonder why he should bother trying in school. So he stops trying, leading to further reduction in learning outcomes. Like the Aspirations Trap, the Self-Confidence Trap then realizes itself in a self-fulfilling prophecy. Some of the most effective interventions focus on developing the self-confidence of the poor and marginalized in society or include this as a key feature of programming in areas like schooling support and microenterprise development.

The Hopelessness Trap

When I was growing up, I used to watch a show after school called *The Banana Splits Adventure Hour*, which featured a cartoon segment based on *Gulliver's Travels*. One of the Lilliputians in the cartoon was a character called Glum, whose dialogue in perilous adventures with his peers mainly consisted of commentary like, "We'll never make it . . . We're doomed . . ." Because Glum believed all was hopeless, it was always left to someone other than Glum to rescue the group of Lilliputian cartoon friends from peril. Glum's hopelessness rendered him useless. Hopelessness can be paralyzing.

The Hopelessness Trap differs from the Aspirations Trap and the Self-Confidence Trap in that one may have aspirations and a generally positive perception of capability, but dark and powerful outside forces, or just plain old bad luck, are always perceived to thwart one's best efforts. Hopelessness becomes a learned response over time, sometimes referred to in psychology as "learned helplessness." For a long time, a series of unfortunate events or obstacles may have caused a person to remain in poverty. But the Hopelessness Trap can endure even when circumstances change and things really aren't hopeless anymore. Yet the perception continues that they are. The Hopelessness Trap takes root when hopelessness becomes a self-fulfilling prophecy. If there is no hope, then why bother? Of course, if one stops trying, then the worst often does happen, and pessimism wins.

Category IV Development Traps

Internal constraints can occur at an individual and independent level, as they often will in developed countries where greater opportunities exist. However, the Aspirations Trap, the Self-Confidence Trap, and the Hopelessness Trap can all translate into Category IV traps at the collective level as they become embodied in communal belief, custom, and culture from which it is difficult for any individual to deviate. I will discuss these together.

Let me first start with an example that differentiates Category IV traps from Category III traps. Although it has its own set of interesting issues, my community of the San Francisco Bay Area is one of the most intellectually, socially, and economically vibrant areas in the world. Jobs are ubiquitous, especially for people with reasonable technical skills, and the main things that bug us are the symptoms of worldly success: too much traffic and high housing prices. The Bay Area brims with aspirations, self-confidence grows on trees, and one could hardly describe the region as hopeless. However, there are thousands who have been left out of this general prosperity who themselves experience a grave sense of hopelessness. Our area may have the worst homelessness problem in the industrialized world, and there are far too many individuals and families who have fallen through the cracks who are mired in poverty traps best described as the Class I and Class III traps mentioned above. Yet the existence of these tremendous social problems among individuals, families, and subcommunities in the Bay Area does not mire the region in a collective development trap.

The situation is much different in the developing world. In the village where Mayan Partners works among the indigenous Quiché population, there is a collective set of internal constraints in the village that continually reinforce each other. One of these we have noticed is a lack of self-confidence in people's ability to solve their own local problems. This may stem from the remnants of colonization or from years of civil war, both reinforcing the idea that indigenous Mayans are incapable of meeting their own challenges.

The challenge of economic development becomes far greater when internal constraints become embedded in a community. I heard a missionary speak not long ago about the challenges of community development work with the Cheyenne Indians on a reservation in South Dakota. Years of injustice against the Cheyenne had infused a sense of hopelessness and helplessness into the culture of the reservation. The sense of hopelessness is so pervasive, unemployment so ubiquitous, alcoholism so rampant, domestic abuse so commonplace, that it has made it hard for people to even conceive of a different life. Here the optimism of a single individual threatens the last refuge of communal psychological comfort, the thought that "nothing was possible anyway."

In such a context, collective internal constraints create a trap where it becomes impossible for any single person to deviate from a community-wide pessimism: aspirations are ubiquitously bleak, collective self-confidence is low, and hopelessness becomes embedded in the collective psyche of the culture. It becomes exceptionally difficult for any individual living in such a community to think differently because deviation from pessimistic group-think is painfully difficult. Dreams of a better life are hard to sustain when everything and everyone around you seems to shout that such dreams are impossible for you, anyone in your community, or anyone who looks like you. Any aspirations of a young Cheyenne on a depressed reservation, or an African American youth in an urban ghetto, or a Quiché teenager are all too easily quashed.

Collective internal constraints often originate through different forms of historical oppression and injustice, but they can persist even when the rules of society change and new opportunities emerge. Policies such as affirmative action in the United States may have addressed some of the external constraints faced by African Americans in the United States, but they have not resulted in economic convergence between whites and blacks in our country. This is partly because they failed to address some of the collective internal constraints that developed when external constraints were especially severe. South Africa ended apartheid, but the gap between whites and blacks persists, partly from centuries of blacks being taught that they were inferior to whites. Laws have been enacted since 1949 in India to prevent discrimination against the Dalits, a group of people considered part of the "untouchable" classes, but even as it has taken decades for enforcement of these laws to take root, it will take even longer to remove the internal stigma faced by groups like the Dalits in Indian society.

Perhaps hardest is the challenge of working with communities who simultaneously face collective external economic constraints and collective internal constraints. Development work among such groups can be painfully slow, and practitioners can become frustrated when the relief of external economic constraints—building schools, paving roads, providing microcredit—fails to yield the expected results. But understanding the formidable challenges in these contexts may provide some sense of liberation through a readjustment of expectations. Measurable change takes place in these situations, not over years, but over generations.

Being able to identify a community as existing in a Category IV trap nearly always suggests an approach not only broadly based but also holistic in nature. Interventions need to penetrate deeply into a community to be effective, while simultaneously addressing both internal and external constraints. In such contexts, many of the traps discussed here may be operative simultaneously, just as a person in poor health may suffer from multiple infirmities. For practitioner work to be effective, the different issues must be patiently identified and diagnosed, with corresponding interventions, where each is likely to be necessary but insufficient in themselves. This is yet another reason why understanding the different poverty traps that exist in a particular context is so imperative, and why holistic interventions that address both external and internal constraints together can be critical to realize genuine impact.

Part 3

EFFECTIVE AND INEFFECTIVE POVERTY INTERVENTIONS

Chapter 6

AN IMPACT FRAMEWORK FOR SHREWD SAMARITANS

One of the most popular schools of thought in global ethics today is a movement called *Effective Altruism*. Founded on the work of Princeton philosopher Peter Singer, it offers a self-contained system of principles for responding to global poverty. Singer's books, *The Life You Can Save* (2009) and *The Most Good You Can Do* (2015), lay Effective Altruism's theoretical groundwork. They are worldwide best-sellers, leading *Time* magazine to call Singer one of the "100 most influential people in the world."

Effective Altruism has encouraged people to give generously and maximize impacts from giving; there is no greater fan of "bang for the buck" than Singer. Indeed, there are so many things to like about Effective Altruism that they come close to outweighing its detractions. The Effective Altruism movement has had such a powerful effect on the way globally concerned people have reflected on and responded to issues of global poverty that it is critical to review it: the good, the bad, and the ugly.

Singer's case begins in *The Life You Can Save* with a scenario that provokes the following question: Would you sacrifice your new business suit to dive into a pond to save a drowning child? The right answer is, of course you would. Ruining your suit is nothing compared to a child's life. But then Singer's got you: this choice has logical implications for your response to global poverty. If you could save an impoverished child's life for the cost of a new suit—and Singer argues persuasively that you could—then why don't you?

Singer's argument rests on a cool, calculated utilitarianism. If you believe that every life has equal value, then the life of each child in sub-Saharan Africa matters as much as your own. A few hundred dollars may buy a frivolous luxury for you but yield the basic necessities of life to the impoverished child, so the only consistently ethical response is to make such a transfer. And in the extreme version of Singer's world, we should only stop giving when we ourselves become so increasingly desperate that our need for the next dollar becomes equal to that of the poorest person on earth.[1]

This is hard stuff, maybe even crazy stuff. Even Singer himself admits that he doesn't go that far. (Instead, he claims to give about one-third of his income away to the most effective charities he can find on the web.) In its best light, Singer's argument can be best summed up as, "We should all give more, and give more effectively." And to this point, I am attracted to Effective Altruism. It presents an internally coherent framework for weighing the "needs" of rich people relative to the greater needs of the poor. It forces us to think through logical inconsistencies in our choices, and it leads many people in the right direction with their giving.

But there are profound problems with Effective Altruism. The moral basis of Effective Altruism is "consequentialism," a philosophy in which noble ends are used to justify means that many would find morally unacceptable. Since all lives are equal, Singer relegates our commitments to those close to us, our family and friends, to mere sentimentality, and he argues that they should be no greater than to a person overseas. Many also have trouble with Singer's assertion that the value of life stems from the ability to experience happiness and pain, from which flows his moral case for infanticide.[2] In some ways to his credit, Singer boldly propels his consistent train of reasoning full speed ahead, even when the train tracks lead it cascading over the edge of a cliff. Thus, even as Singer successfully takes us through the respective states of Ignorance and Indifference to Investigation and Impact, his path leads us back to a kind of twisted Idealism. As a philosophical framework to guide our actions to address global poverty, Effective Altruism is not the rock on which we want to build our house.

Addressing Global Poverty Through a Framework of Human Dignity

I want to offer an alternative to Effective Altruism that instead places human dignity and human flourishing at the forefront of our concern for the global poor. The roots of the Human Dignity framework lie in Catholic social teaching with even deeper roots in Judeo-Christian texts and ethical traditions. It is a framework that has been adopted either consciously or unconsciously by most mainline Protestant and evangelical global poverty organizations.[3] Echoes of the Human Dignity framework even appear in other world religions such as Islam[4] and Buddhism,[5] and a secular version of it underlies the United Nations' development roadmap toward the year 2030.[6] A considerable amount of public funding supports faith-based organizations espousing the Human Dignity framework: World Vision and Catholic Relief Services are two of the largest recipients of funding from USAID.[7]

Some of the growing interest in the Human Dignity framework is driven by a concern that international development that places human dignity on the back burner can quickly become dehumanizing. Governments, donors, and NGOs can become too easily attached to a metric in which human dignity becomes subservient to a score sheet of economic and welfare outcomes. As my colleagues at Notre Dame, Paolo Carozza and Clemens Sedmak, write in their introduction to a new volume on human dignity, "Development work without sensitivity to human dignity is blind, and an understanding of human dignity without paying attention to human experiences and practices is empty."[8]

So what exactly is human dignity? The Judeo-Christian belief is that human beings have intrinsic value as creatures that are in some way made in the image of God, or the *Imago Dei,* as portrayed in the first chapter of the book of Genesis. Our human identity as "chips off the old block" of the Creator is reflected in:

1. the delegation of stewardship over the earth, its resources, and animal life;[9]
2. an elevated consciousness and ability to self-actualize and reason;[10] and
3. an agency permitting moral choices that exceeds that of other created life.[11]

In this way, human dignity is fundamental to human personhood. As Harvard's Donna Hicks describes, "Honoring the dignity of others has nothing to do with any of their unique qualities or accomplishments. . . . It is a birthright."[12] But human dignity can be violated. This happens to all of us in small ways through petty insults and minor humiliations. But tragically, also in more severe ways. Extreme violations of human dignity, such as poverty, brutality, oppression, or other forms of suffering and degradation, occur when the *Imago Dei* is severely compromised.

Good interventions recognize and affirm human dignity, redressing its violations. When we buy a meal for the homeless man, we recognize his dignity and communicate to him his intrinsic value. When we sponsor a fresh-water well in a remote village, we affirm the dignity of the villagers to drink without becoming sick. When we help the exploited child prostitute off the street into a warm and supporting environment, we redress violations to her dignity. As such, the work of recognizing, affirming, and redressing violations to human dignity is that of elevating human beings to their status as made in the *Imago Dei*. Recognition of human dignity is perhaps the most fundamental quality of a Shrewd Samaritan. It reflects a deep, penetrating insight into the value of every human being.

Related to human dignity is the concept of "human flourishing," which is related to the status of human beings as the *Imago Dei* but emphasizes human outcomes. As human dignity is restored, people begin to flourish, developing unique gifts and talents. They begin to express their individual creativity in ways that benefit others, and in small but important ways, reflect the creativity and goodness of the Creator. Some of the fruit of human flourishing is exchanged in markets as goods and services to the mutual benefit of all. As a result, helping the poor to participate in markets can facilitate important aspects of human flourishing.

The relationship between human dignity and human flourishing is somewhat analogous to the secular relationship between relief and development. Redressing violations of dignity is the rectifying of a negative; fostering human flourishing is the promotion of a positive.

Human flourishing is captured in the Hebrew word *shalom*, which conveys the idea of human beings living in wholeness, wisdom, prosperity, creativity, and tranquility. Living in *shalom*, people exist in a state of harmonious mutuality with neighbor, nature, and Creator.[13] Barriers to *shalom* and to human flourishing exclude the poor from social relationships, from having a voice in decisions that affect their welfare, from a fruitful and sustainable relationship with the earth and its resources, and from participation in the natural exchange within markets—or it forces them to participate in ways that violate their human dignity.

The Human Dignity framework does not contradict the best principles of Effective Altruism. Rather, it subsumes them. Altruism and effectiveness are important to the Human Dignity framework. We cannot help those in need if we are not altruistic, and we are unhelpful if we are ineffective. Both are necessary but often insufficient for human flourishing. The great Russian writer Aleksandr Solzhenitsyn seemed to touch on this as he reflected about his life in a Soviet prison camp, "I came to realize that the object of life is not prosperity as we are made to believe, but the maturity of the human soul."[14] The end is not perpetual material accumulation but *shalom* and human flourishing.

But most human beings do not flourish living in destitution. This is why achievements in areas such as health, educational, and economic outcomes are extremely important goals. Yet they are *intermediate* goals, not ends in themselves. Obviously not: Hitler's Germany had one of the most healthy, educated, and technologically advanced populations in history, but no *shalom*.

A Human Dignity framework shapes not only the motivation and objectives of poverty work but the nature of it as well. Not just our goals themselves but our interventions, our *means*, must acknowledge and affirm human dignity. Consider the difference between carelessly tossing a five-dollar bill at a homeless person (a violation of human dignity) with handing him the money, stooping down to look him in the eye, and wishing him well (affirming his human dignity).

Moreover, the end goal of human flourishing is not purely definable in material terms. As Carozza and Clemens suggest, it is not best understood as an "outcome" like we might think of in terms of specific goals for graduation rates, eradicating a disease, or growth in GDP, although these may form important components to human flourishing. The tangible and material are important to global development within a Human Dignity framework; malnutrition, disease, and ignorance are violations of human dignity. But the spiritual, ethical, social, psychological, nonmaterial, and intangible are central too.

As an example, consider the construction of an infrastructure project, say of a dam to control flooding and generate electricity, where the project would involve a mass relocation of a subgroup of people while perhaps benefiting the majority of citizens overall. A consequentialist framework would evaluate the dam project based on the outcome of a financial cost-benefit analysis. A Human Dignity framework would consider a positive result from a cost-benefit analysis as one condition for undertaking the dam project. It would also ask other questions: Does the uprooting and relocation of indigenous communities cause a violation to human dignity that exceeds the gains to human dignity that would accrue from building the dam? Is it possible in the process of relocation to find ways that minimize disruptions to relationships and community life? Such an approach aligns an assessment of costs and benefits more closely to human dignity and human flourishing rather than strictly in terms of material gains and losses.

Another example is a decision we made recently in Guatemala with Mayan Partners. We had developed a pattern of holding health clinics on visits, where doctors and nurses in our group would attend to hundreds of patients in a church or school classroom. Upon some reflection, we decided to switch to undertaking home visits to the sick, partly because they were sicker than those who could make it to the clinic, but also because it allowed us more time and care with each patient in a way that we felt was more consistent in affirming their dignity. With the clinic, it felt like we were running them through a mill. Efficiency is important, but it is not the paramount value. Our ultimate responsibility is not to efficiency but to love people as we love ourselves.

A Human Dignity framework values empathy, mutuality, and accompaniment.[15] It avoids blanket interventions that may be ineffective outside context. Rather it listens, studies, and responds to the poor within the context of their articulated problems, needs, and aspirations. One specifically neglected characteristic of the Effective Altruism movement is the absence of mutuality. Singer's narrative of the helpless drowning child and the hero-savior summarizes the approach well. The poor have nothing to offer the rich and must be saved by them. The role of the rich, in contrast, is to funnel cash through NGOs to the poor. Here there is little emphasis on mutuality or partnership. The poor are assumed to have little to offer; they are the recipients, and the rich are the givers. Yet even secular research has demonstrated how a patronizing approach becomes disempowering.[16] Human Dignity seeks partnership, accompaniment, and mutuality, perhaps even at some sacrifice to material objectives.

The Human Dignity approach views giving as an integral part of human flourishing. In the counterintuitive math of heaven, givers likewise receive, perhaps even more than they give.[17] The Christian belief is that, as we enter into relationship with the needy and the poor, in some mysterious way we actually commune with Christ himself: "Whatever you did for one of the least of these brothers and sisters of mine, you did for me."[18] In my experience, this phenomenon seems at times to transcend actual belief. Christ often seems to meet the giver in the act of giving, whether they know it or not, and is manifest in a kind of mysterious joy. Some of the richest and most rewarding aspects of people's lives, whether they consider themselves secular or spiritual, often come from accompaniment of the needy and the poor through their adversity. If the secular view is really true, that the material is what ultimately matters, one wonders why this would be so.

The Christian view leaves little ambiguity regarding motivation to serve the poor: in serving *them*, we directly serve *Him*. While a more torturous process of reasoning is required to create a prescriptive link between atheism and altruism, serving the poor is an action congruent with Christian belief at the most fundamental level. The statistics connect the dots: Faith-based NGOs disproportionately populate the international development world. About 60 percent of US NGOs working in international development are faith-based, the vast majority of them Christian.[19] It also explains why many faith-based development efforts of organizations like Food for the Hungry, Hope Worldwide, Compassion International, and World Vision are difficult for governments and secular efforts to replicate. This is simply because so much of their labor is supplied by in-country volunteers from local churches. The cost of motivating paid employees to replicate care for children with the same energy of church-based volunteers, at a Compassion International tutoring center, for example, is prohibitively high.

Personally, even more than carrying out fruitful research projects (from which I genuinely derive great satisfaction), I receive something greater from visits with our partners and friends in western Guatemala. Moreover, many of us in Mayan Partners feel that we receive more than they do from the partnership, although the balance on their side is greater in purely material terms. Serving the poor, especially in a direct way, is not the "cost" it is identified as in the secular utilitarian framework. We find joy when we align our will with our Creator's purpose for our lives—to put it in a California way, as we "surf His wave." In giving, we begin to imitate our Creator, and as a result we find joy. Part of human development is to help create the capacity for the poor to give in new ways as well and to help them realize the divine joy in giving.

A Practical Examination

What are the practical implications in the difference between the two approaches for poverty work? Let's divide poverty interventions into two categories based on whether they require a behavioral response by beneficiaries. Many medical- and health-related interventions such as deworming medicine, vaccines, restorative surgeries, and the like yield undisputed biological benefits within a population. Decision making within the Effective Altruism and Human Dignity frameworks parallels most closely in this domain. For health interventions, we generally want to save or prolong the most human lives that we can, balanced with normal concerns for quality of life. We should give generously to many of these efforts, simply conscious of the large impact our giving will tend to have over a population.

For other types of interventions where behavior, response, and relationship are more deeply interconnected with the intervention (such as in microfinance, cash grants, the formation of village cooperatives, and approaches to education), the two frameworks are more likely to diverge in both ends and means.

Health interventions alone—for all their magnificent benefits—will not create broad-based prosperity. Similarly, educational and enterprise interventions—for all their magnificent benefits—will not necessarily develop the character and set of others-centered values required for people to successfully lead communities and nations. While health, education, and enterprise are critically important, if we ever begin to look at human development in this purely technocratic sense, we have missed the larger picture of development as human flourishing.

Moreover, while staying with this larger picture, it is impossible to say whether purely health-related interventions yield a bigger long-run impact on the trajectory of a country than one that results in the development of thoughtful and morally developed citizens who bring a commitment to a higher level of civic leadership and governance. The argument can be made that early childhood interventions, nurturing of children into their teens, and the inculcation of intellectual curiosity, grit, and moral values may very well produce the larger impact. They may be more likely to lead to the elevation of the moral and ethical leader—an Abraham Lincoln, a Martin Luther King Jr., or a Nelson Mandela—whose leadership transforms an entire society. However, because these impacts are hard to forecast and measure, they are hard to pick up in studies like randomized controlled trials. Yet they are critical to the destiny of a people group or nation.

Compassion International, for example, is a child-sponsorship organization deeply rooted in the Human Dignity framework. Its goals of child development are similar in some respects to other organizations' in terms of health, education, and other typical and measurable outcomes. But they differ in other ways. As much as the organization cares about broadly based educational and health outcomes, they also care about the development of character and the kind of leadership that is able to transform societies, which forms the basis for its leadership development program. They also care about fostering community. Organizations with an Effective Altruism approach tend to focus on providing material inputs: school buildings, desks, textbooks, and so forth. In contrast, Compassion invests in thousands of hours of tutoring, nurturing, and encouraging. The end result from this approach is not merely a series of input-output statistics but the development of community leaders with character and moral compass.

I have also become sympathetic to Heifer International's "passing on the gift" approach, in which they ask beneficiaries of a heifer to pass on the first female calf to another local family in need.[20] An Effective Altruist and even some economists might scoff at this approach. They might argue it is inefficient if economies of scale or the existing know-how from raising the first heifer can be realized to produce more benefits when the calf stays in the first household. But the goal of Heifer's approach is to turn *receivers* into *givers*; it is laden with an understanding of human dignity that is missing in the materialist approaches.

Even economics Nobel laureate Amartya Sen's conception of "Development as Freedom" begs the question: freedom to do what? Whether someone uses his greater economic freedom to watch online pornography or care for others in his community is a decision on which Sen is unwilling to place a value judgment. The Human Dignity framework is not. We are unafraid to value choices on how people leverage their prosperity, or what "human development looks like." We intervene on behalf of the poor that they in turn may flourish, including directing their own talents and resources toward the welfare of others.

A Human Dignity framework also can help guide us around some of the thorny questions related to how to *do* interventions. One of these is the problem of patronization. Patronizing the poor may undermine human dignity by teaching people that they are incapable of providing for themselves. Other instances may justify a degree of patronization, especially in the complicated areas of health and medicine, but we must always be wary of it.[21]

Another of these difficult questions relates to boundaries. Part of the problem with the Effective Altruism framework is that, like people living in the idealism phase, it contains no internal boundaries and no guide for setting them. A framework without boundaries is an unsustainable framework. In thinking about giving in this misguided way, people undermine their own dignity in the alleged interests of others. If the purpose of your life is to help others to flourish, then it is important to establish principles around the giving of your time and your money that allow you to do this sustainably.

Jesus calls us to go the extra mile out of our zone of comfort, perhaps well outside it. But the "extra mile" remains a finite distance. Even Jesus established boundaries. He often withdrew from the crowds to spend time alone. He limited his close contacts to a dozen men, several women, and a few closer friends such as John, Peter, and Mary Magdalene. Only in going to the cross did he fully allow his boundaries to be violated.

How much should we sacrifice the needs of our own families to help the poor? To answer this, I think it is helpful to take the perspective of a third, disinterested party, what the economist Adam Smith called "the impartial spectator," someone whose judgment on matters of ethics you believe to be right and true, yet is impartial to the matter at hand.[22] If that impartial spectator would say you are neglecting important needs of your family by giving too much, then you are probably giving too much. If your giving is so negligible that it doesn't even put the tiniest crimp in your lifestyle choices, then an impartial spectator might suggest that you are probably giving too little. I refer to money here, but the same could be said of time.

People must discern these boundaries for themselves, for we all have different tolerances in different areas. For some, the trials of living in the inner-city are not a big issue. For others, like me, they can be draining. Some people are terrified by cross-cultural situations, improvised toilets, and foreign languages. Others, like me, are energized by them. Everyone is different, but the principle is the same: find the place to give where you find life, and you will flourish if you can give there in a sustainable way. In the next chapters, we will discuss how to give in an effective way as well.

Chapter 7

MICROFINANCE, ENTERPRISES, AND CASH GRANTS

With a better understanding about the causes and consequences of poverty, we have the foundation to begin to talk about cures. If our goal is to release people from poverty traps and to foster human flourishing, what interventions are effective at doing this?

In these next two chapters, I will discuss the evidence for the effectiveness of twenty global poverty interventions. All of these are fairly common, but I chose many of these to be ones that ordinary people support financially or with their time. Another criterion I had in choosing the twenty is that they have been rigorously evaluated through randomized controlled trials or other types of rigorous quasi-experimental studies.

My goal here is not to share my opinions as much as to try to build a bridge between the scientific studies on the impacts of these interventions and you, the potential advocate, donor, or volunteer.

How to Distinguish Good Studies from Bad Studies

How do we tell which studies are good and which are bad? The main point to keep in mind is the old adage "correlation is not necessarily causation." Good studies estimate the "causal effects" of programs. They do this by measuring differences between the outcomes of program beneficiaries and a "counterfactual," or what would have happened to beneficiaries if the program didn't exist. It is easy to measure outcomes on program beneficiaries. The tricky part is knowing what would have happened to beneficiaries if the program hadn't been there. Good studies create good counterfactuals, and bad studies create bad counterfactuals.

Bad impact studies will often carelessly compare program participants with nonparticipants. You should beware of some organizations that try to convince donors of the impact of their program from doing exactly this. These studies may yield upwardly biased measures of impact because those who take the initiative to participate in the program may have been better off than nonparticipants anyway. This may lead you to support an ineffective program. The reverse can be true as well: some programs may target the poorest individuals for their program, and so comparing the outcomes of beneficiaries and nonbeneficiaries would bias impact estimates downward. This could lead you to reject programs that are actually doing good work. Bringing the most disadvantaged up to the level of everyone else could mean the organization is actually doing great work!

Other nonprofits present results to potential donors using before-and-after comparisons with program beneficiaries themselves. Beware of these as well, because the status of a beneficiary before program participation does not typically create a valid counterfactual to her outcome afterward. For example, an entrepreneur may take a microloan when an economic opportunity presents itself; it is easy to then falsely attribute an increase in income to the loan rather than to the opportunity. This very problem led people to overestimate the impact of microfinance for decades.

Randomized controlled trials (of a decent size) generate good counterfactual outcomes. Because program beneficiaries are chosen randomly, there is no reason to believe that their outcomes would have been any different from the (randomly nonchosen) control group. When experimentation is impossible, good researchers use quasi-experimental designs that are able to simulate a control group in the absence of the experimental ideal.[1]

The Shrewd Samaritan Rating System

Because I have always found the work of a movie or music critic to be rather alluring, I will partially live out this unrealized fantasy by rating each poverty intervention on a five-star system. Actually, each intervention will receive *three* ratings. The first is the effectiveness of the intervention: the degree to which rigorous scientific evaluation has found the intervention to be *effective* to do what it is supposed to do, irrespective of cost and of how much we might expect the intervention's impact to yield wider benefits that might be associated with human flourishing and broader well-being. There are some interventions where there remains significant uncertainty and debate about whether they work. I will note these in the text.

The second evaluates the relative *cost effectiveness* of the intervention: to what degree the intervention fosters broadly defined human flourishing relative to its cost. Because it is unfair to compare expensive interventions to cheap ones, the rating for cost-effectiveness gives a rough gauge of benefit relative to cost. A mostly ineffective intervention is unlikely to get any stars unless it is at least somewhat effective and really, really cheap.

In general, the number of stars an intervention receives for cost-effectiveness will depend on three factors: a) how effective good research demonstrates it to be in its domain of impact (e.g., how much deworming medicine eradicates worms); b) how important its domain of impact is in the larger picture of human flourishing (e.g., how much being worm-free is vital to human flourishing); and c) how much it costs.

For those who like equations, human flourishing cost-effectiveness is then $(a \times b)/c$. This rating is not just "bang for the buck" effectiveness divided by cost, which I will call "Bang-2" for short, but "bang for the bang for the buck," or what I will call "Bang-3." Interventions with a high Bang-3 rating have a big impact on human flourishing relative to their cost.

My third rating is for "generalizability." Some interventions are highly effective, but only when local conditions are suitable. At the extreme, they are Goldilocks interventions, very sensitive to context, where conditions have to be "just right" for them to realize impacts. With such an intervention, targeting the right beneficiaries is critical. Other interventions work pretty much everywhere, and one does not have to be quite as sensitive to context.

These ratings represent what I believe to be the current consensus in the development field about impacts; ratings will (hopefully) change in subsequent editions of this book as new evidence rolls into scientific journals.

Under my rating system for effectiveness, if rigorous studies consistently show that researchers cannot find statistically significant impacts from an intervention, the intervention gets zero stars. If scientific studies lean slightly toward showing modest positive effects, the intervention gets one star; leaning slightly further, two stars. Interventions that consistently show modest effects receive three stars; those that consistently show strong effects, especially if they are long-term effects, receive four. The most effective poverty interventions, those that overwhelmingly show statistically significant, large, and long-term effects—what we might say consistently yield "transformative effects" to beneficiaries in proper context—receive five stars.

What Works in Microenterprise Interventions?

In this chapter I will focus on interventions designed to boost small enterprises, which employ over half the workers in the developing world (52 percent compared to 41 percent in rich countries[2]). The development of microenterprises in low-income countries is critical for a number of reasons. First, they represent a means of livelihood for a disproportionate number of the global poor. Second, a society full of little capitalists helps to create a business-oriented middle class that allows an economy to flourish. Microenterprise interventions have presented a challenge to policy makers and practitioners for decades, and it is only recently that researchers have begun to discover which ones work—and which ones don't.

Microcredit
Effective: ★★☆☆☆ Bang-3: ★★★★☆ Generalizability: ★★★☆☆

There are few poverty interventions in the developing world that have run the gamut of the popularity cycle as thoroughly as microcredit. Microfinance institutions provide financial services to the poor and are most known for providing microcredit—small loans to entrepreneurs in the developing world. They also often provide a vehicle for savings and, more recently, insurance. Until the 1980s many practitioners scoffed at the idea of making small loans directly to the poor. The common wisdom was that the poor wouldn't repay.

They would simply use their loans for food and then default. The small loan size would never justify the legal hassle of recouping the loan. Thus, small loans were never made in the first place.

In 1983 the Grameen Bank, founded by Muhammad Yunus, became the first major lending institution that proved the global poor were bankable. Its group-lending methodology and minuscule default rate began a revolution. The innovative BancoSol in Bolivia showed, in 1992, that microcredit could be commercialized, and legions of imitators followed. The awarding of the Nobel Peace Prize in 2006 to Yunus for his work in microcredit only added to its recognition and popularity. The number of borrowers spread exponentially across the globe, growing from 13 million in 1997 to well over 205 million by 2010.

For years the development field lived in a microcredit lovefest. Economics Nobel laureates loved microcredit because it helped overcome a natural failure in credit markets that disproportionally hurt the poor, creating its clear intellectual foundation. Liberals loved microcredit because it was targeted at the poor, typically at women, often at artisans. Conservatives loved microcredit because it promoted capitalism and self-reliance. There are few things in the world that bring the political right and left together, but microcredit has been one of them. That is, until research began to show it didn't help poor people as much as we thought.

There were hints early on that the impact of microcredit wasn't living up to the anecdotes of entrepreneurial success stories emblazoned on microlender webpages. Flaws in the seminal empirical study that had shown large and significant impacts from the Grameen Bank's microcredit program[3] had made it the favorite whipping child of young aspiring development economists, who were beginning to prefer randomized controlled trials for evaluating poverty programs. One of the earliest of these, a study in Thailand, failed to show impacts on an array of household and enterprise outcomes from microcredit lending.[4] This led to more and larger studies, culminating with a coordinated study of microcredit through randomized trials in six countries—Bosnia, Ethiopia, India, Mexico, Morocco, and Mongolia—that give us the best current evidence on microcredit's effectiveness on borrowers.[5]

There are nuances with microcredit impacts, and Shrewd Samaritans need to learn to live with these nuances. On the positive side, these studies show microcredit is good at fostering entrepreneurialism. There is evidence that it increases the size of small businesses, the hours that entrepreneurs devote to their businesses, and their freedom to expand them. It also allows households to smooth out shocks to their income, which often pose a bigger threat to poor households than low income itself. The studies also find little evidence to feed the narrative of the few microcredit critics, who had begun to paint a picture of chronic damage done to borrowers through luring them into a state of perpetual indebtedness. This is all good news.

The bad news from these studies is that microcredit is far from the poverty elixir its advocates touted it to be. While there is evidence that microcredit exhibits transformative effects for a small group of borrowers, it also suggests that its impact for the average borrower is nothing close to transformative. None of the six major studies finds strong evidence for increases in overall income, consumption, or female empowerment. Although there are usually positive impacts on microenterprise income, this often comes at the expense of wage income, as the household shifts its time away from working for others and toward entrepreneurial activity.

The public takeaway from this set of studies has been that the intervention does not live up to its billing, but there are a couple of reasons to remain cautiously optimistic about microcredit.[6] First, in the six countries where the randomized trials were carried out, three of them (Mexico, Bosnia-Herzegovina, and Mongolia) were already saturated with microcredit, and in these countries researchers found its impact on income to be essentially zero. But in the three other countries (India, Morocco, and Ethiopia), microcredit was much less widespread, and the estimates of income impact were larger. Since impact is likely to be higher among the motivated entrepreneurs who jump at the first microcredit loans than those who only take it up later, some of the studies done in saturated areas probably underestimate its benefits, although they do tell us that the impact of the twenty-seventh microlender in an area is basically nil.

The second reason for some optimism about microcredit is that these randomized trials measured the impacts of microcredit on borrowers, not on the economy as a whole. If microcredit causes borrowers to spend more time in their enterprises and less time in the labor market, and they create jobs in microenterprises, tightening in the labor market ought to push up wages for everyone. There is growing evidence to support this.

Sometimes the best way to study the effects of an intervention is to see what happens when it suddenly gets taken away. This is just what happened in 2010 when, in response to a crisis of overindebtedness, the government of the Indian state of Andhra Pradesh shut down all the state's microcredit institutions. Approximately US$1 billion of microcredit activity disappeared overnight. Economists Emily Breza and Cynthia Kinnan studied the impacts on the economy, and they found that downward pressure in the labor market caused wages to fall by 6 percent, household income dropped, and there were significant reductions in consumption.[7]

I give microcredit two stars for its relative low average impact on borrowers, but four stars for Bang-3. Microcredit is a relatively cheap intervention, requiring only modest subsidies, and to the extent that it raises wages and fosters creative entrepreneurialism, it has an impact on human flourishing apart from its small impacts on income. Like most development economists today, I am convinced by the Breza and Kinnan study that if you took it away, the poor would be measurably worse off.

More recently in the microfinance world there has been a decreased emphasis on microcredit and an increased emphasis on microfinance services more broadly. While financial inclusion is on the rise, reaching 69 percent of the adult population in 2018, up from 62 percent only four years earlier, there are 1.7 billion adults today who still do not have bank accounts.[8] Recent research has emphasized the importance of financial inclusion and formal savings, showing that simply giving people vehicles to save can increase investment in productive assets.[9] Mobile banking technology, now common with the M-Pesa system in East Africa, allows impressive access to financial services that did not exist previously.

Other efforts have attempted to package microfinance with different forms of insurance, particularly health and crop insurance. While there have been some successes in this area, both practitioners and researchers have found that take-up of most forms of formal insurance is low in the developing world. People are typically embedded in reciprocating insurance networks among extended family and friends to which they are already obligated. They may see formal insurance as an added cost with little benefit. Moreover, there is often a distrust among the poor of formal institutions, especially when they find themselves making a series of insurance payments before any tangible payoff becomes noticeable.

If microfinance doesn't seem to have transformative impacts on microenterprises, then what does? This is an important question because small enterprise growth is directly linked to the welfare of hundreds of millions of households in the developing world. I will review several other microenterprise interventions more briefly.

Microenterprise Business Training
Effective: ★★★☆☆ Bang-3: ★★★☆☆ Generalizability: ★★☆☆☆

At least by rich-country standards, business practices among microenterprises in the developing world are notoriously poor. Inventory from unwanted products often wastes away on shelves while high-demand items are out of stock. Business accounting can be so intermixed with family finances that it is unclear whether or not the enterprise is even profitable.

Formal business training offers the chance for entrepreneurs to manage their enterprises more productively. Early studies on business training failed to show significant impacts on business outcomes,[10] but since then there have been a number of larger studies that have offered more promising results, including a randomized controlled trial in rural Kenya among 3,537 female entrepreneurs. Coauthors David McKenzie of the World Bank and Susana Puerto found as a result of the training that women realized 18 percent higher sales and 15 percent higher profits than the control group, stemming from a combination of improved customer relations, the introduction of new products, and generally better business practices.[11] Life satisfaction also increased among those receiving the training, indicative of positive impact on our Bang-3 measure of human flourishing relative to the cost of the intervention.

Interestingly, other work of McKenzie's suggests successful entrepreneurship may be at least as influenced by personality as business practices. A study in Uganda randomizing a three-day workshop on developing an entrepreneurial mindset (as opposed to formal business practices) found positive impacts on entrepreneurial success twelve months after the intervention. But whether entrepreneurial drive itself can be augmented by practitioners remains a subject of research.[12] Taken together, the most recent evidence on business training appears much more positive, but there remains some uncertainty over the generalizability of its impacts.

Entrepreneurial Mentorship Programs
Effective: ★★★☆☆ Bang-3: ★★★★☆ Generalizability: ★★★★☆

In cases where formal business training is ineffective, part of the problem may be that low-income entrepreneurs have difficulty relating lofty academic business concepts to the daily reality of their enterprise. Some have proposed that a one-on-one approach may be more effective. Recently, practitioners and researchers have begun experimenting with entrepreneurial mentorship programs. Here a more established entrepreneur meets regularly with one or more younger, less-experienced entrepreneurs in a similar line of business: A female entrepreneur with an established dressmaking shop meets with a young woman who recently has started a home-based sewing business. A middle-aged man operating a successful convenience store mentors a younger man starting one in his own neighborhood.

Mentors can affect the outcomes of mentees' enterprises by 1) increasing their interest and desire for entrepreneurship; 2) serving as role models and expanding mentees' view of their own possibilities; 3) modeling successful personality traits; 4) individually tutoring the mentee in specific business skills, such as accounting, finance, and marketing; and 5) transmitting valuable information about suppliers, competitors, and market opportunities.

Research that rigorously studies the impact of business mentoring is still at an early stage, and there remains substantial uncertainty about impact. But two newer studies indicate reason to be optimistic about a significant Bang-3 impact. The first, a randomized trial carried out by Notre Dame economists in Kenya, randomly assigned 372 young entrepreneurs into three groups, where one group received business training, another group received mentorship from an older and more experienced entrepreneur in the same business for at least one month, and a third (control) group received neither.[13] The businesses of the mentees were much healthier—four times more profitable and three times more likely to have at least one employee. While the impact of formal business training in their experiment was negligible, profitability in the enterprises of the mentored entrepreneurs increased by 20 percent over the seven months after the official mentoring period. Even more encouragingly, nearly half of those assigned to mentoring were still meeting with their mentors seventeen months later, and among these, the increase in profitability was even higher and more sustained.

Why did the mentoring program work? Unlike the formal business training, mentorship tailored useful information specifically to the entrepreneur's situation. Because mentors were only paid a small stipend (US$10) for their participation, the program was able to increase profits by US$1.73 for every dollar spent, making it impressively cost-effective.

A second study, by MIT-trained economist Jeanne Lafortune and her coauthors in Chile, studied two similar interventions in the context of a microenterprises training program.[14] Both a "role modeling" component and a "technical assistance" component to their randomized trial proved significantly more effective than the basic business training, raising overall household incomes by about 15 percent after twelve months. The role modeling was particularly cost-effective. Lafortune and her coauthors conclude what many young entrepreneurs may lack is simply the inspiration from a role model to move their businesses forward. The mentoring intervention is also quite generalizable; potential mentors and mentees exist everywhere. For interested donors, Mentors International (.org) is an NGO that provides mentoring and business training along with credit to microenterprises in six countries.

Microenterprise Grants
Effective: ★★★★☆ Bang-3: ★★★★☆ Generalizability: ★★★★☆

The early thinking about how to rapidly stimulate growth in microenterprises was that microcredit was superior to small business grants. Loans were sustainable and grants were not, promoting dependence and unsustainable outcomes. In some respects, the tables have turned on this one. While it has been difficult in randomized trials to find significant long-term impacts on income from microcredit, it has not been with business grants.

One of the key challenges of microenterprise practitioners is getting entrepreneurs to create jobs. Most microenterprises in poor countries contain one worker—the entrepreneur himself.[15] Understanding the secret sauce needed to turn these solo entrepreneurs into employers is a fundamental challenge for development researchers and practitioners.

There is strong evidence that microenterprise grants, especially when combined with some form of mentorship and training, are quite effective for supercharging microenterprises. The University of Chicago's Chris Blattman and his colleagues worked with ten to forty members of 535 village-based groups in Uganda who submitted formal proposals for cash grants related to vocational training and microenterprise start-up.[16] Among those randomly selected to receive business grants, business assets increased 57 percent and profits increased by 38 percent. Hours of employed labor were also 38 percent higher, where about one of four entrepreneurs receiving a grant hired a new employee, extending the benefit of the cash transfers to others in the villages.

Even more impressive impacts from business grants are found in a second study in Nigeria where David McKenzie carried out a study in partnership with the YouWiN! business plan competition.[17] Based on business proposals, organizers of the competition chose a group of 1,841 semifinalists from 24,000 submitted applications, from which McKenzie and his team randomly selected 729 winners to receive US$50,000 grants. These were given as cash payments, conditional on achieving basic milestones at different stages.

Impacts from the business grants to these small- to medium-sized enterprises were transformative. After three years, entrepreneurs chosen to receive the grants were 37 percentage points more likely to be in business than those in the control group, 23 percentage points more likely to have more than ten employees, and they added about five employees more than the control group. Sales and profits were also significantly higher. The Blattman et al. and McKenzie studies reveal the kind of large impacts from grants that we once thought could be realized through microcredit alone. They also paint a picture of the transformative effects of microenterprise grants when properly targeted at talented entrepreneurs with high aspirations.

Business grants can be powerful stimulators of economic growth in microenterprises, and there is evidence that impacts on enterprises can last five years or more.[18] While the implementation is generalizable, impacts do vary depending on context. Although a grant obviously costs more than a loan, grants have far bigger Bang-3 impacts, so an argument can be made that they are reasonably cost-effective. I give microenterprise grants four stars because in practice they are often combined with other supportive interventions. Silicon Valley–based Village Enterprise implements a highly effective microenterprise program that does just that—providing a cash grant along with entrepreneurial training and mentoring.[19]

Unconditional Cash Transfers
Effective: ★★★★☆ Bang-3: ★★★★☆ Generalizability: ★★★★★

If cash transfers for business grants are effective, perhaps it would be equally effective to provide the cash with no strings attached? Cash transfers, both unconditional and those conditional on business investment and investments in education and health of children (which I will review in the next chapter), have become some of the most popular and carefully scrutinized poverty interventions. Unconditional cash transfers—cash given to the poor to use as they best see fit—have captured the imagination of academics and policy makers, but at the cost of some controversy. The controversy revolves around whether the poor use cash transfers responsibly, investing them in enterprise and the future of their children—or as critics charge—they lure the poor into lives of drunken idleness. Compelling new research has begun to shed light on these questions.

Many Americans and Europeans tend to associate unconditional cash transfers with postwar welfare programs that many claim have disincentivized work and created a dependent underclass. Indeed, there is evidence of these effects in rich countries. Some of the most convincing is from researchers who studied the long-term effects of the 1970s Seattle-Denver Income Maintenance Experiment.[20] The program gave thousands of randomly selected families in the two cities about $26,000 for three to five years. The study found that adult work hours dropped by 12 percent, and recipient households earned $1,600 less per year on their own. Even more, the deleterious effects on work seemed to persist in the data for decades. Separate research has found similar work-disincentivizing effects from other American and European welfare programs.[21]

So what about evidence from cash transfers overseas? Many worry that the oversees poor will spend unconditional cash transfers irresponsibly. Like most economists, I maintain a reasonably firm belief in carrots and sticks, and unconditional cash transfers lack both. So don't the overseas poor misuse free money?

Actually, there is considerable evidence that they don't. A World Bank meta-study from nineteen countries examined whether recipients of cash transfers increase spending on "temptation goods" such as alcohol and cigarettes.[22] The study actually finds the opposite result, a *decrease* in expenditures on alcohol and tobacco, perhaps because of a reduced need to medicate feelings of hopelessness with alcohol. Another important meta-study by researchers at MIT finds no evidence that cash-transfer programs in six developing countries decreased the propensity to work.[23] Why there exist such notable differences in the effects of cash-transfer programs between rich and poor countries is an important and unresolved question.

Some of the best evidence for the positive impacts of unconditional cash transfers comes from a rigorous impact evaluation of GiveDirectly. The study, a randomized controlled trial led by Princeton's Johannes Haushofer and the University of Chicago's Jeremy Shapiro, found after one year that the transfers increased recipients' asset holdings by 58 percent, mainly through investment in small businesses and animal herds—exactly what we would hope to see in rural East Africa, where herds are a measure of wealth, a means of insurance, and a sign of prestige. There was a marked decrease in the number of days children went to bed hungry and greater expenditures on their schooling. The transfers also increased reported happiness, life satisfaction, and reduced stress, as measured by the level of cortisol found in recipients' spit.[24] All of this suggests big Bang-3 impacts. On the downside, non-recipients report significant dissatisfaction from not being selected. And a three-year follow-up study finds lasting effects on asset accumulation but waning effects on most of the other outcomes.[25] As a result, there is strong evidence that unconditional cash transfers create short- to medium-term impacts on measures of human flourishing, but less evidence to support their long-term effects.

Nevertheless, one of the most useful aspects of unconditional cash transfers is that they provide a benchmark for the relative effectiveness of other programs. Development economists Craig McIntosh and Andrew Zeitlin carried out a study among three randomized groups made up of seventy-four villages, each in Rwanda.[26] The first group of villages received a multifaceted intervention from Catholic Relief Services: intensive nutrition and sanitation components, an agricultural livelihood intervention, and the formation of savings groups. The second group of villages received a cash grant for $114, the cash equivalent of the cost of the multifaceted intervention, while others in this group received a bigger cash grant of $500. The third group of seventy-four villages served as a control. What they found was that neither the multifaceted intervention nor the small cash grant had a significant impact on the primary goals: child growth, household dietary diversity, maternal or child anemia, household consumption, or wealth within the one-year period of the study, although savings increased in the multifaceted intervention and cash-equivalent recipients paid down substantial household debt. But the more generous $500 cash transfer led to increases in consumption, improvements in dietary diversity, greater height-for-age, a 70 percent reduction in child mortality, and higher savings and assets. In short, the more generous cash transfer was three times as expensive as the Catholic Relief Services intervention but far more effective.

The evidence in favor of giving cash is now strong enough that World Vision, the largest Christian nonprofit development organization, today uses unconditional cash transfers as a major component of its work. And because of the cost-effectiveness of cash transfers, World Vision has a future commitment to deliver half of all its humanitarian assistance as cash rather than in-kind giving.[27] But because the evidence for long-term effects is less clear than some other very effective interventions, I award the intervention four stars instead of five. What is clear, however, is that the poor in developing countries tend to use cash well, and that unconditional cash transfers create a solid benchmark for gauging the relative effectiveness of other interventions, many of which we will consider in the next chapter.

Chapter 8

WHAT WORKS
IN EDUCATION
AND HEALTH?

With the little bits of Spanish she spoke, my then seven-year-old daughter Allie had made her first friend in Guatemala. Her name was Blanca, and Allie brought her to meet us. Allie explained that Blanca had a hurt on her toe. She pointed to it. I looked at the toe and saw a festering infected toenail covered in small flies. They couldn't afford a doctor, her mother explained to us, because the family lacked the money. So we drove Blanca to the doctor, who fixed up the toe. We learned Blanca couldn't afford other things, too, even the six dollars per month it cost to attend our middle school in the village, which is why she had to attend the public school. (And in Guatemalan public schools, teachers tend to show up about every other day.) Lack of quality health care and poor education will likely affect Blanca for the rest of her life.

The very challenges faced by Blanca—income, health, and education—make up the equally weighted components of the United Nations' Human Development Index. They are the big three. In the last chapter we examined economic interventions. In this chapter we will look at interventions targeting education and health, along with a few other areas. Most economists view improvements in education and health as essential building blocks for economic prosperity. These are also areas in which there are opportunities for ordinary people to give their time or money.

Education Interventions

Educational interventions are critical because if they are effective—increasing years of schooling and hopefully learning—the effects may last a lifetime. As a result, educational interventions that are high Bang-2 ("bang for the buck") tend to have a high Bang-3 ("bang for the bang for the buck") as well, except in places where the value of schooling is reduced due to the paucity of economic opportunities, where educational interventions may have high Bang-2 but low Bang-3. When children actually learn in school (not to be taken for granted, as we shall see), and the macroeconomy is strong enough to provide opportunities to those with higher levels of schooling, interventions that strongly boost schooling levels can be transformative.

The following are efforts to increase both the quantity and quality of education.

Conditional Cash Transfers
Effective: ★★★★☆ Bang-3: ★★★☆☆ Generalizability: ★★★★★

In 1997, Mexican president Ernesto Zedillo presented economist Santiago Levy with a task: to design a country-wide poverty intervention that would improve health and education among impoverished Mexican families. Levy designed and introduced *Progresa*, a radical program for its time that provided cash rewards to families for keeping children in school, giving them regular medical checkups, and attending nutritional education meetings. Levy randomized its rollout across villages so impacts could be easily scrutinized. And these have been scrutinized arguably more than any single poverty program in history. The early evidence was strong enough in both education and health that *Progresa* (later renamed by successive presidents as *Oportunidades* and then *Prospera* to politically capitalize on their successes) has been replicated in more than thirty countries across the globe, a testament to its generalizability.[1]

These impacts extend particularly well to other Latin American countries and, to a more moderate extent, to other developing countries. One meta-study covering eighteen countries found conditional cash-transfer programs to lead to reductions in poverty in seventeen of them and consistently outperform programs such as employment-guarantee schemes.[2] Another meta-study of forty-six evaluations of eleven conditional cash-transfer programs in Latin America found that they significantly boosted consumption of recipient households.[3]

But the main purpose of conditional cash-transfer programs is to boost education, and the effects measured in most studies are solid in this area. One of the most famous, on the impacts of *Progresa* itself, found it added 0.66 of a year of grade completion to children in the program, seemingly modest but a large impact compared to other schooling interventions.[4] Studies on conditional cash transfers consistently show moderate to strong impacts on educational outcomes that border on long-term, transformative effects in some contexts.[5] Paying moms to keep kids in school pays off, not just in higher levels of consumption for poor households in the present, but in the future if economies are healthy enough to provide opportunities for the better-educated kids. It can be done not only by governments but also by nonprofits where these government programs don't exist.

International Child Sponsorship
Effective: ★★★★★ Bang-3: ★★★★☆ Generalizability: ★★★★★

My study with Paul Glewwe at the University of Minnesota and Laine Rutledge, a doctoral student at the University of Washington, on the impact of Compassion International's child-sponsorship program was carried out in six countries: Uganda, Guatemala, Philippines, India, Kenya, and Bolivia. We presented the results at the World Bank, Stanford, Berkeley, USC, Cornell, and at a number of academic conferences, receiving feedback from dozens of other researchers on statistical modeling and data analysis. The final results, spread across several published papers, indicate nothing short of transformative effects on the sponsored children—both on the ways they conceptualize their lives in terms of hope and aspirations, and on their life outcomes as adults.

We found the average impact on grade completion is about twice as high as the *Progresa* program in Mexico, about 1.2 years. Overall, sponsorship makes children 27 to 40 percent more likely to complete secondary school and 50 to 80 percent more likely to complete a university education.[6] The program displayed positive and significant impacts in every one of the six countries, but it had the biggest impact in sub-Saharan Africa. In general, wherever existing economic conditions are worse, Compassion's impacts seem to be bigger. In countries where existing outcomes are higher among boys, the impact on girls is larger; in countries where the existing educational outcomes are higher among girls, the impact on boys is larger. International child sponsorship is the great equalizer.

The impacts of the program extend beyond school attendance. We found that child sponsorship means that when the child grows up, he or she is 14 to 18 percent more likely to obtain a salaried job, and 35 percent more likely to obtain a white-collar job. When they become adults, many of the Compassion-sponsored children become teachers instead of remaining jobless or working in menial agricultural labor. We find that child sponsorship increased adult income by about 20 percent. Formerly sponsored children live in better-constructed houses, and they are more likely to have electricity in these houses and own a mobile phone.[7] They are more likely to grow up to be leaders, both community leaders and leaders in a wide variety of denominations of local churches.

There are some important qualifications to our study of child sponsorship. First, while we have extensively studied Compassion's program, which emphasizes the nurturing of individual children, we have not studied the impacts of programs such as those operated by World Vision, Plan, and Save the Children, which use funding given in the name of the child to provide community-wide benefits. This is *not* to say that many of the interventions undertaken by these organizations are ineffective, but they are not the well-defined sponsor-to-child set of benefits received that we measure in Compassion's program. Second, while Compassion's child sponsorship demonstrates long-term transformative effects, it is not an inexpensive program, and its cost-effectiveness is not on the plane of inexpensive health-related interventions discussed later, which display significant effects on child morbidity for pennies on the dollar. But child sponsorship is very effective and should be considered by donors who value holistic human flourishing. (It's fun to exchange letters with sponsored kids too.)

New School Construction
Effective: ★★★☆☆ Bang-3: ★★★☆☆ Generalizability: ★★☆☆☆

If schooling outcomes are key to development, perhaps it would pay to build more schools? Data from one of the biggest school construction efforts in US history finds that school construction in low-income urban areas significantly raises student test scores (and home values).[8] The earliest research looking at the impact of school construction on educational outcomes in a developing country is by leading development economist Esther Duflo, who finds modest but significant impacts from the new schools—each primary school that was built (per 1,000 children) yielded an increase in grade completion of 0.12 to 0.19 years of schooling accompanied by a 1.5 to 2.7 percent increase in wages in adulthood.[9]

The Indonesian context is critical—the case of an up-and-coming Asian economy in which schooling was likely to be in high demand, which probably drove construction in the first place. A more recent study examined the rollout of new schools in rural villages that did not have a school in the Ghor province of Afghanistan. The new rural schools dramatically increased enrollment rates by 35 percent for boys and 51 percent for girls, probably higher for the latter because girls are often not allowed to travel outside a village. Test scores, especially for girls, increased markedly.[10]

Thus, in the proper setting, school construction can yield big educational dividends, but like many schooling interventions, context is likely to matter greatly. The three stars for Bang-3 assume that new schools are built in areas where they are greatly needed. In rural areas of poor countries, schools are often very sparsely located, especially secondary schools, so creating a new school nearer to the homes of potential students may reduce dropout. In fact, this was precisely the motive for the new middle school we helped fund with Mayan Partners in 2002. But in these areas aspirations for schooling are also often low so that building a new school does not guarantee classroom seats will be filled. Even with the new middle school located square in the middle of the village, we still have a hard time convincing parents that it is worth sending their kids to seventh grade, especially their daughters. The physical presence of schools is part of the issue, but so is the demand for schooling, how much learning happens when children arrive, and opportunities when they graduate.

Improving School and Teacher Quality
Effective: ★★★★☆ Bang-3: ★★★★☆ Generalizability: ★★★★★

Construction of schools is wonderful, but children still have to learn. More important than more schools is *better* schools. While the average adult in developing countries today is more schooled than the average adult in advanced countries in 1960, many if not most students in poor countries attend schools of such low quality that learning for many virtually comes to a standstill after third grade.[11] Data from large swaths of the developing world, including South Asia and most of sub-Saharan Africa, indicate more than half of children completing primary school are unable to read even the most basic texts or solve the simplest arithmetic problems.[12] There is a global crisis today in which hundreds of millions of children attend school—all helping to achieve United Nations goals for school attendance—but learn virtually nothing.

There are several means of improving school and teacher quality that have shown to be consistently effective in randomized trials. Patrick McEwan of Wellesley College is the author of a definitive study on the factors that turn schooling into learning.[13] Four schooling interventions he notes consistently show large impacts across dozens of international studies: 1) providing teachers with better formal training to enable them to provide effective classroom instruction; 2) reducing class sizes so that teachers can tailor teaching to student needs; 3) performance incentives for teachers; and 4) training teachers in the use of computer technology. Interventions that were found to be mostly ineffective included school-based nutritional supplements and the training of school administrators and supervisors. I give stars at the top based on the effective interventions, which are moderately cost-effective relative to others and with considerable potential for big Bang-3.[14]

Free Laptops for School Children
Effective: ☆☆☆☆☆ Bang-3: ☆☆☆☆☆ Generalizability: ☆☆☆☆☆

With the advent of One Laptop Per Child, it has become an attractive intervention for many concerned donors to donate free laptops to poor children overseas. My only qualm with assigning zero stars to free laptops is the remote possibility that it could be visually mistaken for five stars. Studies in the US have failed to show any measurable improvements in student learning or educational satisfaction with giving kids laptops,[15] so it is puzzling that we would expect them to do more overseas.

Researchers at the Inter-American Development Bank studied the impact of One Laptop Per Child, in which laptops were randomly allocated to one thousand primary school children via a randomized trial in Lima, Peru.[16] Results of the study show no impact from the laptops on learning, no impact on cognitive skills, accompanied by lower academic effort as reported by teachers. The only positive impact found in the study was that children develop better facility with the donated green and white XO-1 laptop computers. Other encouraging news is that alterations have been made to the laptop so that children can no longer use them to browse pornography.[17] To some well-intentioned people it is impossible to imagine their lives without their laptop, so they believe it is of the utmost importance for the poor to have them too. The One Laptop Per Child program reminds us of an important lesson: our good intentions need filters.

Health Interventions

Clean Water
Effective: ★★★★☆ Bang-3: ★★★★☆ Generalizability: ★★★☆☆

The clean water intervention is one of the toughest to evaluate. When boreholes tap plentiful sources of clean water, and the source is maintained well (no pun intended) and used sustainably, there is arguably no better intervention than clean water. Yet sub-Saharan Africa is littered with fifty thousand defunct boreholes,[18] many drilled by the most determined and well-meaning NGOs, many lying uncovered waiting to swallow up innocent animals and children.

While there has been improvement in recent years, the need remains great: The World Health Organization (WHO) estimates that at least 2 billion people use a drinking water source contaminated with feces and 844 million people lack even a basic drinking-water service. This includes 159 million people who are dependent on surface water, a terribly unhealthy source of water for human consumption. Dirty water is bad for human beings—very bad. It results in a WHO-estimated 842,000 people, mostly children, dying each year from diarrhea related to unhealthy drinking water.[19] In a recent study I was part of with researchers at UC Berkeley on the effects of introducing infant formula into developing countries, we estimate that when it was introduced in areas with unclean water, it killed approximately 66,000 infants a year.[20]

In places with dirty water, providing clean water can prevent a host of human suffering, stave off legions of child health problems, and dramatically reduce infant mortality.[21] A World Health Organization study estimates that the availability of clean water in a rural village reduces infant mortality by 35 percent to 50 percent at a cost of roughly $10 per person per year.[22] So the potential for a big Bang-3 is enormous, but clean water systems must be done right, and they are highly dependent upon complementary improvements in sanitation. Unless there is clean movement of water all the way from well to mouth, the impact of simply drilling more boreholes diminishes substantially.[23] Organizations who do good work in the WASH area are Charity: Water and Living Water. Donated funds to good WASH NGOs are used to drill wells, lay pipe, install pumps, and develop the kind of integrated system of water and hygiene that can have big impacts on health and mortality.

Deworming Treatments
Effective: ★★★★★ Bang-3: ★★★★★ Generalizability: ★★★☆☆

Intestinal worms, or *helminths*, enter into the human body through the mouth or the soles of the feet and live off the iron in human blood, rarely killing the host but causing both acute and long-term health and cognitive problems. Brains don't develop well in childhood without iron to help them grow. About 1.2 billion people, nearly all poor, are infected with intestinal worms.[24] Deworming, the administration of albendazole or other oral drugs to remove infestations of intestinal worms, is considered by many to be the most cost-effective poverty intervention known today. Albendazole and other deworming medications are cheap (50 cents a dose) and strikingly effective with cure rates approaching 100 percent, yielding an extraordinarily high Bang-2. And rigorous studies have documented substantial impacts on overall adult health, education, and even cognition *from* childhood deworming, giving it a big Bang-3 too.

The most celebrated study on the effects of deworming was carried out by development economists Edward Miguel at UC Berkeley and Michael Kremer at Harvard, who found that a randomized deworming treatment in Kenya reduced school absenteeism by 25 percent at a cost of $0.50 per year.[25] Follow-up studies after ten years show astonishing long-term effects on these randomly dewormed Kenyan children. Men who were treated as boys had higher rates of schooling and better jobs. Women who were treated as girls were 25 percent more likely to have attended secondary school.[26] Children who had been randomly dewormed at an age of less than one year showed cognitive gains equal to more than half a year of schooling.[27] Preliminary results on this sample fifteen years later continue to show positive impacts on employment and earnings (approximately 15 percent higher) among the dewormed.[28]

Not all evidence and experts support mass deworming as a cost-effective strategy,[29] but the weight of the evidence has led most policy makers, including the World Health Organization, to view deworming as a critically important intervention, especially given the low cost of deworming medications. For example, one important meta-study finds deworming to be thirty-five times more effective per dollar at promoting healthy weight gain for children than school feeding programs.[30] Four of GiveWell.org's top-rated charities focus on deworming.[31]

There are caveats: One is that deworming needs to occur repeatedly to keep kids worm free; it is not a self-sustaining intervention.[32] Moreover, unlike more general interventions such as WASH, improving schools, or child sponsorship, the effectiveness of deworming is very contextual. Eradicating worms produces large impacts only where there are worms to be eradicated, but there are numerous such places in the developing world.

Mosquito Nets
Effective: ★★★★☆ Bang-3: ★★★★★ Generalizability: ★★☆☆☆

Malaria is neither a bacteria nor a virus, but a parasitic infection transmitted through bites of mosquitos. It has a devastating effect in the developing world, with the latest WHO statistics reporting 212 million cases, 90 percent of which are in sub-Saharan Africa, and 429,000 deaths from the disease.[33] Malaria is a leading killer of children in developing countries, accounting for nearly one in five deaths of children under five in sub-Saharan Africa.

Fortunately, like worm infestation, malaria infection can be prevented cheaply and effectively. Insecticide-treated bed nets cost only $5 to $10 each. New modern nets last for years without needing to be re-treated, and they reduce instances of malaria by 50 percent and malaria mortality by 20 percent. There is strong evidence that actually giving the nets away in mosquito-infested areas is an extremely cost-effective strategy for combating malaria.[34] One recent randomized trial in Zambia found the distribution of free insecticide-treated nets to increase agricultural output by 14.7 percent, likely from simply reducing malaria infections.[35]

As a health intervention it doesn't approach the nearly 100 percent effectiveness of albendazole in combating intestinal worms, but it is nevertheless highly cost-effective. And like deworming drugs, it is obviously sensitive to context; malaria is common in the developing world, but infection is only about a third as common as intestinal worms. It is an easy intervention to sponsor online. Two of GiveWell's top charities are in the anti-malaria business, the Against Malaria Foundation and the Malaria Consortium. Other worthwhile malaria-fighting NGOs include NetsForLife and NothingButNets.net, endorsed by Warriors basketball star Steph Curry, so it's got to be a sure-shot intervention.

Clean Cook Stoves
Effective: ★★☆☆☆ Bang-3: ★★★☆☆ Generalizability: ★★☆☆☆

According to the WHO, about 40 percent of the world's population cooks with biomass fuels like coal, wood, or animal dung. This results in not only deforestation but also major health problems from indoor air pollution. Nearly four million people die from illnesses that can be traced back to polluting cookstoves using solid fuels and kerosene. Most of these deaths occur among women, who spend a disproportionate amount of time around the stove, and their children who develop pneumonia from hanging around their skirts down near the smoke.

One of my researcher-heroes is Kirk Smith, professor of Global Environmental Health at UC Berkeley, and the world's leading expert on indoor air pollution, publishing more than four hundred academic papers documenting the problem and solutions to it. The principal solution Smith advocates is clean-burning woodstoves, even those that continue to burn wood. Once on a visit to his office, he showed me his latest new gadget: the *Turbococina*, developed in El Salvador, which uses 95 percent less wood and, at 900°F, burns it so efficiently that the stove doesn't even need a chimney. These and the many other types of improved stoves reduce deforestation and indoor smoke, dramatically reducing a family's exposure to harmful particulate matter.[36] There is mixed evidence, however, on the effectiveness of improved stoves. In one important meta-study, research results on improved stoves consistently and significantly report reduced indoor smoke (Bang-2) and that this indoor smoke reduction significantly reduced cough, chest pain, and breathing difficulties that would significantly affect human flourishing (Bang-3).

But these impacts critically depend on whether people use the stoves correctly and adopt them in the long term. A 2016 study by Esther Duflo and her colleagues finds that effects from a stove introduced in India failed to generate long-term health benefits; households used the stoves inappropriately and irregularly, with usage declining over time.[37] This reflects our experience in a small intervention and study we carried out with Mayan Partners in the village where we work in western Guatemala, where we used a public lottery to randomize the introduction of forty ONIL wood-burning stoves (US$150).[38] While we found major reductions in wood use and respiratory problems, nearly all of the households had abandoned the stoves two years later. The reason? The Guatemalan women reported that they didn't cook their husbands' tortillas fast enough. Now the stoves sit in the corner bearing potted plants. This is an intervention whose impacts vary substantially depending on product, usage, and context. Those wishing to learn more about the introduction of clean cookstoves globally can visit the Global Alliance for Clean Cookstoves at cleancookstoves.org.

Reparative Surgeries
Effective: ★★★★☆ Bang-3: ★★★☆☆ Generalizability: ★★★★☆

Many children worldwide are born with birth defects such as cleft palate, clubfoot, or vision impairment. Cleft palate, for example, occurs in about one in seven hundred births, congenital cataracts in about one in twenty-four hundred, and clubfoot in about one in a thousand.[39] While in rich countries these types of conditions are typically repaired through surgery at birth or as they arise, they are often not in poor countries, leaving those who suffer from them disadvantaged socially, educationally, and economically. These surgeries potentially produce life-changing benefits, but they cost the equivalent of several hundred dollars or more, which many poor families are unable to afford.

One study carried out on the work of Smile Train estimates that cleft-palate surgery results in benefits between $16,000 to $42,000 for a surgery costing only a few hundred dollars.[40] Another study carried out across low-income countries found that the routine Ponseti treatment for clubfoot on infants costs an average of $167 and was effective at curing the condition without major surgery. A study on the average costs of cataract surgery in developing countries reports costs in the $150 to $400 range for sight restored, depending on severity and context. These studies are not perfect because they do not estimate causal effects on life outcomes, but they strongly suggest transformative impacts on recipients. Reparative surgeries seem to compare decently in terms of cost-effectiveness with other public health interventions, and they are generalizable to wherever these conditions are diagnosed: in a small but significant fraction of the population nearly everywhere.

Other Types of Interventions

Comprehensive Poverty Graduation Programs
Effective: ★★★★☆ Bang-3: ★★★★☆ Generalizability: ★★★★★

Recently, some NGOs have been experimenting with "kitchen sink" programs, which offer a multifaceted intervention to help the ultra-poor scale the ladder of prosperity. These programs provide some combination of the following to ultra-poor households identified to be living on less than (per person) US$1.25 per day: 1) transfer of an animal or other productive asset; 2) training in how to use that asset; 3) a finite sequence of cash grants; 4) school fees, uniforms, and supplies for children; 5) access to savings and/or a source of credit; 6) health information; 7) a case worker/life coach. The most celebrated comprehensive approach is the Bangladesh Rural Advancement Committee (BRAC) program discussed in Chapter 2.

The BRAC intervention incorporates most of the above and was evaluated by economists affiliated with the Jameel Poverty Action Lab at MIT via randomized controlled trials in a six-country study, where each of the elements was tailored to the local country context.[41] One year after the program ended, asset holdings, consumption, and food security dramatically increased among program beneficiaries on average across countries, as did total time working, household income and household savings, women's economic participation, physical health, and mental health.

Comprehensive interventions are not cheap. The cost of the BRAC program ranged from US$1,538 per household in India to US$5,742 in Peru. But there is near-unanimous agreement among researchers and practitioners that comprehensive interventions are effective, highly generalizable, and scalable across contexts. Indeed, child sponsorship is likely to be so effective because it embodies this kind of comprehensive intervention. The main caveat is that at least in some contexts, cash transfers may be more cost-effective.[42]

Early Childhood Interventions
Effective: ★★★★☆ Bang-3: ★★★★★ Generalizability: ★★★★★

Research has uncovered a fundamental truth about child-related poverty interventions: the earlier, the better. This is because the most important phases of brain development occur before age three. During this time the human brain undergoes a series of layered developments that are extremely sensitive to poor nutrition and stress. For this brain development to occur properly, babies and toddlers need good nutrition, a stress-free environment—and lots of nurture, holding, and hugs.[43] Most parents provide these things instinctively for children, but mothers in poverty, especially young mothers, often don't or can't. Public health experts estimate that about 200 million children in the world do not get enough of these things for their brains to develop to full cognitive capacity by adulthood.[44]

Early childhood interventions are typically holistic—incorporating nutritional, educational, health, and parental coaching components—and are critical to replacing the missing elements required for healthy brain development. Both domestically and internationally, early childhood programs are one of the few slam-dunk successful interventions that consistently show sustained, cost-effective impacts. Some of the most well-known evidence comes from domestic programs, but there is ample evidence that such impacts are highly generalizable.

One well-known study by University of Colorado physician David Olds had trained nurses to visit randomly selected teenage mothers of at-risk children through the Nurse-Family Partnership program. Follow-up results were stunning. After two years, Olds and his team found an extraordinary drop in emergency room visits by toddlers of the treated group.[45] Children were growing up in more stable environments. Fifteen years later they found, relative to the control group, a near 50 percent reduction in child abuse by the parents in the program, while their children were 40 percent less likely to run away from home, had 45 percent fewer arrests, had 37 percent fewer lifetime sex partners, smoked 40 percent fewer cigarettes, and spent 44 percent fewer days consuming alcohol.[46] The most recent data, two decades after the intervention, shows both mothers and children to have significantly lower rates of mortality.[47] The Rand Corporation performed a cost-benefit analysis on the program, finding that each $1 in nurse visits to a young at-risk mother yielded $5.70 in benefits.[48]

After winning the 2000 Nobel Prize in Economics, the brilliant University of Chicago econometrician James Heckman reinvented himself as an early childhood intervention expert.[49] Much of this has involved targeting his substantial econometric firepower at data from the Perry Preschool Project, implemented in 1962 as an early precursor to the US Head Start program. The program emphasized active learning, character building, conflict resolution, and socio-emotional skills. Long-term results from the Perry project are as dramatic as those from the Nurse-Family Partnership. Heckman and his colleagues find extraordinary reductions in crime and arrests among Perry children by age forty and vastly higher levels of education, employment, and income.[50]

There is widespread support for early childhood interventions globally. A meta-study of thirty early childhood interventions in twenty-three countries finds large impacts on overall cognition, behavior, general health, and schooling completion.[51] My favorite overseas early childhood intervention is World Vision's Go Baby Go! Parenting Programme, which does all the right things, focusing on the first one thousand days of a child's life, implementing parental coaching, and integrating nutrition, safety, and nurture. With proven impacts from a randomized controlled trial sponsored by the Gates Foundation, it is a big Bang-3 program that is eminently worth donor support.[52]

Shoe and Clothing Donation
Effective: ★☆☆☆☆ Bang-3: ★☆☆☆☆ Generalizability: ★☆☆☆☆

TOMS Shoes is famous for their One-for-One program. If you buy a pair of TOMS, they donate a pair of shoes to a needy child overseas. How much does this help recipient children? TOMS wanted to find out. So in 2011 they invited a group of us to carry out an evaluation on their overseas shoe giving. Our study involved a randomized controlled trial, where we allocated TOMS-donated shoes among 1,578 children in rural El Salvador.

Three months after giving the shoes to about half of these children, we collected data to test how receiving the shoes affected the way they spent their time, their school attendance, their health (especially of their feet), and their psychology. We found that receiving the shoes did not significantly impact any of these.[53] This being said, the children appreciated the shoes, and they wore them extensively (often to the point of wearing them out—which didn't seem to take very long). Unfortunately, we also found some evidence of aid dependence among children receiving the shoes. They were about 12 percentage points more likely to say that other people should provide for their family's needs. Of course, this is probably not the lesson we want kids to grow up with.

To TOMS's credit, they responded to these results by pledging to give shoes more often as a reward for good school attendance so that children feel like they earn them, and they responded positively to our suggestion that they begin to manufacture their donor shoes locally in some of the poorest countries. They also have offered an array of new products, including European-looking sunglasses, for which someone in a developing country receives glasses (or even cataract surgery) when you purchase a pair. This program is more likely to have transformative impacts.

Another criticism of overseas clothing donations is that they undermine local clothing markets. For example, a well-known tactic of T-shirt sellers before the Super Bowl is to create thousands of victory T-shirts for both football teams, half of which are ready to explode onto the hysteric streets of the winning city at hefty prices. The T-shirts prematurely celebrating the victory of the loser are then sent to poor countries for a tax write-off. A research paper investigating the impact of a similar product, used clothing imports, found that they undermined local markets in Africa, responsible for 50 percent of the decline in employment in that industry from 1981 to 2000.[54] In our TOMS study, we found limited evidence of market undermining from the shoe donations. One domestic sale of shoes in local markets was lost for about every twenty pairs of donated shoes, but the result was mild and statistically insignificant.[55] Nevertheless, most economists regard clothing donations as ineffective at best, failing to address root issues of poverty.

Farm Animal Donation
Effective: ★★★★☆ Bang-3: ★★☆☆☆ Generalizability: ★☆☆☆☆

One Christmas several years ago, instead of buying my dad a necktie for Christmas, we decided to buy a goat. He was delighted with the goat, mainly because it wasn't for him. Instead, we gave it in his name to a poor family in Kenya. It became a Christmas tradition in our family: giving each other fun farm animal gifts that benefit the poor. Sending gift catalogues to potential donors with barnyards of farm animals to choose from has been a staple of organizations like Heifer International for decades and has become increasingly replicated by other organizations. It is an incredibly effective marketing strategy. What could be more fun than donating a cuddly alpaca in your sister's name to a Peruvian family for Christmas?

Perhaps Bill Gates's answer to that question is giving away chickens—lots of them—by partnering in 2016 with Heifer to give away 100,000 chickens to impoverished families in Africa. "Our foundation is betting on chickens," says Gates.[56] But does giving an alpaca or chickens (or a cow, sheep, goat, pig, rabbit, or bees) to a family overseas create an effective poverty intervention? It has become a controversial question.

The answer isn't as straightforward as either proponents or opponents like to argue. On the positive side, farm animal donation can be part of an effective holistic poverty intervention approach, such as those implemented by BRAC and other first-rate NGOs. Moreover, even when we study animal donation in isolation, there is evidence of impact.

A few years ago Cornell agricultural economist Chris Barrett and I carried out a project with our graduate students to study the effect of a Heifer International intervention that gave away pregnant heifers and meat goats to impoverished rural families in Rwanda.[57] The heifers, much more popular than the meat goats, were not your passive, run-of-the-mill bovine. They were a Swiss breed that could best be described as turbo-charged milk machines, producing fifteen to thirty times the milk volume as the skinny local cows. Our study found big impacts from both Heifer's heifers and from their goats. Dairy consumption increased threefold for families receiving the heifers, and meat consumption doubled among families receiving the goats, noteworthy Bang-2. Most of the increase in dairy consumption came from Rwandan families eating yogurt they created from the milk, necessary because poor refrigeration prevented most from bringing the milk to market. But what effect does higher dairy consumption have on long-term health and human flourishing, i.e., Bang-3? We found this increase in dairy consumption to be so strong that it actually reduced *wasting* (weight relative to age) among children in the goat families and *stunting* (height relative to weight) among children in the milk-cow families. While we have reason to believe the context in Rwanda was "just right" for the heifer transfer (local recipients knew how to take care of the cows but didn't have them), any intervention reducing wasting and stunting is a big deal. Several other larger studies have documented significant effects from livestock transfer programs, showing substantial impacts on self-employment, income, and consumption.[58]

Nevertheless, there is a debate over the cost-effectiveness of animal donation relative to simply giving families cash. This debate is summarized in a *Foreign Affairs* article by Paul Niehaus and Chris Blattman, citing that the total costs of heifer, family training, and heifer delivery in our study were $3,000 per animal (not the $500 listed in the Heifer catalog).[59] This is a lot of cash for a Rwandan household, roughly double the per-capita GDP at the time of the study. Niehaus and Blattman make the case that families could have been better off with a series of equivalent cash grants. Quick to respond in a subsequent issue of the journal, Heifer CEO Pierre Ferrari argues that cash doesn't allow the poor access to better breeds of heifers, nor does it replicate the holistic nature of its "passing on the gift" program and its positive effects on community development.[60] It is a debate that will continue to be the subject of "horse race" experiments between cash and in-kind giving, but the burden of proof today lies with in-kind donation programs to demonstrate their effectiveness relative to giving cash.

Fair-Trade Coffee
Effective: ★☆☆☆☆ Bang-3: ★★☆☆☆ Generalizability: ★★☆☆☆

Fair trade guarantees a minimum price to certified growers who meet a set of standards related to environmental practices, wages to laborers, and other requirements. Meeting these standards embodies nontrivial costs to growers, along with the direct cost of certification itself by Fairtrade International. The reward to coffee growers for certification is a minimum price ($1.40 per pound to growers for hard bean arabica and US$1.70 if the coffee is grown organically). A social premium of $0.20 is added to the price that growers receive to be used for investment in the community, often in the coffee cooperative itself.[61]

A great deal of new research has been done on the impact of fair-trade coffee. One carefully executed study by University of California researchers illustrates why fair-trade coffee is not the elixir it is brewed up to be. The problem lies in the design of the fair-trade system. When global coffee prices plunge and fair trade is able to bring growers higher prices, more and more coffee growers choose to become certified, reducing the share of coffee beans that can be marketed at the higher price through fair-trade coffee channels, thus lowering benefits to growers. In this way the advantages of fair-trade coffee thus become whittled away so that in the long run, fair trade no longer offers a price advantage over good old free trade. The authors of the research use fourteen years of fair-trade coffee data from Guatemala, which confirm that the laws of economics work in the expected ways. Even in times when it should be most effective, the design of fair-trade coffee undermines itself, and the net price advantage to individual growers from belonging to a fair-trade network falls to essentially zero.[62] In this way most economists view the system itself as flawed because of its poor design.

To the extent that fair-trade coffee is unable to increase Bang-2 (consistently raising prices for growers' coffee year in and year out) it is unlikely to have a big impact on Bang-3 (human flourishing from higher incomes). Most of the evidence on fair trade tends to weigh on the side of insignificant-to-small positive impacts, where positive impacts certainly occur in the low-price cropping seasons that redistribute profit away from intermediaries to growers.[63] In *The Taste of Many Mountains*, I try to give a fuller picture of the issues surrounding fair-trade coffee, but most economists view any modest benefits generated by the enormous fair-trade apparatus as dwarfed by other more proven interventions, and arguably by *direct* trade, in which coffee companies contract directly with growers to produce specialized, high-quality beans. But given the sensitivity of coffee prices to world supply, if we really want to raise prices for coffee growers, we should try to *reduce* the supply by encouraging movement into economic activity away from coffee, not promote growing more. Fair trade is not a bad intervention; it's just not one that Shrewd Samaritans get excited about.

Chapter 9

COMMON THEMES
AROUND WHAT WORKS

It is easy to become lost in the forest of global poverty and poverty programs. But like Hansel and Gretel, let me retrace our bread crumbs through the forest along the path that we have traveled (and hope that the crows haven't eaten them up).

Along this path we often walk through stages of ignorance, indifference, idealism, investigation, introspection, impact—the six *i*'s. We moved past the stages of idealism and ineffectiveness by investigating the causes of global poverty, why rich countries are rich and others remain poor. We learned about the sources of poverty and inequality in rich countries, and then about the nature of poverty traps: how people, places, and countries get stuck. Here we see how an intertwined set of geographical, economic, political, social, and psychological factors underlie the emergence of both poverty and prosperity. We introduced the concept of human flourishing as a goal for poverty and development work, and then in the last two chapters we examined an array of global poverty interventions to understand the degree to which different approaches are effective at intervening in this complex web of factors to break the poverty cycle.

What are the common themes that run through approaches that work? In this chapter I'd like to discuss five themes that stand out to me in the enormous body of research on poverty interventions. To summarize these briefly, they are 1) the cost-effectiveness of selected health interventions; 2) the younger the child, the better; 3) cash transfers as a benchmark of effectiveness; 4) the effect of holistic, integrated development; and 5) the value of faith-based interventions.

The Cost-Effectiveness of Selected Health Interventions

If one's primary goal is to save lives, there is simply nothing one can support that is more effective than a selected handful of inexpensive health interventions. The very cheapest among these include deworming and the provision of insecticide-treated mosquito nets, both of which received five stars for cost-effectiveness. The consensus among experts, including those at GiveWell, is that among properly targeted populations, both of these interventions have high Bang-2 and are tremendously effective at doing what they are designed to do. Deworming medicine like albendazole and praziquantel kills worms. Insecticide-treated mosquito nets help keep people malaria free. And the results of being worm free and malaria free in places like sub-Saharan Africa are substantial: big gains in general health, schooling, and productivity, so that so that these interventions also have a big Bang-3. The main issue with these preventative health interventions is that they are effective only where malaria and worms are prevalent, and there are many areas on the planet where they are not. But if a donor's goal is to have the greatest impact on health per dollar Somewhere On Earth, this is a great area to invest resources.

Some may have noticed I did not include an evaluation of vaccines among the twenty; vaccines are more typically the work of governments and large multilateral organizations and less-often driven by individual initiative. However, research indicates they yield health benefits at least as large as deworming and bed nets. Sachiko Ozawa at Johns Hopkins University and his collaborators at the Gates Foundation (which heavily supports vaccinations) estimate the average economic return to ten different common vaccines in ninety-four low- and middle-income countries to be sixteen times greater than cost. It is forty-four times over cost with the highest return vaccine, the one for measles.[1]

The Younger the Child, the Better

The second theme surrounding effective interventions relates to the age at which we intervene. Let us set aside the very cheap and cost-effective health interventions for a moment and focus on quality of life, especially as it relates to social integration, happiness, general welfare, and other aspects of human flourishing. Here the rock-solid consensus among economists is that early childhood interventions are far more effective than later-life interventions. Economist James Heckman presents a graph that illustrates the return to investments in human capital and captures decades of research on the returns to different policies and programs that seek to increase what economists call "human capital," which are the productive resources of the people that allow them to participate to lesser or greater extent in economic life.[2]

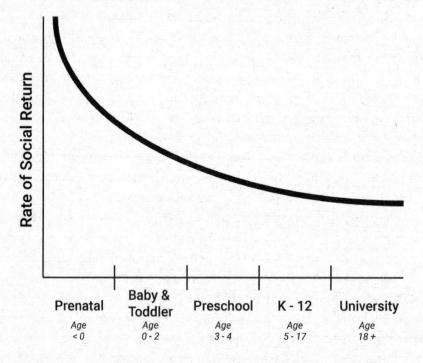

Figure 4: The Heckman Curve

Heckman argues that great benefits could accrue to society from diverting resources away from colleges, universities, and other forms of vocational training toward early childhood interventions targeted at children ages zero to three, and even prenatal investment. Nobel Laureate Heckman is a brilliant economist, one of the brightest minds on the planet, and virtually no one disputes his data. So why don't we just do what he says?

Part of the problem lies in two types of cognitive bias. One is what behavioral economists call "salience bias," a phenomenon related to the old saying "the squeaky wheel gets the grease." It is a bias that also probably explains much of why our attention is heightened toward addressing the tangible problems close to us. To put it bluntly, in-utero babies don't cause society that much trouble—and neither do infants and toddlers. High school dropouts, gang members, the homeless, and the unemployed—they are another story. Their problems, needs, and anger at their unfulfilled aspirations grab the attention of politicians, media, and everyone else. But the best research tells us that the genesis of these more salient problems are largely early childhood problems, just all grown up. On the positive side, we don't see all the socio-emotional skills becoming nested in the brains of three-year-olds at a quality preschool. The fruit of these skills—patience, grit, and self-control—seem to be part of the ingredients to successful learning and life, not becoming fully realized in the data until adulthood. But as the seeds of character are planted by parents and preschool teachers at an early age, they tend to germinate in the life of a well-adjusted adult. The causal relationship is hard to detect without decades-long science, but it is there. (There is little doubt that preschool teachers are far more important to society than university professors like me.)

The second reason we don't invest enough in early childhood is related to "present bias," the tendency to emphasize immediate costs and rewards at the expense of our long-term objectives. There is a delayed return to early childhood investments. We don't see their fruit for years, something the research of Heckman and his colleagues has demonstrated repeatedly, so we discount the benefits far too heavily. How many politicians will support programs that will only bear fruit decades after their reelection cycle has passed? Not enough.

Part of being a Shrewd Samaritan is being conscious of psychological phenomena like salience bias and present bias. They result in a misallocation of resources toward addressing pressing problems rather than more cheaply preventing the same problems from happening in the first place. Shrewd Samaritans favor cheap, preventative interventions over expensive interventions that address full-fledged dysfunction only after it has hit the fan.

I am always surprised by how many effective poverty interventions simply replicate what many would consider to be "good parenting." But where this is difficult, early childhood interventions that promote and even try to replicate good parenting, that uphold the value of the nurturing family, that provide safe spaces for children's minds to develop socio-emotional skills, and that provide crucial interventions for children at the earliest stages need far more domestic political support than they currently enjoy. And they must comprise a greater fraction of the budgets of overseas NGOs working with the global poor.

Cash Transfers as a Benchmark of Effectiveness

The growing consensus among economists is *not* that cash transfers should supplant all other forms of development aid, and it would be a mistake to interpret the exciting new research on cash transfers as saying so. An emerging consensus is, however, that governments and NGOs who like to give the poor "things" need to demonstrate that these "things" yield a bigger benefit than an equivalent cash transfer.[3]

There are good reasons behind this consensus. The first is the demonstrated effectiveness of cash transfers—at the very least, yielding substantial short- and medium-term benefits in consumption, enterprise investment, and general well-being. The second is a feeling by many that cash allows greater dignity to the poor in allowing them agency over their own choices rather than having those choices imposed by others through in-kind gifts. A third reason is forwarded mainly by economists: there is every reason to believe that cash is more efficient, both in terms of transaction costs and in terms of its flexibility in allowing the poor to use cash in the way that they best see fit.

But it is important to delineate the exceptions where in-kind gifts and interventions *may* yield bigger benefits than cash. One exception is when there are spillover benefits to the rest of the community. That individuals will likely undervalue these benefits to neighbors in decisions about how to spend cash provides a solid rationale for certain types of in-kind interventions. Vaccines, deworming, mosquito nets, and other health interventions are clear examples. If your child is dewormed, then if my child accidentally steps in the dust of his feces, your child's worms do not enter through the soles of my child's feet. If your family sleeps under an insecticide-treated bed net, you are a lot less likely to get malaria, and then, as your neighbor, so am I.

A second class of interventions in which the case can be made for in-kind programs over cash occurs with public goods, such as infrastructure and public sanitation, and common pool resources, like fresh-water wells. It has been long understood in economics that these types of goods tend to be under-supplied and inefficiently consumed within private markets. Cash can never solve the kind of collective action problems that are inherent to public goods and common pool resources. They are the purview of governments, skilled NGOs working closely with governments, or local collective action.

The third relates to interventions in which potential beneficiaries have poor information. For example, low-income parents in developing countries appear to chronically underestimate the returns to schooling.[4] This also may be the case with some kinds of new technologies, for example, where an NGO may be justified in providing a free high-yielding seed or fertilizer so that farmers may gain information about its viability.

But we must be careful of this later justification. For example, when we introduced clean wood-burning stoves through Mayan Partners in Guatemala, families lacked clear information about how well they would perform. As it turned out, by all of the technical metrics of the stove, in terms of their effects on indoor air pollution and in reducing wood usage, they performed to spec-ifications. But in the end, they were rejected for other practical and cultural reasons. The families in our village would have probably been better off with an equivalent cash transfer.

And while some may argue that in-kind gifts forcing investment over con-sumption can be justified in the face of people's present bias, these arguments are often forwarded by those whose giving is ruled by simplistic jingles like, "Give a man a fish and he eats for a day, teach him to fish and he eats for a lifetime." But when children are malnourished, a lack of food today can result in cognitive impairment that lasts for a lifetime. In general, we need to lean toward trusting the poor with most of these consumption-versus-investment decisions. Cash delegates this agency and authority to them and away from patronizing benefactors. Shrewd Samaritans understand the benefits and lim-itations of cash.

The Effect of Holistic, Integrated Development

Although it has been a guiding principle of many development practitioners for some time, economists have begun to discover holistic development. Until relatively recently, economists relegated issues such as trust, identity, character values, spiritual beliefs, self-esteem, temptation, self-control, aspirations, and hope to psychologists, theologians, and faith-based development practitioners. This has changed.

MIT economist Esther Duflo began to argue in a series of 2012 lectures about the paramount role hope and aspirations play in the lives and behavior of the poor.[5] Hopelessness among the poor, she argues, is accompanied by low aspirations, which diminish investment in just about everything—education, one's own skills, small businesses, even fertilizer on crops—all of which perpetuate poor outcomes. Over the last decade, economists are taking baby steps in understanding how social, psychological, economic factors, and spiritual worldview work together to create poverty traps. And there is increasing evidence that approaches that simultaneously address internal and external issues can be effective at helping free people from them.

The comprehensive poverty intervention program carried out by BRAC, and studied by Duflo and her colleagues, was a watershed discovery in social science. BRAC's holistic intervention, while secular in nature, realized significant impacts on all ten poverty indices the researchers tracked, including food security, household income, and health. Why did the program work? She suggests the multipronged intervention increased hope among the recipient population, encouraging them to invest more of their own resources in economic activity. The life coach may have been key as well.

In a similar way, my coauthors and I are convinced that it is the holistic nature of Compassion International's child sponsorship intervention that lies behind its success. When we originally sought to understand what lay behind the success of the approach, we asked Compassion directors what they thought was responsible. "That's easy," they replied. "Hope." "Hope?" It was a nebulous concept to us at the time, but we decided to investigate. In a series of follow-up studies, instead of formerly sponsored children, we began to look at currently sponsored Compassion children in different countries around the world.

As part of this research we gave 540 children living in the slums of Jakarta, Indonesia, a box of twenty-four colored pencils and asked them to "draw a picture of yourself in the rain."[6] About half of these children were sponsored. The others were siblings of sponsored children on the wait list. We then digitally coded the pictures based on twenty drawing characteristics psychologists have found to be correlated with better or worse mental health. For example, a self-portrait that is frowning or crying is correlated with depression, a missing mouth with insecurity, choosing light colors with optimism, holding an umbrella with self-efficacy. Samples of these drawings are shown in Figure 5.

This would help us test whether Compassion was making a difference, not only with providing tangible benefits like school fees and uniforms, but also through the four thousand hours staff and volunteers spend with each child over an average of ten years. This is time they spend tutoring sponsored children, nurturing them, and reminding them that they are loved by God. What we found from analyzing these pictures was that child sponsorship was responsible for increasing an index of hope by about two-thirds of a standard deviation—which, for the layperson, is a whole lotta hope. We also saw that the Compassion children had higher levels of happiness and self-efficacy.[7] Human nurturing creates human flourishing.

Other work in development economics has begun to show impacts from understanding the holistic relationship between "soft" phenomena such as psychology, worldview, and outlook and tangible economic opportunity.[8] Eager to test whether hope and aspirations could elevate the impacts of microfinance, I moved with my wife and two young daughters down to Oaxaca, Mexico, where we lived in a small Zapotec village for half a year while I set up a randomized controlled trial that we would call the Oaxaca Hope Project.

U.C. Davis's Travis Lybbert, Irvin Rojas, and I worked with *Fuentes Libres*, a Mexican NGO affiliated with the Evangelical Covenant Church, who had anecdotally reported anemic results from their microfinance lending program. We randomized a "hope" intervention among 780 women in Fuentes's fifty-two community banks, using a biblically based curriculum designed to boost women's hope: aspirations, ability to conceptualize pathways out of poverty, and sense of capability. To do this we worked with Skywalker Studios' E. J. Holowicki, award-winning documentary film producer Robert Machoian, and his film studies students at California State University at Sacramento to

HAPPINESS: 17TH PERCENTILE   HAPPINESS: 92ND PERCENTILE

SELF-EFFICACY:
8TH PERCENTILE

SELF-EFFICACY:
94TH PERCENTILE

HOPE: 7TH PERCENTILE   HOPE: 85TH PERCENTILE

Figure 5: Children's Drawings

create an inspiring documentary featuring four of the most successful women in the program.[9] Then we showed the film to half the groups. We also created refrigerator magnets for these women with verses from the Bible reinforcing our three components of hope and upon which they could write goals related to their business and family. Every time they took a trip to the fridge, the magnet would remind them of their goals.

After one year, we measured the impact of the hope intervention. It significantly increased aspirational hope. Women in the treatment groups were more confident of their own abilities and better able to conceptualize pathways to success for their businesses. There were also significant increases in the time women spent in prayer and in church attendance. We saw gains in the performance of their microenterprises. All of our six measures of business performance were higher in the treated groups, some marginally, others significantly. Women in the treated groups added a net increase of eight employees to their small businesses—a figure that sounds small, but few women had any employees at baseline and the net gain in the control group was zero.

We have been convinced from results of the experiment that holistic interventions, which focus not only on providing tangible economic opportunities but also on social, psychological, and even spiritual factors, can have tremendous potential relative to interventions that focus on economic, educational, or health interventions directly and alone. This approach recognizes that often what matters is not just economic opportunities but people's self-perceptions of their ability to respond to these opportunities. A holistic approach values the role of identity and culture in shaping economic outcomes. As theologian Al Tizon writes in his book *Whole and Reconciled*, a holistic approach flows out of the desire of a loving God to "mend, heal, restore, renew, re-create, and make whole—the world and everyone in it."[10] A holistic approach views economic development as a means to a broader concept of human flourishing, not as an end in itself.

The Value of Faith-Based Interventions

This brings us to a question of many religious as well as nonreligious people: does religion make a difference in economic outcomes? Of course, material prosperity is not the primary goal of Christianity, which is love of God and neighbor. Nor is it the primary goal of most other world religions for that matter. But the originator of this line of inquiry was early-twentieth-century author Max Weber in his *Protestant Ethic*.[11] The question over the effect of religion on economic development lay relatively untouched for decades, until recently when empirical methods reached a level of sophistication required to begin to successfully address it.

How religious faith affects the phenomena we associate with economic development is not a straightforward question. On one hand, religious faith may foster passivity. At the core of one type of faith may be the belief that God orchestrates all events, where one's principal role is relegated to faithful bystander with an eye toward heaven. This kind of spiritual worldview tends to be correlated with chronic poverty. On the other hand, religious faith may emphasize God's provision of opportunity and both the wisdom and agency to make positive choices. This kind of spiritual worldview fosters a disposition that is favorable to economic development. Different world religions emphasize one relative to the other, but even within Christianity we find a range of beliefs across the passivity/proactivity spectrum.

In the last decade there has been a flurry of exciting research that has sought to follow Weber and understand the relationship between spiritual beliefs and economic outcomes. Among the unconverted, religious belief often begins through missionary work. So researchers have found that a good place to start is examining the impact of historical Christian missionary activity and how it has affected the path of economic development centuries later. Harvard economist Nathan Nunn finds strong and enduring impacts on literacy and level of education from historical Christian missionary activity in colonial Africa.[12] Nunn uses *The Stations of Missionary Societies*, a large 1924 volume documenting the history of missions across the continent, to help establish geographic centers of historical Catholic and Protestant activity. He then makes use of the modern survey across Africa to test whether those with ancestors living close to Christian missions during the colonial period are more educated today. As it turns out, he finds both historical Catholic and Protestant missions to exhibit a powerful effect on modern-day literacy all across Africa. The effect of the Catholic missions, he finds, is somewhat weaker and limited mainly to men. The effects from the Protestant missions is stronger, where the vast majority of their effect is on the literacy of women. This, he explains, seems to be consistent with the emphasis Protestant missions placed on people learning to read the Bible themselves and on the education of women.

Influential studies in the top political science journals have moved beyond impacts of missions on literacy and have documented their effect on the evolution of democracy in developing countries. One study by Tomila Lankina at the London School of Economics and Political Science and her coauthor Lullit

Getachew examines the impact of Protestant missions on democratic development in India.[13] They look at the percentage of historical Christian converts in an Indian district and its current effect on citizen participation and electoral competitiveness. They summarize their findings well:

> Protestant mission curricula, which included modern subjects and put a premium on critical and abstract thinking . . . helped equip the most downtrodden—women, the lower caste, tribal, and untouchable groups—with practical skills and confidence to escape the clutches of a hierarchy that had kept them at the bottom. . . . Where missions had been active, mission schooling thus had human capital, social mobilization, and civic activism effects extending far beyond the community of converts.[14]

These types of results appear to extend across countries. Baylor's Robert Woodberry uses centuries of data detailing the location and intensity of Protestant and Catholic missionary activity in 142 developing countries. Using a set of democracy scores for these countries from an established political science database,[15] Woodberry looks at the historical effect of centuries of Protestant evangelism on the emergence of democratic political systems of government.[16] Woodberry writes:

> Protestant missionaries also transferred ideas, skills, and networks that made nonviolent, indigenous anticolonial, nationalist, and pro-democracy movements easier to develop and sustain. In addition, a significant minority of Protestant missionaries directly promoted democracy and equality through their teaching, translation, and support of nationalist organizations.[17]

His analysis controls for colonization by different countries, geography, disease prevalence during the time of missionary activity, and literacy levels before missionary activity began. He also argues that Protestant missions account for more democracy formation than Acemoglu and Robinson's explanation originating in settler mortality. What Woodberry's results show is that evangelistic Protestant missionary activity explains about half of the variation in democracy across the developing world, an overwhelming impact for any single variable. The impact is consistent across continents and other subsamples, when using alternative measures of democracy and employing sophisticated statistical checks to ensure that the relationship is a causal one and not merely correlation.

Other fascinating research reveals impacts on *economic* development from Christian missions. Researchers from the Hong Kong University of Science and Technology studied the effect of Protestant missions on the emergence of economic prosperity in China during 1840–1920.[18] After the country's loss in the first Opium War in 1842, Protestant missionaries flooded into China from Britain, the United States, and other Western countries. Though clearly a primary goal was Christian conversion, to this end missionaries in China built hundreds of hospitals and schools. These, however, acted as conduits for the flow of information: new ideas, new concepts, and new technology, which significantly advanced economic development.

What about the impact of Catholic missions? New research by economist Felipe Valencia Caicedo at the University of British Columbia studies the impact of Jesuit Catholic missions among the Guarani, an indigenous tribe living in modern-day Argentina, Brazil, and Paraguay.[19] This early tribal evangelization by the Jesuits, made famous by the 1985 movie *The Mission* starring Robert DeNiro and Jeremy Irons, was carried out from 1549 to 1767 and included thirty missions spread across the South American intersection of the three countries. The Jesuits were certainly interested in Christian conversion, but in contrast with their Franciscan brethren, also heavily emphasized schooling and economic development through the adoption of new agricultural technologies. The Jesuits were not around to see the long-term fruit of their labor. They were expelled from the region in 1767—part of their expulsion from Spain and Portugal and all of their colonies (the basis for the movie) by the Spanish king Charles III, who wanted to curtail Jesuit power in the New World.

Caicedo creates a novel data set that combines archival information about the location and scope of the missions with present-day economic outcomes. He finds no economic impact from the Franciscan missions, which did not as strongly emphasize education and economic development. But educational attainment was vastly greater in the areas of Jesuit missions among the Guarani, even in the centuries after Jesuit expulsion. Moreover, he estimates that educational levels *today* are 10 to 15 percent higher in areas that encompass the 250-year-old Jesuit missionary presence. There is also more broad use of higher agricultural technology, translating into incomes that are 10 percent higher than they would be otherwise.

These are remarkable impacts on secular development outcomes from Christian missions, but do they have implications for today? And there is a question about whether Christian missions merely facilitated the flow of Western ideas and technology or if Christian spiritual principles specifically played a major role in economic development.

Leading scholar in economics and religion Laurence Iannaccone wrote not long ago, "Nothing short of a genuine experiment will suffice to demonstrate religion's causal impact." In 2016, economist Dean Karlan and his colleagues decided to launch just this kind of experiment.[20] Karlan, a self-described agnostic Jew, assembled a group of three researchers that also included an evangelical Christian (James Choi at Yale) and an avowed atheist (Gharad Bryan at the London School of Economics). This was clearly a team that, on the whole, was not going to be accused of bias either for or against religion. The researchers studied the impact of International Care Ministries' "Transform" program, which works with more than ten thousand evangelical churches in the Philippines. In the Transform program, the local pastor leads thirty families in a weekly thirty-minute lesson in spiritual values, focusing on the gospel message and Christian living. Another component of the program provides practical health and livelihood information to the family to help stimulate microenterprise and keep children in school and well-nourished.

The three researchers asked ICM to run its normal Transform program, with its combined spiritual values and "secular" health and livelihood program, in a randomly selected eighty communities. In another eighty randomly selected communities, ICM introduced only the health and livelihood components, and in another eighty communities ICM ran only the spiritual aspects of the program. The fourth group of eighty communities received no intervention and served as a control group.

Six months after the conclusion of the Transform program, the researchers surveyed the 6,276 families participating in the experiment. The results gained national attention and surprised many researchers and practitioners, both faith-based as well as secular: those who received evangelical religious training not only felt like their lives had grown spiritually but also experienced a 9.2 percent increase in household income compared to those in the experiment who did not.[21] The researchers believe that the Christian teaching aspect of Transform increased *grit*, that elusive quality of persistence that helps people overcome life's small and large challenges and that keeps people focused on long-run objectives. It is the first experimental study testing Weber's *Protestant Ethic*, and it provides some evidence that the impact of Christian missions is a channel not just of Western ideas but of biblical principles themselves.

The spiritually based, holistic approach to human development is not new. For all the myriad mistakes, sins, and failures in the history of Christian missions, it has been an approach common to missionaries for centuries, Protestant and Catholic, from the Guarani in South America, to tribal peoples of sub-Saharan Africa, to the rural poor of the Philippines. Taken together, there is an increasing body of evidence that spiritually based, holistic interventions yield long-term impacts, not just on spiritual beliefs but on "secular" economic outcomes. It also gives us a fuller understanding of human beings and how they flourish. While there is more research that can be done to better understand the mechanisms behind holistic, integrated development, it is exciting to see mounting evidence of its fruit.

Heart and Mind in Our Parables

What can we learn from our two parables about holistic thinking? The Good Samaritan and the Shrewd Manager respectively represent *heart* and *mind*. But the Samaritan was not all heart and no mind. And the Manager was not all mind and no heart. Heart is more salient with the Samaritan: risking his life to save the injured man when the bandits could have been using him as bait, walking the dusty miles while the man rode on his horse, paying the innkeeper for his care, offering to cover additional expenses. These were intentional risks and sacrifices of his own well-being for that of another (heart), but with wisdom, boundaries, and an awareness of the limits of resources (mind). When it was time for him to finally tend to his own affairs, he substituted some of his money for his time and was on his way.

Like any good Econo-Man, the Manager's actions are deliberate. He understands the nature of reciprocating relationships, of give-and-take. He entertains no naïveté about the uses of worldly wealth. His hope is that some giving now will result in some taking after he gets sacked, an open door here, a welcome mat there. But there are interesting subtleties at play in the cultural context. Listeners of the parable would understand the master's debtors to be not just indebted but poor, and reciprocating relationships are far more important and more common among the poor than the rich.[22] While the rich can take their economic lumps in solitude, an unexpected economic shock for the poor induces a desperation that forces them to rely on a neighbor. In his high position as the master's steward, the manager probably had little use or respect for the poor and their social networks. But his actions reflect his own preparation and willingness to take his place in the social milieu of reciprocating relationships among the poor, in the table fellowship made up of outsiders, tax collectors, and sinners, the "lost but found" that populate the larger narrative of Jesus.[23]

Without heart we are unmotivated to engage the poor and needy. Without mind, we do so ineffectually. Heart and mind are the twins of fruitful engagement with our global neighbor. As Jesus told his followers as he sent them out among the villages of Israel, "I am sending you out like sheep among wolves. Therefore be as *shrewd* as snakes and as *innocent* as doves" (Matthew 10:16).

While the balance between heart and mind is fundamental to our engagement with the world, it is also a goal of this engagement. We should labor for the economic capacity of the poor, but for the capacity of their hearts as well, that they would use this growing economic capacity to love and care for their own neighbors. In some respect, this is the only kind of development that is sustainable.

Part 4

BECOMING
A SHREWD
SAMARITAN

Chapter 10

GIVING OUR TIME
AND MONEY

I am an economist and am thus enamored with charts and graphs. I find that the most useful of these help us neatly synthesize data and ideas. They organize our thinking. The chart below attempts to organize our thinking about giving away our time and money.

We can engage in acts of compassion independently or they can be within an organized structure. They can be spontaneous and short-term, often in response to a specific and immediate need. Or they may be more strategic and planned, often forming a longer-term commitment to a person or group. Finally, compassion for others typically involves contributions of either time or money—and often both.

	Spontaneous, Short-Term	Strategic, Long-Term
Independent	*Time:* Help confused migrant find housing *Money:* Buy handicraft made in remote village	*Time:* Serve as "big brother" to at-risk youth *Money:* Support missionary friend's orphanage in Tanzania
Institutional	*Time:* 1 week in Nepal with Doctors Without Borders *Money:* Online donation for earthquake disaster relief	*Time:* Serve as foreign missionary or aid worker *Money:* Provide cash grant for microenterprise

Figure 6

The chart above creates categories for these distinctions, but none of these eight categories is better than the others. One might be tempted to place the strategic, long-term commitments on a higher pedestal, but it is wrong to assume that strategic compassion trumps spontaneous compassion. Indeed, the example Jesus gives in the Good Samaritan lies in the upper left individual/spontaneous quadrant, involving both the Samaritan's time and money.

Both strategic and spontaneous love of neighbor are of great value, and individuals tend to engage in one over the other based on their natural gift-edness and personality traits. In psychological indices that measure sensing versus intuition, those who tip more highly toward the sensing side tend to be more prone to spontaneous acts of compassion. These are the people who are the first to notice the needy person on the street, the one left out in the crowd. In contrast, those with a more intuitive personality trait will tend to favor strategic approaches to compassion. These are the people who spend more of their time developing creative approaches to meet the needs of the world. My wife, Leanne, and I make a good team because she is more sensing and I am more intuitive. She is better than I am at recognizing the needs in context. I usually develop the larger idea, the general approach, and the structure. The needs of the world require both strategists and "spontanists," if that could be a new word.

Sometimes we tend to put those who work independently above those who work within an institutional structure. Our culture is enamored with individual achievement. However, it is easy to be influenced too strongly by romantic visions of poverty work. While individual acts of compassion are laudable, especially spontaneous ones, work in the context of an organized institutional framework facilitates accountability, interdependence, specialization, learning, the ability to scale, and a number of other outcomes that challenge the solo operator.

Institutions also tend to represent commitments. A church without any organized programming, for example, is often a church without commitments to the welfare of any definable group of people. Nongovernment organizations (NGOs), at a basic level, represent a commitment to charitable work and a definable group of people that supersedes the whims of an individual. Although our culture tends to value the individual effort above the institutional effort, it is important to bring this back into balance.

Time Well Spent

My friend Jodi is married to a popular pastor here in Berkeley and leads a nonprofit organization working with Burmese refugees in nearby Oakland. We met for coffee recently to talk about her work, which as one might expect, is somewhat chaotic: many refugees, many issues, many needs. But one of her challenges is that the refugees come with different degrees of preparedness for life in our country. Some are fairly comfortable with the language and culture and have brought with them skills that will play well in the labor market; others appear pretty lost in America, speak little English, and have few marketable skills—a group comprised of many older women. Life in America is simply a giant shock, and culture prevents them from getting out of the house to dive into the melting pot. Still others enter the country with professional skills of different kinds, but their English isn't good, and they are still uncomfortable in American culture. The last group, she described, are the opposite. Their English is decent and they have caught on to the culture well, but they have few skills, characteristic of many of the younger men and women.

So the question was how the organization should divide its time between the different individuals and families. Economists love these kinds of questions, and as I thought about it, I ended up drawing the following chart on her coffee napkin:

	Cultural/Soft Skills	Lacking Cultural/ Soft Skills
Hard Skills	*Group 1:* Help match with employers in local tech industry	*Group 2:* Center offers course in work-based language and culture
Lacking Hard Skills	*Group 3:* Enroll in vocational courses at local community college	*Group 4:* Create support groups made up of this group to meet at center

Figure 7

Jodi also mentioned that, along with the obvious importance of doing good work, the organization would like to create some success stories for its donors so that funding could continue to support the work. This seemed to create a triage situation for the allocation of the organization's time among the different groups. Because networks in this type of community tend to be close-knit, income is often widely shared. Therefore, the organization's time might be best spent first on the low-hanging fruit in Group 1 with both hard and soft skills. Getting this group into decent jobs should be priority number one—so that their income can support others in the family network. The organization should focus its time on Group 2 next, since soft skills in language and culture are arguably a little easier to pick up than hard skills. If possible, the organization could help people in Group 3 enroll in vocational training courses at one of the good community colleges in Oakland.

What to do with Group 4 posed an interesting challenge. If Jodi's organization were to allocate its time teaching these older women both English and hard skills, not only would it be an uphill battle, it would use up the organization's resources, and key breadwinners might still be unemployed. But at the same time, their dignity is just as important as the others'. Perhaps the best approach would be to simply help these women support each other in the transition. So rather than using a lot of the organization's time to try to impart a bunch of different skills to Group 4, she thought of simply organizing times and spaces for them to be together, perhaps to sew or bake and just generally support each other.

As I thought more about it, I believe this framework has some general implications for the way Shrewd Samaritans can think about how to use their time. While keeping an eye on the dignity and worth of everyone, it is good to prioritize time where there is the sense that it is likely to bear fruit. This is particularly true when those who have been helped in a group can then, in turn, care for others.

The tension that always must exist here is that sometimes we are called to simply "be" with people, without expectation of bearing fruit. This might be the case when we spend time at the side of one with a terminal disease or little chance of "transformation," but we hope merely to affirm their human dignity. There is a mentally disabled man in our church in Berkeley who many of us spend time with as our friend, listening to his thoughts and stories, engaging with him, not because we expect transformation but simply to affirm his dignity and place as a member of our community.

Giving Our Money Away

Ryan Loofbourrow is a homelessness guru, a recognized leader in the urban poverty field. Most of his adult working life has been devoted to finding effective solutions for homelessness in greater Sacramento County, where a disproportionate number of homeless call home.

Ryan is also my brother-in-law.

During the holidays, we have been known to conversationally isolate ourselves from the holiday chatter to engage in wonky conversations about poverty interventions. It's a guaranteed buzz killer at any Christmas party, and other family members usually head for the eggnog when this conversation starts up again. The problem is that there is nothing either of us finds to be more interesting.

Much of what our conversation stems around is effective giving. We want to give, especially during the holiday season, when the spirit of giving descends on America (along with the December 31st tax-deduction deadline). We want to move from Idealism to Impact, but not all poverty interventions and not all types of giving get us there. As seen in the previous chapters, some of it is effective, some of it is ineffective, and some of it can be downright destructive in any number of ways.

Consider, as an example, the recurrent focus of brother-in-law Ryan's and my yuletide conversations: how to best help the American urban homeless. Unlike cash transfers given to the poor in developing countries,[1] the most reliable studies indicate that a significant fraction of the cash given on the street to homeless people in North America is spent on tobacco, alcohol, and narcotics.[2] Using firsthand survey data, a team of empirical sociologists estimated the average monthly income among panhandlers in urban Toronto to be $638, about half of which came through panhandling. Of this, $200 on average was spent on food, $112 on tobacco, and $80 on alcohol and narcotics.[3]

The decision about giving money to people on the street presents an ethical dilemma because it pits two widely held values against one another. Both of these values have deep roots that are embedded in Western religion and culture. The first is *justice*, by which individuals receive based on merit—e.g., "A little sleep, a little slumber, a little folding of the hands to rest, and poverty will come on you like a thief,"[4] and "The one who is unwilling to work shall not eat"[5]—where the status of being poor may be a deserved consequence of moral lapse. The second is *mercy*, defined as compassion without regard to merit—e.g., "A generous person will prosper; whoever refreshes others will be refreshed,"[6] and "Give to the one who asks you, and do not turn away from the one who wants to borrow from you"[7]—where generosity to the poor is identified as a paramount virtue.

While acknowledging the dilemma, our default response should lean toward giving. Why? Because both biblical values and economic reasoning lead us there. First, Jesus is clear on the subject, and this alone should be sufficient for those who identify as Christians. Second, the Good Samaritan teaches us to love our neighbor *as ourselves*. As we "love ourselves" throughout the day, we are constantly reallocating small amounts of cash between the activities of our lives in ways we believe will make us better off: wallet to cash register, ATM to wallet, and back again. If reallocating a little cash to our needy neighbor obviously helps our neighbor more than it hurts us, then in this kind of giving we are literally loving our neighbor "as ourselves"—by carrying out the same kind of small reallocation that we do every day to care for our own needs.

Moreover, one can make the case that handing a homeless person $5 is a pretty efficient transfer. It involves zero administrative costs. It gives a person agency to use the money in the way that, at least in his own view, will be the most helpful. The data show this could include buying alcohol to medicate pain or feelings of hopelessness. And while medicating hopelessness with alcohol does (kind of shockingly, actually) have some biblical precedent,[8] enabling self-destruction is a reason one might choose not to give. We also might choose not to give in particular situations because we feel it would reward manipulative behavior or intentional indolence, or create an unhealthy dependence. But that some of the money given to people on the street is used for alcohol and drugs may not be a good enough reason not to give. The vast majority is spent on other basic needs, and these are choices made by the receiver, not the giver. The overall biblical message is that those who can give are accountable for giving, and those who receive are accountable for how they use it.[9]

Research suggests that there are far better ways to help the homeless, but they involve more substantial resources than the average street handout. Ryan and many of his colleagues who work with the homeless favor an approach called "housing first." While other approaches use housing as a kind of carrot to incentivize sobering up, "housing first" takes the opposite approach. The model is based on the evidence that the extreme stress endemic to homelessness and the constant need to find food and shelter cause homeless people to make poor decisions in other areas. "Housing first" prioritizes permanent shelter to provide stability and reliability, freeing up mental bandwidth for people to make better decisions.

This idea that people make better choices when they are housed and well fed has strong support from behavioral economics. Harvard behavioral economist Sendhil Mullainathan's book *Scarcity* with Princeton psychologist Eldar Shafir describes a series of experiments in which subjects voluntarily went without food and were asked a set of questions that required significant thought. The same subjects performed better when they were well fed than when they were hungry. They performed especially badly when they were hungry and experimenters gave them food-related questions (e.g., "If Bill had six juicy bacon cheeseburgers and gave three to Larry, how many . . ."). In another experiment, dieters who were subjects in a hidden word search game were much slower finding the next word in the puzzle after discovering the word *DOUGHNUT.*

We can learn two important lessons from Mullainathan and Shafir's research. The first is that while in some cases bad decisions can lead to poverty, poverty also causes people to make bad decisions. Those of us who lead "respectable" upper-middle-class lives would make the same questionable decisions that are made by the chronically homeless if we were constantly preoccupied with satisfying basic needs like food and shelter. Understanding this should increase our level of empathy toward the homeless. They are us, but poor. Secondly, giving the poor sufficient resources to meet basic needs will measurably improve their prospects at leading productive lives.

Giving can be legitimately based on mercy or on merit. Giving can be transformative, such as is the case with housing first, restorative surgeries, providing critical medicines, or internationally sponsoring a child. But giving can also be destructive, where it may enable harmful behaviors,[10] undermine markets,[11] and exacerbate government corruption.[12] Giving also may be neutral, such as giving shoes or laptop computers to children overseas—not harmful, but ineffective at solving root problems.

Four Types of Giving

I want to classify types of giving into four distinct categories, each of which has important consequences for how our giving impacts the poor. Figure 8 tries to summarize types of giving and the different impacts our giving may have on the poor. As shown by the arrows in the diagram, giving cash (or in-kind donations) to the poor has different effects in different contexts among different populations.

Alms-Giving

Alms-giving is giving out of mercy and compassion toward others. It is giving to those who are unable to function in society without the help of others, either directly, through a nonprofit organization, or through the state. It is a necessary, appropriate, and biblical response toward a category of the poor who, through no fault of their own, are unable to survive without leaning on others in society: the widow, the orphan, the mentally disabled, those with severe psychological problems, and others with little realistic or immediate possibility of being self-sufficient. Alms-giving is not generally transformative; it simply fulfills a posture of mercy toward the disadvantaged that is required of all Christians and of any good society.

Ineffective Giving

While alms-giving is not directed toward empowering the poor, other types of giving seek to move people from a place of dependence toward independence. This can be done effectively or ineffectively. Ineffective giving can take many forms. When donors give in-kind goods that don't line up with the needs or aspirations of the poor, it usually results in ineffective giving.

Economists talk of "binding constraints," those factors that are truly impeding forward movement toward an objective. Ineffective giving is directed at something other than binding constraint, and consequently it has no effect on forward movement. For example, as mentioned in Chapter 5, poverty traps can involve both internal and external constraints. If the binding constraint causing the trap is internal, but giving focuses on external constraints, it will be ineffective—and vice versa.

For instance, a spiritually based program may increase a person's motivation to escape poverty, perhaps through messages that provoke a genuine inner

ABOUT OUR GIVING

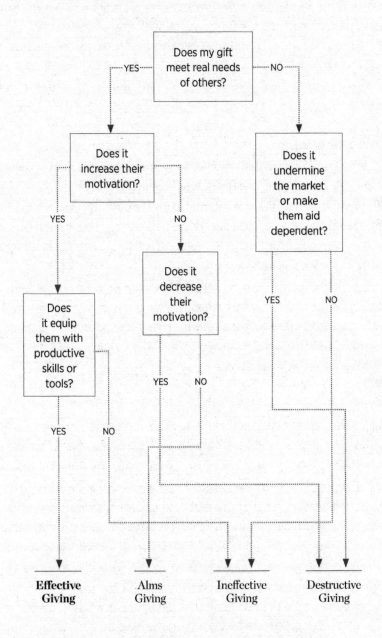

Figure 8: Different Types of Giving

transformation, but fail to equip that person with the practical skills needed for upward economic mobility. Ineffective giving also occurs when an intervention offers helpful skills and tools for earning a living but ignores inward issues if they in fact represent the binding constraint. Perhaps a person doesn't need cash, credit, or vocational training as much as healthy self-esteem balanced by humility, understanding a respect for authority, the ability to work in harmony with others, overcoming a psychology of victimization or entitlement, or help in establishing goals and aspirations.

Destructive Giving

Destructive giving enables dysfunction and undermines human dignity. It undercuts the functioning and development of markets by flooding economies with free goods. It occurs when misguided giving undercuts the motivation to work. It breeds cultures of dependence on the state or on charitable organizations. It conveys a message to the able poor that they are unable, sapping them of their motivation and self-esteem.

Steve Corbett and Brian Fikkert's *When Helping Hurts* is the go-to reference for avoiding destructive giving.[13] By our best intentions we can both demotivate and disempower the poor with giving to support interventions that fail to recognize the capacity of the vast majority of the world's poor to lead lives of dignity and self-sufficiency.

Effective Giving

Effective giving moves individuals who are either "willing but unable" or "unwilling but able" to a place of being both willing and able to achieve economic self-sufficiency. Givers focused on reducing poverty should choose some of the high Bang-3 interventions listed in Chapters 7 and 8 that have rigorously demonstrated impacts. By giving part of our income to programs and organizations (or cash directly!) to places where there is rigorously demonstrated impact, we can move beyond "feel-good giving" that may be ineffective or destructive toward giving that genuinely makes a positive difference.

Finally, it is important to remember that people have varying amounts of money and time across their life stages. As the figure above shows, when we are younger and when we are seniors, we typically have more time, perhaps also when we are newly married but the babies haven't arrived yet. But as anyone

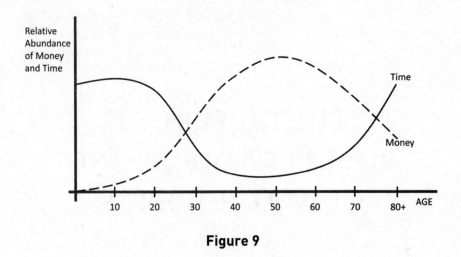

Figure 9

who has been through that life stage knows, time becomes scarce when young children are in the picture (and money may be fairly scarce too). But as we move into middle age, the data show income tends to increase until roughly our mid-fifties on average, and then as we move into retirement, we again have more time (but income generally goes down). So being conscious of our life stage is important as we consider whether it is our time or money we give, and we should not feel guilty when we find ourselves in the midst of a life stage when it is difficult to give as much as we would like of one or the other.

Chapter 11

THE DIFFERENT ROLES IN ADDRESSING GLOBAL POVERTY

When giving talks to college students, I find that most are looking to align their lives with a cause greater than themselves. Many could not be more enthusiastic about playing a role in global poverty alleviation. Enthusiasm isn't the problem. The problem is *what* role. Particularly for young adults who are making vocational decisions, the maze of options and opportunities can become paralyzing. In response, I have developed some vocational bins in the larger space of international development and poverty work. Each represent important roles that individuals can play in the larger effort of helping people to flourish and live with dignity across our planet. These roles I call Investigators, Givers, Advocates, Creators, Directors, and Practitioners.

Before I elaborate on each of these, a few points are in order. The first is that diversity is not just a feel-good concept espoused by California liberals. (Although it is.) Diversity is a biblical concept. One of my favorite passages in the Bible is the twelfth chapter of the apostle Paul's first letter to the Corinthians, where he lays out his diversity argument. Paul teaches us that each person is given specific gifts of healing, helping, teaching, administration, and other spiritual gifts that are crucial to the whole. Each playing her own instrument, the band thrives.

For economists, this argument is not a new one. Early on the founding father of economics, Adam Smith, highlighted the advantages of a division of labor, which many today view as the foundation of human society. Although

Paul's conception of diversity was formulated in the context of the first-century church, the advantages of diversity are supported by good science, where a plethora of new evidence shows that teams made up of a diverse collection of individuals are more creative and more productive than teams of people who are all the same.[1] So while we might be tempted to elevate the role of the big donor, the role of the academic who makes a major discovery about a poverty intervention, or the leader of the NGO implementing a transformational intervention, all of the roles are vital. Moreover, even though our vocation is likely to lie mainly in one role, it is good for us to be active to some degree in all six.

Investigators

My primary role is as an Investigator, so I'll begin there. Among all the different approaches, policies, and programs aimed at reducing poverty, a primary role of the Investigator is to find out which actually work. Investigators are often academic researchers with an interest in global poverty, for whom the balance of their time not devoted to research is given to teaching. Other development researchers are based at institutions such as the World Bank, domestic nonprofit research institutions such as the International Food Policy Research Institute or the Center for Global Development, or they are affiliated with secular or faith-based NGOs overseas such as Oxfam, CARE, Food for the Hungry, or World Vision.

While many investigators working in the poverty area try to answer questions related to "what works," others investigate causes of poverty, while still others create frameworks for issues related to ethics, meaning, and motivation that underlie our thinking about global issues. Many of the latter with backgrounds in philosophy and theology, such as Peter Singer, Ron Sider, and Bryant Myers, have made vital contributions in helping us understand our responsibilities and relationship to the poor.

Most investigation in the "what works" area is carried out by people with master's or doctoral degrees in economics, statistics, political science, sociology, public health, education, and related fields. People with PhDs tend to take the lead on research projects, directing teams of people with master's degrees and field assistants. Poverty research is sometimes viewed as glamorous work, but it is mostly *hard* work.

The work of the modern Investigator increasingly lies in trying to figure out if x causes y. This sounds rather banal, but for a true Investigator nothing is more exciting. Here the x's are often poverty interventions in economic development, health, or education, although sometimes the x's are *causes* of poverty like malnutrition, corruption, wars, and monsoon floods. The y's, in contrast, are welfare-related outcomes we care about, like children's health, learning in school, microenterprise growth, the number of days children receive adequate food, and so forth. Relevant combinations of x's and y's create the basis for research that pushes out the frontier of our knowledge about causes, consequences, and cures for global poverty.

The trick in all this is in understanding the causality between the x's and y's. Today poverty investigators often run randomized controlled trials (RCTs) to ascertain the level of causality between an x and a y, where the x is randomly assigned to a treatment group within a pool of subjects. When it is difficult or unethical to run an RCT, researchers use quasi-experimental methods, such as comparing the changes in y between two populations over time, one of whom gets the x at some arbitrary point. In other cases, researchers make use of an arbitrary rule delineating program eligibility (such as the "under age 12" rule that determined eligibility for sponsorship by Compassion), and then they statistically compare the y's of individuals on either side of the program eligibility rule.

Whatever technique is used, once Investigators begin to get a handle on the relationships—and the context in which these relationships are operative—then the Investigator's job is well done and the ball lies in the hands of others. Even when we know what works, the task remains of motivating Givers and Practitioners to carry out what is likely to be an effective intervention.

Givers

The work of the Giver is as challenging as any and must rely on a relationship with Investigators and Practitioners for giving to be effective. The problem is that the relationships between actors in the world of charitable giving differ substantially from the normal relationship that exists between the consumer and seller of a product. If consumers buy a product or service that is dissatisfying, the market mechanism feeds this information back to the seller, who either improves the product or goes out of business. With charitable giving to the nonprofit sector, the "buyer" (the donor) is distinct from the "consumer" (who may live far away overseas). So even if the product is ineffective, this information may not be transmitted back to the buyer/donor, replaced instead by a handful of warm anecdotes of some "consumers" who claim to have benefited from the program. Since most development NGOs do not carry out scientific evaluations on their own work, even they themselves may not fully understand the impact of their programs.

Why is it so difficult to identify what works?

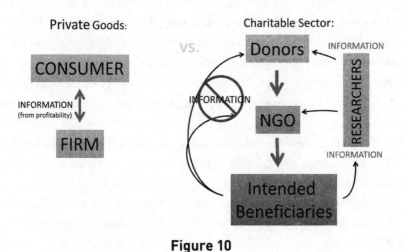

Figure 10

How does a potential Giver know what works?

Whereas Investigators depend on Givers to provide funding for interventions (and maybe for their own research too), Givers must also depend on Investigators to use rigorous impact evaluation techniques for information about effective giving. Anecdotal information from other sources, even from Practitioners, is unlikely to be reliable.

Insights from behavioral economics and psychology help us to understand why this is true. Despite their best efforts, NGOs suffer from the same basic flaws in human nature that afflict the rest of us. One of these is *confirmation* bias, where we tend to accept information that more readily conforms to the way that we think the world is or should be.[2] Human beings find it easier to believe things that they would *like* to be true than things they would like to believe are false. For example, psychologists carried out an experiment among a pool of college students with opinions on affirmative action and gun control, finding not only that they intentionally sought out arguments from sources that would likely confirm their prior beliefs, but also that they were much more likely to interpret any new information toward their own biases.[3] Because most people doing nonprofit work among the poor believe they are doing good and meaningful work, it is hard for even the most candid to provide an even-handed assessment of their own effectiveness even if they truly wanted to.

There are other psychological phenomena that play even more subtle tricks. The human brain is constantly looking for patterns in visual, audial, and statistical phenomena to explain the world and make it less mysterious, a phenomenon called *pareidolia*. People everywhere report seeing images of Elvis Presley in rust stain patterns, tree trunks, and potato chips.[4] The same phenomena manifests when our brains subconsciously seek patterns between cause and effect in our work. When I was growing up, our dog Greta felt that her work was to bark the mailman off our property every time he dropped off the mail. In her mind it worked every time. Undoubtedly due to her remarkable 100 percent success rate, she didn't stop barking the mailman away until the day she died. Patterns can be deceptive.

One of the most common psychological tricks that fool not only Givers but NGOs themselves about their own work is *mean reversion*: people opt for help when things are bad. But if there is one lesson life teaches us, it is that when things are bad, they usually get better. I work out with a doctor friend of mine, Sanjay, who tells me that 85 percent of doctor visits are unnecessary. He says the vast majority would get better anyway. I was particularly impressed with Sanjay's honesty in confessing this to me, especially given that he is a doctor. But if doctors were to measure their effectiveness by the fraction of people who get better after an appointment, they would vastly overestimate their effectiveness. In the same way, the poor do not select into poverty programs randomly. It is often after a terrible calamity or when something has especially gone awry. It is easy then for a poverty organization to attribute any subsequent improvement to their program's effectiveness. Givers need to watch out for this and ask tough questions to nonprofits.

The bottom line for Shrewd Samaritans in the role of Givers is this: focus giving on programs that have scientifically demonstrated impacts. This is the approach of the Gates Foundation and others who truly understand effective giving. The Gates Foundation does not give unless there is evidence of impact or their grant will be used to provide such evidence. There is no other reliable way to make sure your giving will make the difference you intend. GiveWell. org is a good resource for small donors who want to make sure their charitable donations are used in ways that genuinely benefit others. (A shortcoming of GiveWell, however, is that it has a rather limited focus within the more easily measurable space of economic and health outcomes, especially the latter, tending to overlook NGOs and interventions that have longer-term impacts and promote a broader conception of human flourishing.)

Givers furthermore need to be cautious of the "warm glow" that appears to motivate giving more than the actual impact it has on potential beneficiaries. Behavioral economist Clair Null carried out an experiment to see whether people give to charity to maximize the social benefit of their giving or to maximize the "warm glow" effects from giving.[5] She allowed subjects to make donations across a number of well-known poverty-fighting organizations: CARE, Mercy Corps, and Oxfam America. Subjects in the experiment tended to diversify their donations across the organizations despite their similar work. Even when Null made one of the donation recipients blatantly more "productive" (by increasing the matching rate for donations made to that organization), subjects continued to diversify their contributions across the charities based on the positive feelings they received from donations to multiple charities.

The insights from Null's experiment should help Givers to check their motives for giving. A Giver may want to donate to multiple charities for different reasons: to sustain relationships or to show individuals or groups that we support their efforts. But it is worth reflecting why we give to each recipient. In general, it is better to try to focus our giving where it is demonstrated to be effective and let our "warm glow" come from that.

This being said, sacrificial giving can bring great joy and renewal into our lives. I ran an experiment as part of a talk I gave to a group of students at the University of San Francisco, beginning with a modified example of Peter Singer's pond dilemma, where a person must decide whether to ruin his work clothes to save a drowning child. To understand the modification I made to Singer's dilemma, you must first understand that the most precious personal possession of a college student today is his or her cell phone—nothing else comes remotely close.[6]

I posed to the room: "Suppose you were walking by a pond on the way to school," I asked them, even though there are not many ponds in San Francisco, "and you saw a child drowning in the pond. You have your cell phone in your pocket, and you cannot leave it on the bank (suppose there are sketchy people nearby who you believe would steal it). Would you dive into the water, ruining your cell phone in order to save the child?" There were about thirty people in the room. Every hand went up in the room indicating they would eagerly lay waste to their phone to save the drowning child.

But they didn't know this was a setup.

I subsequently presented some statistics on the positive impacts of GiveDirectly's cash transfers. "So if everybody in this room were to give $50, we could dramatically reduce hunger among a desperately poor Ugandan child, perhaps even saving a life." A sense of unease began to manifest in the room. I continued, "A donor has pledged $50 to GiveDirectly for every one of you who is willing to part with your cell phone for two weeks." The unease began to grow, as engaged smiles were transformed into expressions of deep anxiety. They reminded me of the face I saw once on a student who had forgotten to study for a midterm I began to hand out in class.

I held out a basket to collect the phones and put my smartphone in it. "I'm first," I began. In the end, fourteen people in the room put their phones in the basket to be locked in a file cabinet in the Department of Economics for two weeks. I was pretty impressed.

The next day another of my favorite students, Sam, appeared at my office. "Professor, I feel like I'm kind of going nuts." I studied his face for a moment. He was smiling, but it was a rather odd smile, and he actually did look like he was going a little nuts. "Please . . . could I have my phone back?" But in the end, only Sam asked for his phone back, and over the course of the two weeks, I had students email me with their thoughts on parting with their cell phone so that another person could eat. For the younger ones, it seemed to be their first real experience being Givers, at least in a truly sacrificial way. While they reported feeling cut off from friends, the lack of a phone freed up time for personal reflection that had been absent before. They spent more time talking with people face-to-face. And they reflected often on the purpose of their cell-phone fasting—to allow others to eat. I too felt a little disconnected from the world. I ended up in a major San Francisco traffic jam that made me an hour late for dinner, something I could have avoided with quick access to Google Maps on my phone. But it was a small price to pay for the collective solidarity we felt with a family in East Africa who we would never see but whom we could be confident was better off than if the thirteen of us hadn't taken the plunge into temporary cell-phone abstinence.

I met one of my favorite Givers when I had the opportunity to speak a few years ago at the Gathering, an annual conference of large Christian donors. (By large I refer not to height or girth, but to income and generosity.) Attendees at the conference are people of wealth, and they meet each year to talk about the best ways to give substantial amounts of it away. I gave the talk shortly after the publication of our impact study on child sponsorship, and afterward I was approached by a middle-aged man with a warm, Southern drawl who said, "Bruce, I just wanted you to know my wife and I internationally sponsor 31,543 children through Compassion right now." The figure stunned me— first because it was so exact—he had the number right down to the single digits, like an attentive hen keeping track of her eggs. But at $38 per child per month this man and his wife were sending well over $1,100,000 a month to a bunch of fortunate overseas kids. All I could think at the moment was, *Well done, billionaire Bob!* I didn't know how he had made his money, but he had found his niche, as a Giver, transforming lives—31,543 at a time.

Advocates

The book of Proverbs, that ancient Hebrew text written nearly three thousand years ago, contains these inspiring words to those who would stand with the poor:

> Speak out on behalf of the voiceless,
> and for the rights of all who are vulnerable.
> Speak out in order to judge with righteousness
> and to defend the needy and the poor. (Proverbs 31:8–9 CEB)

An Advocate is one who "pleads the case of another," one who "publicly supports or defends the interests of a group." It is a role distinct from the Investigator or the Giver, from the Creator, Director, or Practitioner. The proverb talks about two aspects of being an Advocate: voice and defense. Those living in poverty often do not have a voice. Or if they do, it is often ignored. One role of Advocates is to publicly articulate—give voice—to a community whose concerns have been overlooked by the larger society.

The second role of an Advocate is to defend. If you are part of the great middle class in a wealthy, democratic country like the United States, you probably encounter minimal obstacles defending your ability to obtain sufficient food, shelter, a life free from violence, and other obstacles to a life of human dignity. Those called to be Advocates for the poor are not content with having secured these things for themselves, but they go out of their way to defend the poor in their struggle to lead lives of dignity.

Writing in the *Stanford Social Innovation Review*, Ann Christiano and Annie Neimand list several tips for Advocates that draw effectively upon insights in behavioral science and psychology.[7] They argue that advocates will tend to be ignored if they focus on abstract concepts and statistics, especially when they contradict people's prior-held beliefs, opinions, or identities. Instead, they contend that effective advocates harness the power of story and narrative. Effective advocates focus on creating mental images that evoke action based on emotional responses to narrative rather than trying to achieve intellectual acquiescence to facts, even when there is solid empirical evidence behind an argument (which of course is the only appropriate time to use narrative like this ethically). They suggest that advocates focus on specific communities that are both *influenceable* and *influential*, whose own behavior it is possible to change and in turn influence that of larger society.

I know of no better examples of Advocates than my friends Russell Jeung and Dan Schmitz, who along with their spouses and extended group of friends, have dedicated their lives to a Cambodian immigrant community living in Oakland, California. As Russell writes in his excellent 2016 autobiography *At Home in Exile*, the relationship began with his decision to move in with Dan, who in 1989 had intentionally relocated himself from the affluent San Francisco suburbs into a cockroach-infested inner-city apartment complex.[8] Living in the apartment complex were a network of Cambodian families who had fled the horrors of the Khmer Rouge, taking refuge in East Oakland, an area plagued by poverty, gangs, and drugs.

Inspired by a biblical call to live in solidarity with the poor, Dan along with

Russell, then a doctoral student in sociology at UC Berkeley, immersed them-selves into the community of the fifty-six-unit Oak Park apartment complex. Early on they were robbed multiple times and threatened by drug dealers, but they quickly began to build bridges with their neighbors—especially the kids, who spent a good deal of their time scurrying in and out of their living spaces. Soon they created an after-school tutoring center housed in their apartment, on whose walls, instead of the usual decorative posters and artwork, hung the ABCs. This life of simplicity and service became attractive to other students finishing school at Berkeley, who had a greater interest in the inner-city poor than jump-starting their own professional careers. Gradually they, too, began to take the plunge to live among the refugees in the Oak Park complex. The OPC, the Oak Park Community, an organic Christian community of inner-city refugees and ex-suburban college graduates, was born.

The Shrewd Samaritans in the OPC have used the power inherent to their status and education to give the refugee families a voice that advocates for their welfare. This voice began to emerge at the time of the "Personal Responsibility and Work Opportunities Act of 1996," which cut off food stamp and disability benefits to noncitizen immigrants. This posed a grave threat to the refugees in the Oak Park community, who were unable to work due to language barriers and symptoms of post-traumatic stress syndrome as survivors of the Killing Fields.

As Russell writes, "Working with a larger coalition of Asian American nonprofit organizations, we sought to inform the public about the disastrous consequences of the law. . . . Oak Park tenants boldly shared their stories in a variety of media outlets."[9] Through helping the Cambodians to navigate the legal system, members of the OPC helped the refugees find the public voice that would make their concerns known to decision-making authorities.

They also defended the rights of the refugees against the abusive slumlord who owned their apartment complex. During the winter of 1997, northern California experienced one of the heaviest periods of rain in its history, far heavier than the shoddy Oak Park apartment construction could repel. Water flooded into the apartments, causing sewers to back up and mold to grow on ceilings and walls. In my friend Christine's apartment, a 2x4-foot section of rotted ceiling fell onto her bunkbed. While showering, another member of the OPC, Cameron, leaned against the stall and fell through the moldy wall into the next room. Their neighbors on the first floor had it worst; the apartment sewer backed up, flooding their apartments with human waste. The owner of the apartment complex did little to address the situation. With the help of an attorney named Joe Angel (his true name), Russell, Dan, and the other members of the community mobilized the tenants to bring a lawsuit against the slumlord from which they received $950,000 in damages, mitigating some of the suffering from injuries and illnesses due to the dilapidated conditions.

In their advocacy for the Oak Park residents, the members of the OPC avoided communicating values that cause so many other kinds of activists to stumble. Many activists today try to empower the poor through creating an identity of victimization. In contrast, the OPC has focused on providing opportunity and helping the community to make positive decisions in their interest. A sense of victimization cripples the poor. It stifles the initiative critical for taking proactive steps out of poverty. (Why bother to try if you will always remain a victim?) Other activists stir up feelings of vengeance against a named or unnamed oppressor, or they explicitly or implicitly refer to conspiracy theories as explanations for poverty. Instead of promoting victimization and vengeance, Russell, Dan, and the other Advocates in the OPC have inculcated a more productive set of values—proactivity, reconciliation, and peace.

Creators

About three miles up Interstate 880 from the Oak Park Community lies the national headquarters for the Family Independence Initiative (FII) and the office of its founder, Mauricio Lim Miller. Investigators look at a problem and seek to understand it. Givers mobilize resources to fund a solution to it. Advocates stand beside those experiencing it. Creators develop something new to address it. Mauricio Lim Miller is a Creator and the Shrewdest of Samaritans.

Creators may create a new poverty intervention, a nonprofit organization, or a social business. In 2012 Miller was one of the winners of the MacArthur Foundation's "Genius Grant" award for his pathbreaking new approach to addressing US urban poverty. However, his innovative approach has been celebrated as applicable across the globe.

Miller worked for more than twenty years as a recognized social worker, even being invited by President Clinton to a State of the Union address to sit alongside Rosa Parks. But while he found many aspects of his work rewarding, he also found that tremendous resources were being expended with little result. Poor families generally remained poor and dependent upon government programs. The situation came to a head in 2001 when then-mayor of Oakland, Jerry Brown, asked him to develop a model for urban poverty. Put on the spot, he found himself reflecting more on the failures of the traditional government and nonprofit approaches than on their successes. Instead he found himself returning to the positive steps his mother had taken to lead their own immigrant family out of poverty. At this moment Miller's idea was born.[10]

Miller conceived the Family Independence Initiative (FII) as the anti-program. Indeed, his goal for the FII was that it would replace a whole array of government and nonprofit programs. When a family participates in the FII, the heads of households meet in a house with other neighboring families who have a desire to leave poverty. A member articulates a goal to the rest of the group: obtaining a job interview, increasing savings toward buying a house, improving children's grades in school. All goal achievements must be verifiable to the group, but there is no competition within the meetings. Every family cheers for every other family to achieve its goals. When a goal is achieved and verified, the FII provides a small reward for the achiever—perhaps a new work shirt, a necktie, a school backpack. Miller hates to call the FII a "program." All the important decisions are made by the families; the FII simply provides a structure for goals to be formulated and articulated, social support for working toward those goals, and the modest rewards for meeting them. FII claims remarkable results from the approach: a 23 percent increase in income over two years, 88 percent of students having excellent, good, or improving grades, and a 60 percent decrease in federal assistance.[11]

Impressed with these statistics, but realizing that they came from observation rather than a scientific study, some of our graduate students decided to test the program among 160 female entrepreneurs with a randomized controlled trial in Medellín, Colombia.[12] We found that women allocated to the full FII package of goal setting, social support from peers, and small prizes for achieving goals had increases in business sales that were significantly higher than the control group. Results showed that even simply articulating a goal was helpful; those who did so performed significantly better than those in the control group.

Miller's FII approach offers real prospects for impoverished families, not only domestically but for the overseas poor too. Rather than incentivizing poverty as many traditional programs do, where eligibility is based on demonstrated need, the FII approach rewards movement out of poverty. It creatively harnesses and combines approaches in psychology (goal setting), social support (sociology), and economics (incentives) into a malleable design, each proven in their own fields to be effective motivators. The FII approach provides a minimal amount of structure that gives participants the freedom and dignity of making their own choices. It is an immensely flexible tool, adaptable to a wide variety of contexts.

Another favorite Creator of mine is Scott Harrison. At twenty-eight years old, Harrison became disillusioned with his career as a New York City nightclub promoter, left his lucrative job and hard-partying lifestyle, and sailed to West Africa with Mercy Ships, hospital ships devoted to carrying out medical work and restorative surgeries in low-income countries. In Liberia he witnessed the plight of children affected with disease, learning that many of the infirmities treated on the ship could have been prevented simply by families having access to clean water. The trip altered the course of his life.

After experiencing a spiritual renewal in his Christian faith, in 2006 Harrison founded Charity: Water, a nonprofit devoted to providing fresh water to rural areas across the developing world. Charity: Water raised $1.7 million in its first year. In 2017 the nonprofit raised $50 million—and a total of $300 million since its foundation. By mid-2018 Charity: Water had established 28,389 water projects serving over 8.2 million people. As I mentioned before, development economists and public health researchers are unanimous in their belief that there are few poverty interventions that can be more important than clean water. But historically the problem has often lain with the malfunction of pumps and other delivery mechanisms that litter the land with defunct boreholes. Part of what makes Charity: Water unique is its use of remote-sensing Google technology that monitors water usage and communicates water flow data on whether wells are operating properly. One can literally check on the internet to view water use data across virtually any of the organization's water projects.

While many have created innovative nonprofit organizations, others have created social businesses, enterprises whose objective is a "double bottom line" (a social objective along with profit) or a "triple bottom line" (a social objective, an environmental objective, and profit). Others maximize a social objective that is subject to a constraint that the business breaks even on the profit side.

This is the reverse of the standard objective, which is more typically to maximize profit subject to complying with legal constraints and environmental laws.

Some of these double- and triple-bottom-line Shrewd Samaritans are truly inspirational: Sanjit Roy, raised in a wealthy family in India, created Barefoot College, a network of schools in eighty countries founded on the principles of Mahatma Gandhi and dedicated to making education available to impoverished children.[13] Tom Szaky grew his small fertilizer company into TerraCycle, a multimillion-dollar recycling enterprise that works in twenty countries. The company has diverted four billion pounds of recyclables from waste dumps across the globe and donated $22 million to charity in the process.[14] Notre Dame graduates Xavier Helgesen, Kreece Fuchs, and Jeff Kurtzman created Better World Books, an online bookstore funding global literacy dedicated to the triple bottom line, and especially to promoting literacy worldwide. Many social enterprises with double and triple bottom lines are now labeled as "B-Corp" businesses, a certification that ensures that they comply with rigorous and specific standards of social and environmental performance, accountability, and transparency.

Directors

Directors are those whose primary role lies not in investigation, material giving, or advocacy but in overseeing and administrating the good work of organizations. Perhaps surprising to some, in the passage I mentioned before, the apostle Paul actually describes administration as one of the spiritual gifts.[15] The Greek word he uses in this passage is *kubernesis*, which connotes a gift not only of administration but also of some form of leadership, which is why here I prefer the term *Director*.

The most effective NGOs have great Directors. These are women and men who are passionate for work among the poor but who are not necessarily operating on the front lines. Instead they fill vital administrative roles at the top or middle of an NGO's organizational chart. In a poverty-focused NGO, work is usually chaotic and unpredictable. It is common for people to fill a variety of administrative and leadership roles and to interface routinely with Givers, Investigators, Advocates, Creators, and Practitioners. It is a vocational calling for the multitasker who might consider him- or herself to be a jack-of-all-trades, but master of organization, follow-through, and the ability to work well with others. These are the talents held by Directors that are keys to an organization's effectiveness.

One of my favorite Directors is David Sutherland, CEO of International Care Ministries (ICM) in the Philippines, who supported the first randomized trial on the effects of spiritual programming on economic outcomes among the poor. Formerly Chief Financial Officer at Morgan Stanley, he has overseen the direction of ICM since 1999, now as full-time Chairman and Global Chief Executive Officer, taking the NGO into its current role as one of the most nimble and innovative poverty organizations on the planet.

What makes David the paragon of a Shrewd Samaritan in an NGO Director role? In my few years of interacting with him in the Investigator/research role, I have noticed that what sets him apart in the role is that his commitment to excellence is nested in a unique amalgamation of gifts. These include a genuine love for the poor in the Philippines, a deep intellectual curiosity, and his ability to fully relate to and engage the Giver, the Investigator, and the Practitioner. His intellectual curiosity about the important questions related to poverty interventions has allowed him to forge relationships with top research economists, including Dean Karlan, founder of Innovations for Poverty Action, who has led much of the pathbreaking poverty research in partnership with ICM described in earlier chapters, transparently documenting the impact of ICM's work in top academic journals. His strong relationships with the financial community in Asia have allowed him to scale up successful interventions with confidence of their effectiveness. The result is ICM's excellent development work, vetted by some of the top researchers in the world, and a holistic development approach that has gained immense credibility in both secular and faith-based development circles.

Practitioners

Finally, there are those whose role is to be the hands of the body touching those in need. In development circles, we tend to call people in this role "Practitioners," although this title is a bit formal. Anyone can be called to the Practitioner role, whether as a full-time professional, a volunteer, or a calling within another formal profession. Practitioners are those on the front lines—aid workers, teachers, missionaries, social workers, health specialists, water specialists, agriculturalists, logistics experts, and microcredit officers. They are people working directly with children, low-income families at home or overseas, refugees, or victims of disasters. Practitioners are those who care directly for the poor.

One of my favorite Practitioners is Isabeth Zárate. Isa is the Chief Operations Officer for *Fuentes Libres* in Oaxaca, Mexico. *Fuentes Libres* is an NGO affiliated with the Evangelical Covenant Church that works with poor and abused women in a variety of interventions, but most tangibly in their wide network of community banks. Members of the community banks meet once a week to make their loan payments, deposit money for savings, and discuss challenges with their microenterprises and life in general. Isa oversees the community banks and the younger women from *Fuentes Libres* that technically serve as their loan officers, but in reality they serve more as advisors and life coaches.

In the time we lived in Oaxaca and worked with Isa and her coworkers at *Fuentes Libres*, I couldn't help noticing some compelling attributes that Isa possesses as a Practitioner. For one, Isa seems to understand that the real impact of the work of *Fuentes Libres* isn't in the borrowing and lending. Of course, she understands the importance of practical interventions, access to credit, developing women's business skills, and so forth. But more than this, I see from her work that Isa understands that ultimately transformation is not primarily about programs that provide "things" for the poor, even good things.

Good Practitioner work is largely about creating and redeeming relationships. Being able to grasp this fundamental idea is what makes Isa a Shrewd Samaritan. The impoverished women with whom Isa works have weak economic relationships—with lenders, with buyers, with markets as a whole. They often are single mothers who have been abused in relationships with men. Their relationship to extended family is often strained. They lack defined roles in the community.

At *Fuentes Libres*, Practitioner work is about encouraging an impoverished female entrepreneur to develop a better relationship with her customers in the market, teaching them to thoughtfully study their customers' needs. It is about fostering quality relationships between her and other women in the community bank—the trust they build to overcome the obstacles that they face together. It is about her relationship with her husband or the man in her life, and about creating love and stability in the home. It is about relationships with her children, the impartation of values that prepare them to be successful adults. Isa understands that the most successful interventions are fundamentally about relationships: business relationships, social relationships, and family relationships—creating them, strengthening them, deepening them.

Healthy relationships are the genesis of prosperity and human flourishing. They manifest in the positive expectations of supportive family, in the emulation of the successful behaviors of parents, in trust-filled networks that extend beyond the family.

Something else I appreciate about Isa is that when you walk into her office, you feel loved. Over the decades of my professional work as a development economist, I have probably walked into the offices of hundreds of development practitioners. Although I almost always feel welcomed, not too long after the first handshake the vibe that a visitor often begins to receive from the Practitioner is "I'm really, really busy, and I'm really, really tired."

Isa is busy and tired. But as I work on my laptop across the hall and listen to her talk with the women from the program who come and sit in her office, I know that they feel loved too. Like the very best of those working with the poor, Isa seems to have been able to internalize some other famous words of the apostle Paul: "If I give all I possess to the poor and give over my body to hardship that I may boast, but do not have love, I gain nothing."[16] I'm convinced that Isa feels that if she doesn't do work among the poor in a spirit of love, then it doesn't count. Undoubtedly there must be some days when Isa doesn't feel up to it. There must be days when she has low energy or feels grumpy or stressed, because even though I'm still slightly uncertain, I lean toward believing Isa is actually human and not angelic. But unlike most other humans in her role, she never seems to let her agenda for the poor eclipse her love for the poor. People like Isa have taught me that at its root, being a successful Practitioner is about helping people create successful relationships and doing so in a spirit of love.

The following table may help some who are considering which of the various vocational roles in international development and poverty work— Investigator, Giver, Advocate, Creator, Director, Practitioner—may be best suited for them. In the second column is a short summary of what each role involves professionally, and the third column shows the most common types and levels of university training that are associated with each. The last two columns try to match personality types (based on the Jungian-based traits found in the Myers-Briggs categorization with which readers may be familiar) and the "Big Five" personality traits (which are more scientifically based and used in academic psychology) that are important to each role.

Some people may feel called to multiple roles. In my own case, I'm mainly devoted to the Investigator role, but also to some degree as a Giver and as a Practitioner with Mayan Partners.

Six Vocational Roles in International Development

Role	What do they do?	Common Degrees	Personality Types*	Key "Big 5" Personality Traits**
Investigator	Experimental design and data analysis on poverty interventions. Ascertain effectiveness of policies and programs.	M.S./Ph.D. in Economics, Statistics, Analytics, Psychology, Education, Sociology, Political Sci, Public Health	INTJ "Scientist" ENFJ "Pedagogue"	Openness Conscientiousness
Giver	Provide resources for practitioners and investigators needed for implementation.	Any college or graduate degree that enables one to earn sufficient income to give much of it away	ISFJ "Conservator" ISTJ "Trustee"	Agreeableness Openness
Advocate	Stand in solidarity, give voice to concerns of the poor. Often transplant to live in community in impoverished areas.	J.D. (Law), Psychology, Master of Divinity, Counseling, Community Development, Sociology, Social Work, English	ESTP "Promotor" INFP "Questor" ENFP "Journalist" ESFJ "Vendor"	Extraversion Conscientiousness

Role	What do they do?	Common Degrees	Personality Types*	Important "Big 5" Personality Traits**
Creator	Innovate new types of poverty interventions, programs, non-profit organizations, social enterprises.	Master of Business Administration, Master of Public Administration, Non-profit Management, Computer Science	ENTP "Inventor" INTP "Architect" ISFP "Artist" INFJ "Author"	Openness Extraversion
Director	Administer the people and resources of non-profit organizations to promote effective poverty work.	Graduate degree in Organizational Leadership, Master of Business Administration, Master of Public Administration, Non-profit Management	ESTJ "Administrator" ENTJ "Field marshal" ISTJ "Trustee"	Conscientiousness Agreeableness
Practitioner	Carry out hands-on, front-line work among the poor in economically, spiritually, or technically supportive ways.	Teaching, Nursing, Master of Divinity, Agriculture, Social Work, Engineering, Construction, Water Resources, Community Development	ENTJ "Field marshal" ESFP "Entertainer" ISTP "Artesian"	Conscientiousness Extraversion

Figure 11

* Based on Myers-Briggs four-letter categorizations of E or I (extrovert or introvert), N or S (intuitive or sensing), T or F (thinking or feeling), and J or P (judging or perceiving) where labels are "vocations" that conform to the psychological motive base of each corresponding personality type. Reference: David Keirsey and Marilyn Bates, *Please Understand Me: Character and Temperament Types* (Del Mar: Prometheus Books), 70–79.

** The "Big Five" personality traits are Openness (curious vs. cautious), Conscientiousness (organized vs. easygoing), Extroversion (outgoing vs. reserved), Agreeableness (friendly vs. challenging), and Neuroticism (sensitive vs. confident). See Lewis Goldberg, "The Structure of Phenotypic Personality Traits," *American Psychologist*, 48:26–34.

Which Role?

Let's reflect for a moment on the roles played by the Good Samaritan—*roles* plural. Initially he was a spontaneous Practitioner, the hands that provided succor to the injured man. But then his role transitioned to a Giver, as he provided the financial resources for the innkeeper to house and care for the man, who then in turn became the Practitioner. Especially if we are working with the poor informally, we might find ourselves helping individuals directly in tangible ways, through giving, and by advocating. But it also may be wise to refer individuals to others who are better advocates than we are.

Whether formally or informally, laboring in the diversity of community and in a network of like-minded people is nearly always the best path to meaningful and effective work.

Chapter 12

THE SEVENTH *i*

In the summer of 2005, my friend Jim Porter traveled to meet me at a café in Guatemala. From a dock near the café, we caught a launch that took us across Lake Atitlan to the small town of San Pedro la Laguna to meet Emilio Battz, a middle-aged Tzutujil pastor overseeing about seventy Protestant churches nestled in the fog of the western Guatemala highlands.

About eight years before, a group from Alaska, *Projecto Fe*, working alongside some Christian employees at eBay, had helped Emilio and his wife, Ester, build *Colegio Bethel* San Pedro. The partnership between eBay, the Alaskan church, and the school had yielded some remarkable results. Colegio Bethel had become one of the best rural schools in Guatemala. Its excellent low-cost education, along with being one of the first schools of its kind to connect to the internet, won praise from all quarters, including a full-page article in the *New York Times*.[1]

Pastor Juan Ajcac, a Quiché-speaking leader of one of the mountain churches, had walked with members of his town, some barefoot, all the way to San Pedro. Word had worked its way up into the mountains about Colegio Bethel. They dreamed of a school like it for their village too. And this was why Jim and I came to San Pedro la Laguna. It was to see if the dream could become something real.

Jim was my college roommate for two years, one of my best friends along with two other guys from InterVarsity Christian Fellowship at the University of California at Davis, Ron Giles and Robb Thompson. Our friendship was instantly bound the first week we all lived together, when after collectively fixing the decrepit vacuum cleaner left to us by our absentee landlord, we proudly exalted together, "It sucks!"

As a roommate, Robb's self-deprecating charm and athletic physique attracted a steady instream of female company to the house, whom we were happy to help entertain. Ron was always up for energizing activities, including spur-of-the-moment road trips and squirt-gun fights with Listerine. Our friendship continued to grow, and (even more remarkably) mature somewhat, since leaving college in 1987. Every year since leaving Davis we have reunited in the Sierras for a winter weekend, including the annual activities of skiing, playing poker, enjoying our favorite beverages, cracking jokes in strange accents bordering on the extraterrestrial, and engaging in much-needed prayer for one another. By 2005 we had all married up to four outstanding women who had succumbed to our charms, and we had started families.

But there was an underlying sense we all shared that our friendship could serve a purpose outside ourselves. After college, I had followed Jim to Eastern University, where we studied together under Ron Sider, Samuel Escobar, and Tony Campolo, renowned men of faith and professors who layered in us a foundation in holistic economic development. I went on to study economics at Berkeley, where at about the same time Robb completed his MBA. We had both the depth of commonality and the background to move our relationships beyond mutual support and self-entertainment. We wanted to create something meaningful that would matter to others, and in Guatemala, Emilio the pastor presented us with this kind of opportunity.

With Emilio, we met with the community leaders, mostly coffee growers and village elders, who wanted the school. It was to be a Christian middle school with grades equivalent to seventh through ninth grades in the United States, open to all children in the village. The families in the village would not pay much, only the equivalent of US$6 per month. The church in Alaska was building the physical school, but they had no funding for teachers or operations of any kind.

We visited the school construction site. Like a long trail of ants, tiny young children to the elderly of the village, the women dressed in the colorful Mayan *güipiles*, were carrying sacks of sand and concrete up to the school. It was obvious that this was a corporate dream shared widely in the village. The middle school was their idea, their desire, their dream. Would we fund it? We would talk with our friends.

We discussed the idea with one another. Then we talked with our UC

Davis alumni friends Kent and Ann Moriarty, who had just returned from riding their tandem bike from the top of Alaska to the tip of Argentina. We figured if they were up for that, they were probably up for anything. We reached further into our network and talked with more of our college friends, and some of them seemed excited about the idea too. Kent came up with the name: Mayan Partners. The partner part of it was important to us: we are not the drivers of the train; we want to partner with the leaders of the village to help fund their own dreams to promote human flourishing in their village.

Mayan Partners started with funding the teacher salaries at the new Colegio Bethel in the village. After the school became stable, we immediately turned to thoughts of scaling up. Why not make it our mission to spread little Colegio Bethels all over western Guatemala? We thought and prayed about it, and wiser heads in our network prevailed, especially Kent's. We would not scale up, we would scale *in*—inside the village. Some of us were reflecting one day in a conference call. How many decent, healthy years do we have left? Maybe thirty? Why not just commit any time, effort, and energy we have left on planet Earth to this one village? That day, in our minds, we basically decided to marry the village.

Along with the new Colegio Bethel version 2.0, we now support the only village community library, help support a preschool, and do some small-scale microenterprise work where we market Christmas ornaments with cool indigenous Mayan designs made by the women of the village.[2] In 2010 *Projecto Fe* got tired of us mooching on their nonprofit status and encouraged us to start our very own 501(c)(3) nonprofit organization. We are small—really small. Our annual income from donations is barely over $50,000 a year. Mayan Partners has about thirty-five regular givers, mostly people in our college-friend network and faithful donors in our respective families and churches. Every dollar donated to Mayan Partners goes to the village. Everyone is a volunteer.

Let me not mistakenly convey the idea that this kind of work is always happy grins and smooth sailing. Administration can be a pain, and even though most of us speak Spanish to varying degrees, communication over three thousand miles can be difficult. Through the years we have dealt with cancelled flights, missing passports, regular episodes of illness and vomiting, busted bus axles, lack of classroom discipline, death threats to our staff with crude pictures of knife-bearing thugs decapitating people, drinking problems, difficulties telling the truth about things, a vice principal who committed adultery then vanished off the face of the earth never to be seen again and was probably murdered, and other sundry lapses on all sides. But we're stuck with the people in this Guatemalan village, and they are stuck with us. We will go through life together like an old married couple—sins, warts, and all.

One of the happiest times for all of us are the summers when a big group of us make the trip together down to Lake Atitlan, cross the lake on a launch, and then take the hour-long trek on the chicken bus up twenty-five switchbacks into the mountains. Usually somebody goes every six months or so, but the larger trips are like reunions between our families and the Guatemalan families. They tell us how much our kids have grown, and we theirs. They love us, and we love them.

The story about Mayan Partners is all about the seventh *i*—*identification*. As individual human beings, we cannot solve all of the world's problems. And we are *not called* to solve all the world's problems. But with the help of those around us we can prayerfully discern our roles, be they as Investigators, Givers, Advocates, Creators, Directors, or Practitioners. Then we can learn to not only identify with and embrace our roles but also learn to identify with the population of those whom we are specifically called to serve. As a group of friends in California, we are learning to identify with the Quiché people in the village, to become more sensitive to their situations, to their needs, and to the dreams they have for their own lives. Even though we are three thousand miles away from each other, we are trying to practice accompaniment in our relationship with them as our friends and brothers. One of the purposes of our lives is to see the lives of these people—in this particular village in the highlands of western Guatemala—flourish.

Why Is Identification Important?

Identification is important because it allows the giving of our time and money to draw on our humanity rather than labor against it. We give more and better when we identify with specific individuals and groups rather than statistics. We learn to come outside ourselves and all our little ambitions and plans. We learn to love. This drives some effective altruists crazy because they would like people's giving to be solely motivated by average treatment effects, but unfortunately or not, our brains just don't work this way. It has something to do with being human.

It is difficult for the brains of most normal people to connect emotionally with data enough to motivate actual giving. This is true even when people believe that the statistics are true. The problem is that while we become emotionally detached to statistics, we are moved substantially by the needs of identifiable, real people.

Psychologist Deborah Small and her coauthors demonstrated this in a series of experiments where subjects could contribute up to $5 to Save the Children.[3] The research team randomly gave half a message with factual information taken from the Save the Children website describing poverty conditions for millions of affected individuals in sub-Saharan Africa (the statistical victim). The others were told the story of one impoverished girl in Mali and showed her picture (an identifiable victim). The subjects in the experiment were moved much more by the identifiable victim, giving an average of $2.83, but only an average of $1.17 to the statistical victim.[4]

Identification is a powerful force. We become absorbed into novels as we identify with the plight of a character. We love a film because we identify with and root for the protagonist with whom we have developed a psychological relationship. We root for him or her to overcome all odds stacked against them. We identify with sports teams, wearing their jerseys, following players on social media, and spending countless hours watching them on TV. We exult when they win, and we feel terrible when they lose.

This human ability to identify leads to some common but fairly useless behaviors (like our identification with sports teams), but it can also be a powerful force for good. Identification allows us to empathize with the plight of others in a way that data and the barrage of information we receive over media cannot. The challenge is finding ways to develop our capacity for identification with global action that is meaningful and effective.

Researchers have experimented with poverty simulators to help people identify with the poor and build empathy for their situations. The most studied of these is CAPS (Community Action Poverty Simulation), a live simulation in which participants have to move through four fifteen-minute simulated weeks of poverty in which they must interact with employers, social services, and community resources in order to meet basic needs. "Spent" is an online simulator in which subjects have to make decisions at very low levels of income over how much food they can afford, whether to take different part-time jobs, paying for housing, health care, and other decisions while walking the poverty tightrope.[5]

Experiments using these poverty simulators typically work by randomizing student participation and then measuring how feelings of the participants change about those in poverty. Results of these experiences commonly find that participants are much more able to identify and empathize with the poor. They find that attitudes become generally more positive toward the poor and their challenges, and that they show an increasing tendency to attribute the reasons for poverty to external causes rather than dysfunctional personal attributes. This change in "attribution" seems critical because it appears to open the door for a person to empathize with those in poverty rather than attributing the person's condition solely to their own choices.[6]

Recently my friend Chad from World Vision came to my office at the university with some virtual reality goggles. We talked for a while. Finally, I asked, "What are those for?" He explained that you could put them on and walk the steps with an African woman traveling miles to fetch water. I had never put on virtual reality goggles. It was a new experience walking the path with the woman, looking around 360-degrees as we walked along the dry, cracked creek with her children. Chad uses the goggles to raise money for water projects, to help rich Americans identify with those needing to walk miles for a jerry can of water, and I bet it works.

Our own nonsimulated painful experiences can lead us to more strongly identify with others in need. Effective altruists often chide those who give out of the result of painful experience rather than as a result of a careful utility calculation. A common example of Peter Singer's is to challenge the breast cancer donation of a person who has lost a close relative to the disease.[7] Couldn't the money have been more efficiently spent to reduce death overseas? Perhaps. But identification with the pain of others, or a desire to prevent for others the kind of pain we ourselves have experienced, is one means through which God seems to be able to redeem suffering for ultimate good. Our own experiences of pain can inspire us to new ways of giving that we would have never considered in the apathy of our unperturbed comfort.

There is a second reason we need to learn to identify with the poor. It is because they are us, only facing different circumstances. There is a tendency for those of us with more education and higher incomes to think that we are better than poor people either because (a) we possess special qualities or (b) we have worked harder. But any "special qualities" we as the rich possess are derived from one of two sources: God's grace (if one is a believer) or if not, the blind genetic lotto. Either way, the special qualities are not of our own doing. And we can dispense with the "work hard" rationale too. Every time I return to the Guatemala highlands and see a sixty-year-old woman carrying a hundred-pound bundle of firewood on her back down a rugged mountain path, I am reminded that I do not work harder than the global poor.

Research in behavioral economics reveals that the brightest academic, the most creative programmer, the most dedicated teacher, or the brightest entrepreneur, lawyer, or physician, if malnourished or under the constant threat of starvation or violence, would act little differently from the poorest beggar on the street in Kolkata or San Francisco.[8] The reality is that most of us are a few consecutive bad breaks away from a plea for assistance on a cardboard scrap.

A third reason we need to learn to identify with the poor is that because even the most materially prosperous among us are also poor and broken in our own way. To accept the Christian message is not to primarily fault the misdeeds of others for the problems of the world, but to first acknowledge that one's own self is a vessel in need of repair. And in this critical step of self-awareness and repentance, Jesus seems to indicate that it is the rich who face the greater challenge in coming to this realization.[9] In our relative prosperity, we attribute our success to our smarts and hard work. We remain unable to bridle our arrogance and pride. We habitually undervalue and underappreciate the contributions of others around us. We value ourselves innately and unconditionally, but we value others based on their accomplishments and status. We choose those around us for what they give us, be it advantage or entertainment. Like the poor, we are broken vessels navigating in circles, and we have to learn to identify with them on equal terms.

How important is it for the rich to commune with the poor? Some would argue that overseas travel is a waste of resources that could be better allocated toward effective poverty interventions. Effective altruists argue that people who can get a high-paying job should spend their time earning money and giving it to nonprofit organizations rather than devoting their time to caring for people. I understand these economic arguments, and spending much of one's time earning to give can be meaningful and effective. But a shortsighted analysis of these trade-offs views them as isolated choices rather than as complementary activities.

Even if we give large amounts of money to health interventions, it is good to engage in relationship with those we are seeking to help. It acts as a check and a confirmation on the statistics, which may only show overall averages and not impacts specific to a particular area, for which firsthand observation may help to resolve specifically local issues and inefficiencies.

Developing relationships with those we are seeking to help makes us more rooted and generous in our giving. Behavioral economics suggests that preemptive actions are often helpful in keeping us committed to long-term goals. As articulating a goal in front of a group helps us stay committed to that goal, contact with beneficiaries of our giving helps us stay committed to our giving. We have noticed this with Mayan Partners. The most committed givers to Mayan Partners are those who have taken a couple of weeks out of their busy schedules to go to Guatemala and meet our friends and partners in the village. Of course, it is the most committed people who tend to go on these trips in the first place, but we notice a renewed excitement for the mission among those who go that lasts many months after the visit. As we physically interact with our partners, we become more deeply identified with them and we are changed as well. We become more fully human, more full of God, more alive.

Some Practical Steps

The global community has made significant inroads into poverty reduction worldwide, but there is a vast work that remains, both at home and abroad. What are practical steps we can take to be part of this effort? I want to suggest seven concrete ideas for meaningful and effective action. All of these are effective in their own domain, but opinions will differ about which to prioritize over others. One can argue in circles whether effective health interventions have a bigger long-term impact than holistic childhood interventions, which tend to shape a strength of character that, if manifest in a single individual in the right circumstance, may impact the course of a nation. This comes nowhere close to being a comprehensive list of effective actions one can take on behalf of the poor. However, based on the most current research, these are likely to be both genuinely effective as well as helpful in leading lives that are more closely identified with the poor.

1. Adopt an Effective Health Intervention

Everyday people have the opportunity to support effective health interventions such as deworming, bed nets to protect families from malaria, clean water, and inexpensive reparative surgeries to correct birth defects such as club foot, cataracts, and cleft palate. In the proper context the first two have an enormous Bang-3. This is likely the same for clean water provision, if integrated with sanitation, and although the data is less certain, almost certainly true for reparative surgeries.

If you choose to adopt one of these interventions, my suggestion is that you read about it, learn about it, and make it your own. Identify with it. If you are able, take at least one trip overseas to visit practitioners engaged in this work, and build relationships with them, especially in-country workers. If you choose to sponsor bed nets, meet some families using a bed net and ask them how it works, how it could be improved, and about other aspects of their lives. See how your own observations match with the results of rigorous studies in the field, and try to keep up with new research and best practices. Not only give, but advocate for the intervention. Consider holding fund-raisers in your home and sharing your interests with friends and colleagues.

2. Sponsor a Child

Sponsoring a child through an organization such as Compassion International that addresses the holistic needs of children has large and significant impacts on their self-esteem, aspirations, happiness, education, future employment, future income, and capacity for community leadership. Child sponsorship is not a cheap intervention, but it is a high-quality intervention that has demonstrated impacts around the globe. We found that impacts on education were largest in countries where existing educational levels are lowest, but significant impacts were found in every country we studied. Economic impacts in later life depend to some extent on the economic opportunities available to those with higher levels of education.

One of the joys of our work with Mayan Partners has been bringing our network of college relationships together to serve with one another in a single village in Guatemala. This has brought new meaning to our existing relationships, and the collective enthusiasm and support of our mutual interest has sustained the momentum of our work. However, one of the most difficult aspects of this endeavor has been the effort involved with the creation of an NGO and all the management involved thereafter and therein.

In a new initiative, Compassion has started to allow networks of friends, groups of high school or college alumni, groups of work colleagues, members of the same church, or any other group to sponsor children in the same village. This kind of arrangement allows you and your group of friends to make regular trips together to visit the village in which your children are sponsored and commit to the welfare of that village in other ways—through other donations via Compassion; through partnership and relationship-building with village residents; and through the collective prayers, energy, and focus of your group. Through this kind of collective sponsorship and identification with one particular village area in the developing world, you may be able to realize the kind of focused commitment we have with Mayan Partners, while letting Compassion deal with the administrative details. If you would like to bring your group (of whatever kind) together in this kind of village partnership, visit www.compassion.com/shrewdsamaritan, where your group can choose children to sponsor in the same local Compassion project in a given country.

3. Support Early Childhood Interventions—Globally or at Home

The benefits of early childhood interventions are so broad and so well documented that there is every reason to believe effort and resources devoted to this area will yield significant long-term impacts on later life outcomes. The best research consistently shows that early childhood interventions promote positive character traits, facilitate later success in school, reduce crime and other assorted types of delinquency and dysfunctional behavior, and generally facilitate well-adjusted transition into adulthood.

For this intervention there are ample opportunities to be committed both globally and locally. Globally, consider supporting World Vision's Go Baby Go! Parenting Program[10] or Save the Children's Early Childhood Development (ECD) program,[11] both of which are vetted by rigorous research. In addition, you can now begin to sponsor children through Compassion International starting as early as age one.

You can also support early childhood interventions at home financially by helping to provide scholarships for at-risk children to attend excellent preschools that focus on nurturing young children, inculcating character values, and incorporating strong parental coaching and involvement. If you are wealthy, consider an endowment gift to a high-quality preschool that will sponsor one at-risk child at the center and can be passed from child to child over the years. You can also serve there as a volunteer. This is an excellent choice for seniors or retired people seeking to be Shrewd Samaritans who impact the youngest generation. Look for a well-run preschool in your area that operates in a manner consistent with your values, and volunteer to help preschool teachers with children who need individual attention. You may not see the benefits immediately, or even in this life, but trust that they will be there. Not to mention, the preschool teachers will mistake you for an angel from heaven.

4. Support Successful Charter Schools

Supporting successful charter schools is a strong complement to domestic early childhood interventions. Because charter schools are publicly funded, they allow low-income children to attend without burdening parents with excessive school fees or the need for scholarships. The rate of college attendance for low-income minority students in charter schools is three to five times that of public schools; some of this is due to creaming the best students, but good research shows the impact of excellent charter schools is real.

Not all charter schools are excellent, and it may take some research effort on your part to find the right ones to support in your area. But research has shown the good ones to be extremely successful not only at putting at-risk children on an academic track for college but also in developing the kind of soft skills and character values that at-risk children will need to be successful adults. The KIPP schools are one such network of schools, but there may be others in your area such as the Sugar Creek Charter School in Charlotte, the Noble Network of Charter Schools in Chicago, and the Alliance College-Ready Public Schools in the Los Angeles area that present some of the best opportunities for at-risk youth to flourish.[12] Good charter schools are worthy of your political support, your volunteer time, and generous donations for helping to bring equity and choice to US public education.

5. *Support Comprehensive Poverty Alleviation Programs*

There are both secular and faith-based comprehensive poverty alleviation programs that are worthy of support. These programs often go under the name of poverty graduation programs, holistic interventions, or integrated development programs. The BRAC poverty graduation program, targeting the ultra-poor, is the most famous and celebrated of these, where randomized trials have found that 75 to 98 percent of BRAC participants worldwide meet poverty graduation criteria in eighteen to thirty-six months.[13] Other NGOs, including Food for the Hungry, have implemented models similar to the BRAC program that incorporate a spiritual focus built around biblical values along with addressing economic and social needs.[14] Their work is built around a theory of change that incorporates a strong emphasis on listening to locally based community leaders about community problems, supporting and mentoring these local leaders as they carry out the work, emphasizing components to its program that are likely to have greatest local impact, then monitoring the results.

6. *Provide Cash Grants*

Of all the microenterprise interventions, providing cash grants for building small enterprises is not the cheapest intervention, but it has the highest and most consistently demonstrated level of impact, especially when accompanied by basic business training and mentoring. When administered well, and when targeted at entrepreneurs with elevated aspirations, cash grants can be life transforming in and of themselves or as part of a holistically integrated development intervention.

Village Enterprise, based in San Carlos, California, has been making cash grants to businesses long before everyone realized how effective it was. A randomized controlled trial run by Innovations for Poverty Action found that their microenterprise development program led to significantly increased enterprise assets and household income. This resulted in subsequent improvements in consumption and nutrition and subjective well-being. Village Enterprise is an innovative NGO doing excellent work that incorporates the best practices of microenterprise development, including personalized business training and mentoring. You can donate or even volunteer to be a fund-raiser for Village Enterprise, raising cash that will create transformative changes for microenterprise entrepreneurs and their families.[15]

7. *Give Cash*

The latest and most current research has shown that you cannot go wrong by making unconditional cash transfers to impoverished households in East Africa through GiveDirectly. GiveDirectly not only was the first nonprofit to harness the new digital technologies for making direct cash transfers to the poor, it is also considered to be a flagship NGO, a paragon of efficiency, proven impact, and transparency. Giving households cash empowers recipients with the decision over how to best use donated funds. It is efficient and effective, significantly increasing food consumption and their investment in herds and small enterprises, and reducing the number of days children go hungry. There is no evidence that the overseas poor spend the transfers on liquor, cigarettes, or other temptation goods, or that it causes them to work less. Although more research is needed to ascertain the long-term impacts after the transfers come to an end, cash transfers have come to represent a solid benchmark for effective giving.[16]

The Big Picture

These all represent microeconomic interventions, and while they each can make substantial differences at the individual level, what kinds of larger economic policies should Shrewd Samaritans support to foster human flourishing? There is always debate over the best macroeconomic policies. People joke that when you ask two macroeconomists about the best policies, you get three opinions. But I will suggest four general policies that have virtually universal support by development macroeconomists and that are consistent with a human dignity framework. While, as individuals, most of us have less influence over macro policies, we should still advocate for them to the extent we can.

The first of these principles regards the importance of ethical leadership and good governance. Altruistic leadership with a genuine concern for the citizenry of a country, especially of those within it who are poor and marginalized, is a rare but powerful force. The emergence of this type of leader is largely a product of the intellectual, moral, and spiritual capital within a nation. Nations rich in character tend to promote high-character people to leadership. Where these attributes are scarce, people look to the power of strongmen to solve their problems. It is why interventions that foster positive adult character attributes, even though their effects are harder to identify in randomized controlled trials, may be equal to or more important than health interventions, which tend to have more obvious impacts.

Second would be favoring both leaders and policies that eschew quick fixes such as printing money and overborrowing to cover deficits. Instead, good governments pursue economic policies that keep inflation low. There is a constant temptation for politicians to seek the political bump from short-sighted economic policies that yield benefits within the electoral cycle while saddling the next leader with their damaging repercussions. While the rich have means for shielding assets to protect themselves from currency instability, nobody is hurt worse by hyperinflation than the poor. Stable currencies are a social justice issue.

Third, we should favor policies that create a ripe environment for entrepreneurship. Nothing stifles economic growth in developing countries as much as a maze of rules, permits, and regulations that keep entrepreneurs from creating and expanding small- and medium-sized businesses. Economic development happens through the actions of entrepreneurs and, while certain economic regulations need to be in place, they should be simple, transparent, and easy for entrepreneurs to comply with and navigate.

Fourth would be a general openness to international trade and investment. Trade agreements should be phased in slowly to minimize sudden disruptions to employment and vulnerable parts of the economy. But they *should* be phased in, because in the long run it is important to allow countries to harness their areas of comparative advantage in trade. Historically, this has led to the kind of economic growth that is able to reduce poverty on a large scale. This does not mean that a libertarian ideological mooring to free markets and unfettered international commerce becomes our guiding philosophy. It is that a Shrewd Samaritan recognizes the enormous power of participation in domestic and international markets to promote human flourishing.

More broadly, what are the values that should distinguish Shrewd Samaritans? We want to harness the passions of our hearts and the power of our minds to advocate for truth, goodness, beauty, and human flourishing in all its forms—in relationship with God, with neighbor, and creation. We take our place in service of a loving God as the fingers of his hands, and as we do, we become part of that great project, the redemption of a broken world.

Light and Love

On our last trip to Guatemala, we approached the village on foot. We walked along the cobbled road, marveling at the lush mountain range, the volcanoes pushed up out of the earth, descending from the rugged highlands to the distant haze of the Pacific coast. As we drew near to the village, we heard music. It was some kind of marching band. The music grew, and after some moments we realized that it was the band from our middle school. They had come to greet us at the gate of the village.

Appearing between the donated trombones and dented tubas, we saw the principal and teachers of the school, families from the village, our friends, our partners. The family reunion had begun. We embraced as the teenagers from the school continued with their marching band music, a little out of tune, but not bad. Rather embarrassingly, I felt tears starting to well up in my eyes. But at the same time the thought occurred to me: *This is what heaven must be like.* It reminded me of the two parables, for in the end both the Shrewd Manager as well as the Good Samaritan identify with the poor and needy. After the final curtain falls for the Econo-Man and eons pass in a flash of light, there they are, the poor, welcoming him to Light and Love.

And maybe at that time more than others, I realized that the economy of heaven really does work backward. I realized that even in our bent state of humanness, in our motives tangled beyond repair, in our vast imperfection, it really *is* more blessed to give than to receive. For whatever our best efforts had brought to that village, we were changed even more.

STUDY GUIDE

Before you engage this Study Guide, please go to AcrossTwoWorlds.net to find self-assessment tests related to:

1. Finding your stage within the six *i*'s (Chapter 2)
2. Discovering your role in global development (Chapter 11)

This guide is built around six sessions of small-group discussion or individual reflection. I have grouped the chapters by the natural divisions within the book, but they can be easily adjusted to different numbers of sessions for discussion or reflection.

Chapters 1 and 2

1. Whom do you relate to most closely in Chapter 1? Which are you more like: Dr. David Yee, someone who naturally prefers relating to others close to home, or a person like airline pilot Mike Burnett, who naturally gravitates toward relationships with people overseas?
2. Are you a person like Melinda Gates who is naturally intellectually curious and proactively engages "big-picture" global issues, or are you better at responding to issues and needs as they come to you?
3. What do you think we are supposed to learn from the two parables at the center of this book? Are you naturally more like the Good Samaritan or like the Shrewd Manager? Do others think the same about you?
4. Take the self-assessment test connected to the six *i*'s on my blog at AcrossTwoWorlds.net. In which stage does your test place you? In general, in what stage do you see yourself at this point in your life: Ignorance, Indifference, Idealism, Investigation, Introspection, or Impact? Why?

5. Is there a group of people who are poor or facing disadvantages to whom you feel prompted to care for in some way? How much do you feel like you understand their needs and how they match up with your own gifts?

Chapters 3, 4, and 5

1. What was something new that you learned about our best understanding of the origins of poverty and prosperity across the globe?
2. If you have visited a low-income country in the past, or if there is a particular country in which you have interest, which of the explanations given (geography, culture, or institutions) makes the most sense to you in understanding the situation of that particular country?
3. What are the different factors responsible for inequality in rich countries? As you look at the region in which you live, which factors seem to be the most applicable to your context?
4. Why do you think interventions such as the KIPP charter schools are so successful? What are the factors that appear to make them so?
5. What are the four categories of development traps and how are they categorized? If you have been overseas to a low-income country, which of these do you think was applicable to the place that you visited?
6. Have you ever felt like your life was caught in a "trap" from which it was difficult to escape, where the very situation you were in prevented you from improving your situation? Does this experience help you in any way to relate to those trapped in poverty?

Chapter 6

1. What motivates you to care for the poor? Is it your faith? Is it your upbringing? Is it simply what you believe to be the right thing to do? Something else?
2. How do you view Effective Altruism? In your own mind, what are its strengths and weaknesses? Using Peter Singer's example of the drowning child, what is the most you would risk or sacrifice in the moment

to save a drowning child? Would you sacrifice the same to save a child at risk of dying overseas?

3. What are the meanings of "human dignity" and "human flourishing"?

4. Do you believe all people are in some way created in God's image? What does this mean to you? Do you find a framework of human dignity and human flourishing helpful for thinking about your responsibilities and engagement with those facing poverty or other types of oppression?

5. If you were approached by a person on the street asking for money, how might considering the situation through the lens of human dignity and human flourishing help you to respond?

Chapters 7, 8 and 9

1. What is the evidence regarding the effectiveness of microcredit? Does it do what it claims to do? Part of what it claims to do? In what ways is it successful, and in what ways less so?

2. If you had $1 million and wanted to stimulate the development of micro-businesses in the developing world, given the evidence on impact of different microenterprise interventions, how would you use that money?

3. What are the most effective educational interventions, and what do they have in common? If a donor asked you where to give financially in order to promote education among the poor, what would you suggest? Are there any notably bad educational interventions that we should avoid?

4. Why do many health interventions yield a very high B-3 (bang-for-the-bang-for-the-buck)? What are the ones that are the most effective across contexts?

5. What are your thoughts on the measured impacts by top academic researchers of missionary work on "secular" outcomes such as literacy and income? Do they surprise or not surprise you?

6. Which do you think is more important: to give to programs that help people be healthy, or those that foster strong character, education, and leadership? Should one be prioritized over the other, or should different people and organizations focus differently?

Chapter 10

1. Look at the matrix in Figure 6. Of the eight different categories of giving over time/money, independent/institutional, spontaneous/strategic, where do you feel the most comfortable? Least comfortable?

2. Comparing an outreach program to the poor that you are aware of with the program for immigrants run by my friend Jodi, can you categorize the different individuals similar to the manner done in Figure 7? How could this help you more effectively use the resources of the program?

3. What are the contradictory feelings you have when someone approaches you for money on the street? Should you give or not give? Under what circumstances? What is the basis for your decision over giving or not giving? How can we best help the homeless in our country?

4. Consider a program you give to and subject it to the criteria in Figure 8. Does it pass the criteria for effective giving?

5. What is your life stage, as portrayed in Figure 9? Where are you in your place in life with respect to time and money? Which of these is most scarce for you now? Which is more abundant? How does your life stage inform your calling to the poor?

Chapters 11 and 12

1. Take the self-assessment test matching your natural gifts and talents with different roles in global poverty development on my blog at AcrossTwoWorlds.net. Where do you score the highest? Is this a role you would have expected you would test high in or not?

2. Natural talent aside, which of the six roles is easiest for you and which is hardest?

3. Do you think one of the roles is more critical than the others, or all they equally valuable? Explain.

4. The seven listed interventions in Chapter 12 are not an exhaustive list of effective interventions, but they have each exhibited large, positive, and statistically significant impacts in rigorous scientific studies. Do

you feel drawn to any of these such that you could be a committed giver of money or time in a sustainable way?

5. What do you think are the best ways to support change at the macro level—political or economic reform overseas or at home? Is activism effective? If so, what kind of activism?

6. How does the story of Mayan Partners impact you? How do you feel about bringing together a group of friends from your church, work group, neighborhood, or online community to support needy children in a single village overseas?

7. Is there a both a role and a group among the poor with which you can identify? Do you think you are at a point to make a commitment to this role or this group? Perhaps in partnership with others?

APPENDIX: SINISTER
TIPS FOR MISSION TRIPS

Originally published in

Christianity Today *(6/18/2015)*

This summer, many of us will head out on short-term mission trips, spending anywhere from a week to a couple of months serving in a developing country with members of our church or para-church group. I plan to help lead a group from InterVarsity to a village where our organization Mayan Partners works in Guatemala.

For many of us, this will be one of the great highlights of the year, despite the challenges of working in difficult circumstances. Many will experience culture shock, argue with teammates about what we should be doing, and/or spend one or more days lying in bed with diarrhea. Missions work in a foreign country opens the door to a variety of trials and temptations that exceed those in the relative comfort of everyday life.

No one more famously wrote about temptation than C. S. Lewis in his classic novel *The Screwtape Letters*. This past November marked fifty years since the passing of Lewis and has been accompanied by numerous commemorations, including the present one.

I began to write a short piece on tips for mission trips from the perspective of a development economist. But upon settling in to write, I was interrupted by a series of cryptic e-mail messages that appeared in my Gmail inbox. Initially perceiving them to be an annoying barrage of spam, I nearly deleted them. Upon a closer investigation, I found them to be written in an ominous red font, indeed appearing to be a list of tips for mission trips—from the other side. . . .

from: sr_diablo@hell.net
to: lucifrito@sector6.mex
date: March 15
subject: Alert and Re-deployment

My Dearest Lucifrito,

Word has reached our office from the North American command that a despicable little team of pimpled teenagers—and the adult buffoons who lead them—are headed into one of our sectors in northern Mexico. Their sojourn will occur during what the Christian humans call "Holy Week" (yes, a time of seasonal depression for us). I am therefore requesting you temporarily to redirect your efforts. Put on hold fomenting reprisal executions among drug traffickers and focus on the work of this group. It should prove a welcome respite from your ordinary labors, and indeed I have decided to count it against your vacation time.

These missioners originate from the Glad Tidings Bible Church of Tuscaloosa. They want to build a church near one of the sectors you patrol. The construction is to be led by a middle-aged civil engineer named Jerry who, despite years of time logged in the Enemy's camp, seems genuinely to believe that churches are things created from building materials, and that the more resistant walls are to seismic tremors (I speak in the physical sense here), the sounder the church. Of course, you must deepen this shallow view. The "church-as-building" notion has proven notoriously effective over the centuries at distracting these people from real church—the community of "love" and "service" (horrid thoughts)—the Enemy wants them to build.

Encourage Jerry to hold his convictions to the point of dispute with the other adult leaders. They unfortunately may attempt to refocus the efforts of the group toward the nurture of individuals. Indeed, as Jerry slams bullheadedly into the project and barks out commands from his scaffold, lead him to feel two things: 1) convinced that the project must be completed and with excellence above all else (even if relationships must temporarily suffer) and 2) a profound sense of pride in the project. Nurture the thought in him that none of the locals could have been capable of such an engineering marvel. The desire to be indispensable has lured many a missioner into the field, and we have frequently been able to exploit such bent motivations for our eternal purposes.

What is even more fortunate (as relayed to me by the North American command) is that the idea to build the church was Jerry's. Indeed, real change—at least of any kind we might be concerned about—nearly always germinates from ideas the Enemy reveals directly to people in the villages themselves. Whatever you do, do not allow the missioners to nurture any of the villagers' own dreams that the Enemy might have given them. Indeed, it is essential that the group forcefully articulate its ideas while gently, but patronizingly, disregarding any ideas from the villagers themselves. Get them to reason, *After all, isn't that why they are poor?*

Encouragingly,
Diablo

P.S. Inform Nuñez in the Tijuana sector that I must speak with him immediately about his failure to forestall the implementation of pollution-control infrastructure on the border factories. Is there no greater joy than witnessing the birth of a disfigured human child?

from: sr_diablo@hell.net
to: lucifrito@sector6.mex
date: April 13
subject: "Honest Communication"

Dearest Lucifrito,

Now that the group has arrived, it is time to act. More than ever, help the missioners feel pleased with themselves about devoting an entire week of their lives to helping the poor. Moreover, focus their thoughts entirely around feeling good about what they are doing, rather than on any effect their work may be having on the villagers.

Also keep the focus of each participant on him- or herself rather than the well-being of his companions and those they came to serve. This plays upon the spirit of the age in the missioner's country, where the feelings and rights of the individual so often trump the general welfare, or even what the Enemy says is good.

Sadly, when one of these little creatures forgets about himself and focuses on the needs of others, the Enemy often rewards them with what he calls "joy." Instead, we must continue to convince the humans that happiness originates from securing their rights and following their impulses. In the end the happiness yielded by these pleasures continually disappoints as the humans are naturally ignorant of the fact that they were designed to love and be loved by others in their midst, and that this is where what the Enemy calls joy originates. In short, keep the focus of each individual on his or her self, and you scarcely can go wrong.

This can often best play out by suggesting they employ "honest communication." Let each member of the team frankly express disappointment whenever the trip fails to meet his or her expectations, whether it's about food, sleeping arrangements, team leadership, or the quality of the devotions. "Honest communication" is particularly important when team members are tired, hungry, and annoyed with one another, and is best expressed in front of the entire group if possible. In this context and with a little luck, "honest communication" will lead to arguments and divisions that can inflict permanent damage to these little idealists, and be extremely profitable to us.

In fact it is useful to encourage each member of the team to be "true to himself" in every way.

Eagerly awaiting your next report,
Diablo

from: sr_diablo@hell.net
to: lucifrito@sector6.mex
date: April 15
subject: Fear

Dear Lucifrito,

You mention that you are happy that some missioners are afraid because one of their countrymen was murdered in a drug deal. Remember: instilling fear is no victory in itself. It is what we do with fear that counts. In the worst case, it can drive them to dependence on the Enemy. The best outcome is that fear manifests itself in condescending remarks about the weakness of local institutions and culture, contrasting those of their home country. Let each of them ignore the fact that they themselves played virtually no role in the creation of the relative prosperity and stability they enjoy at home. But even so, let them gloat with the pride of founding fathers.

Further, create in them a sense of cultural superiority about these differences. Help them to ignore any positive differences. It is through positive aspects of the local culture that the Enemy may be trying to teach a missioner about his own sins and weaknesses: materialism, narcissism, disrespect for family, and overindulgence in media entertainment.

You mention glowingly in your recent letter that Jerry has been afflicted with a case of what the North Americans call "Montezuma's Revenge." I am disappointed, Lucifrito, you gullible fool! You fail to see that this malady has been sent by the Enemy, who is seeking to humble and quiet Jerry so he does not become so domineering and insensitive to others. See to it that Jerry is able to obtain all of the medicine he needs for a speedy recovery.

Con mucho cariño,
Diablo

from: sr_diablo@hell.net
to: lucifrito@sector6.mex
date: April 20
subject: Language

Lucifrito,

You mention that some missioners can't communicate with the villagers
in the local language, principally because they failed to learn even
two words of it before they left. This is good. We know the barriers
and mistrust that can be erected (and amplified) between humans of
different cultures because of a language barrier. It is critical that the
North American missioners fail to understand that even the smallest
attempt to communicate warmth and respect to the villagers in
their local language can quickly lead to growing bonds of trust and
friendship. This is a development we want to discourage at all costs.

To this end, subtly convince the missioners that villagers would be better off
if they are forced to speak in English anyway, since it's practically a universal
language today. This way they can rationalize their own laziness and fear of
appearing awkward. And it only enhances their sense of superiority.

I see from your recent message that Jerry has made a full recovery and
that he is at work on the building again. This is good. Now see to it that he
avoids the salad and uncooked vegetables for the remainder of the trip.

Awaiting a more auspicious future correspondence,
Diablo

P. S. I see that you have been moonlighting. I've been told of the summary
execution of three policemen in the northern zone by the drug traffickers.
Lucifrito, you have foolishly failed on two accounts. For one, two of the
policemen confessed their sins to the Enemy just before their execution,
when they previously had been on safe passage to our father's house.
Second, the shocking nature of the crime has unified the town against
the drug traffickers, filling many with a courage they had not previously
possessed. Have you not yet learned the art of subtlety?

from: sr_diablo@hell.net
to: lucifrito@sector6.mex
date: April 20
subject: Failure

Lucifrito, you incompetent fool,

Not only have you allowed the villagers to join the missioners in the construction of the church, you have also allowed Jerry to learn enough of the local language that he has been able to work side-by-side with the villagers. Even worse, in the course of the budding relationship with a local carpenter, he appears to have even stopped hammering long enough to listen to some of the villagers' own hopes and dreams. How could you have allowed the villagers to actually have a degree of ownership over this ill-conceived construction project? How once again have you allowed the Enemy to turn something that we should so easily have been able to exploit for our good, or at least happily neutralize, for His own Purposes?

Furthermore I see Amber and Kelly have spent the week developing a genuine friendship with some of the local teenage boys, one built around their mutual (though fortunately nascent) love for the Enemy, rather than the skin under their clothes. I get heartburn thinking of the innocent joy these teenagers experienced when leading a game of "duck-duck-goose" with the littlest humans in the village. All of this on the most depressing of all days in the year, when that wretched Son of the Enemy somehow . . . nevermind.

At this point, the best you must do is to ensure that this relationship is one-off. Let this group travel year after year to different sites in the name of "gaining new experiences" rather than committing themselves in any kind of significant partnership with the villagers over years or (our father forbid) decades. This will keep any future experiences pleasantly superficial and relatively harmless. Obviously, the worst-case scenario would be for a long-term commitment in which both parties struggle side-by-side through a close partnership with one another and the Enemy.

I will monitor the situation, and if such eventualities come to pass, I will see to it that the patrol of Sector 6 is entrusted to a spirit with higher levels of temptoral competence, and that you are reassigned to inciting food fights in a preschool cafeteria.

Disappointed in the Extreme,
Diablo

NOTES

Chapter 1: What Is a Shrewd Samaritan?

1. Craig Keener, *IVP Bible Background Commentary: New Testament* (Madison: InterVarsity Press, 2000).
2. Timothy C. Morgan, "Melinda Gates: 'I'm Living Out My Faith in Action,'" *Christianity Today* (July 2015), https://www.christianitytoday.com/ct/2015/july-august/melinda-gates-high-price-of-faith-action.html.
3. Patricia Sellers, "Melinda Gates Goes Public," *Fortune*, January 2008.
4. "Who We Are: Foundation Fact Sheet," The Bill & Melinda Gates Foundation, accessed January 21, 2019, https://www.gatesfoundation.org/Who-We-Are/General-Information/Foundation-Factsheet.

Chapter 2: The Six i's

1. Martin Luther King Jr., "I've Been to the Mountaintop," American Rhetoric, https://www.americanrhetoric.com/speeches/mlkivebeentothemountaintop.htm.
2. Paul Neihaus, "A Theory of Good Intentions" (working paper, University of California at San Diego, 2014).
3. James 1:19.

Chapter 3: What Causes Poverty?

1. Thomas Hobbes, "Leviathan," i. xiii (1651).
2. Greg Laden, "Falsehood: 'If This Was the Stone Age, I'd Be Dead by Now,'" *Greg Laden's Blog*, October 20, 2017, http://gregladen.com/blog/2017/10/20/falsehood-stone-age-id-dead-now/.
3. Ann Liljas, "Old Age in Ancient Egypt," Researchers in Museums: University College London, 2 March 2015, https://blogs.ucl.ac.uk/researchers-in-museums/2015/03/02/old-age-in-ancient-egypt/.
4. John Baines, "Literacy and Ancient Egyptian Society," *Man* 18, no. 3 (New Series, 1983): 572–599.
5. Mary Harlow and Ray Laurence, "Old Age in Ancient Rome," *History Today*

53, no. 4 (April 2003), https://www.historytoday.com/mary-harlow
/old-age-ancient-rome.

6. W. V. Harris, *Ancient Literacy* (Cambridge: Harvard University Press, 1989), 158.

7. Catherine Hezser, *Jewish Literacy in Roman Palestine: Texts and Studies in Ancient Judaism* (Tuebingen: Mohr-Siebeck, 2001), 503.

8. Walter Scheidel, Ian Morris, and Richard Saller, eds., *The Cambridge Economic History of the Greco-Roman World* (London: Cambridge University Press, 2007).

9. Angus Maddison, *Contours of the World Economy, 1–2030 AD: Essays in Macro-Economic History* (Oxford: Oxford University Press, 2007).

10. Max Roser and Esteban Ortiz-Ospina, "Literacy," OurWorldInData.org, revised September 20, 2018, https://ourworldindata.org/literacy/.

11. Maddison, *Contours of the World Economy*.

12. Dr. C. Chandramouli, "Census of India 2011," CensusIndia.gov, http://www.censusindia.gov.in/2011Census/pes/Pesreport.pdf.

13. Max Roser, "Life Expectancy," OurWorldInData.org, 2016, https://ourworldindata.org/life-expectancy/.

14. Roser and Ortiz-Ospina, "Literacy."

15. Maddison, *Contours of the World Economy*.

16. Thomas Malthus, *An Essay on the Principle of Population, 1798*.

17. Roser, "Life Expectancy."

18. "Gross Domestic Product (GDP)," OECD Data, 2018, https://data.oecd.org/gdp/gross-domestic-product-gdp.htm.

19. Max Roser, "Economic Growth," Our World in Data, https://ourworldindata.org/economic-growth.

20. World Bank Group, "Global Poverty," in *Poverty and Shared Prosperity: Taking On Inequality* (Washington, DC: The World Bank, 2016), https://openknowledge.worldbank.org/bitstream/handle/10986/25078/9781464809583.pdf#page=55.

21. Ibid.

22. Jared Diamond, "What Makes Countries Rich or Poor?," review of *Why Nations Fail: The Origins of Power, Prosperity, and Poverty* by Daron Acemoglu and James A. Robinson, *New York Review of Books*, June 7, 2012, http://www.nybooks.com/articles/2012/06/07/what-makes-countries-rich-or-poor/.

23. John Gallup, Jeffery Sachs, and Andrew Mellinger, "Geography and Development," *International Regional Science Review* 22(2), 1999, 179–232.

24. Solomon Hsiang, Edward Miguel, and Marshal Burke, "Quantifying the Influence of Climate on Human Conflict," *Science* 341, no. 6151 (13 September 2013): https://doi.org/10.1126/science.1235367.

25. Frances C. Moore and Delavane B. Diaz, "Temperature Impacts on Economic Growth Warrant Stringent Mitigation Policy," *Nature Climate Change* 5 (12 January 2015): 127–131, https://www.doi.org/10.1038/NCLIMATE2481.

26. Jared Diamond, *Guns, Germs, and Steel: The Fates of Human Societies* (New York: W. W. Norton & Company, 1997).

27. Diamond, *Guns, Germs, and Steel*.

28. Alexis de Tocqueville, *Democracy in America*, trans. and ed. by Harvey C. Mansfield and Delba Winthrop (Chicago: University of Chicago Press, 2002), 525.

29. De Tocqueville, *Democracy in America*.

30. The first occurs when Moses defends himself against charges of theft by retorting, "I have not taken so much as a donkey from them, nor have I wronged any of them" (Numbers 16:15). The second he finds after the prophet Samuel has acquiesced to the demand of the Israelites for a king. Samuel reminds them that a king may not have as much respect for their property as he: "Whose ox have I taken? Whose donkey have I taken?" (1 Sam. 12:3).

31. Pervez Hoodbhoy, *Islam and Science: Religious Orthodoxy and the Battle for Rationality* (London: Zed Books, 1991), 103–104.

32. David Landes, *The Wealth and Poverty of Nations: Why Some Are So Rich and Some So Poor* (New York: W. W. Norton, 1998).

33. Jean-Philippe Platteau, *Institutions, Social Norms, and Economic Development* (Amsterdam: Harwood Academic Publishers, 2000).

34. Pamela Jakiela, "How Fair Shares Compare: Experimental Evidence from Two Cultures," *Journal of Economic Behavior & Organization* 118 (2015), 40–54. Kenyan subjects were rural dwellers in the Busia district of Kenya. American subjects were students at the University of California at Berkeley.

35. Douglas North, winner of the Nobel Prize for his work on institutions, formally describes them as "the humanly devised constraints that structure political, economic, and social interaction" in Douglas C. North, "Institutions," *Journal of Economic Perspectives* 5, no. 1 (1991) 97–112.

36. Daron Acemoglu and James A. Robinson, *Why Nations Fail: The Origins of Power, Prosperity, and Poverty* (New York: Crown Books, 1991).

Chapter 4: Inequality and Poverty in Rich Countries

1. For example, see Joseph S. J. Fitzmyer, *The Gospel According to Luke: Introduction, Translation, and Notes* (New York: Doubleday, 1985); Gilles Bekaert, "The Literary Unity of Luke 16: Almsgiving and Friendship with the Poor" (PhD diss., Graduate Theological Union, Berkeley, 1996); Duncan M. Derritt, *Law in the New Testament* (London: Darton, Longman & Todd, 1970) 48–77.

2. Nadia Whitehead, "The U.N. Looks at Extreme Poverty in the U.S., from Alabama to California," NPR, December 12, 2017, https://www.npr.org/sections/goatsandsoda/2017/12/12/570217635/the-u-n-looks-at-extreme-poverty-in-the-u-s-from-alabama-to-california.

3. The representative countries for Asia are China, India, and Indonesia. For Latin

America they are Brazil, Mexico, and Chile. For Africa they are Nigeria, Ethiopia, and Ghana. And for Europe they are the United Kingdom, France, and Germany.

4. "Poverty by Race and Ethnicity," Henry J. Kaiser Family Foundation, 2017, https://www.kff.org/other/state-ndicator/poverty-rate-by-raceethnicity.

5. Elizabeth Kneebone, "The Changing Geography of US Poverty," *Brookings*, Feb 15, 2017, https://www.brookings.edu/testimonies/the-changing-geography -of-us-poverty/.

6. Cory Smith and Laurence Chandy, "How Poor Are America's Poorest? U.S. $2 a Day Poverty in a Global Context," *Brookings*, August 26, 2014, https://www .brookings.edu/research/how-poor-are-americas-poorest-u-s-2-a-day-poverty-in -a-global-context/. The official poverty line established by the US government is $16 per person per day, and by this standard, 43.1 million Americans lived under this level in 2016 according to the Center for Poverty Research, University of California at Davis (https://poverty.ucdavis.edu/faq/what-current -poverty-rate-united-states), but this overstates the number living in extreme poverty. See US Census Bureau data.

7. An op-ed piece I wrote for the *San Francisco Chronicle* lays out a more detailed case for the myths we believe about immigrants and why we believe them. Bruce Wydick, "Why We Think Immigrants Steal Jobs, Increase Crime," *San Francisco Chronicle*, 7/13/18, https://www.sfchronicle.com/opinion/article /Why-we-think-immigrants-steal-jobs-increase-crime-13071416.php. For an excellent overview of this research see: Mary Waters and Marisa Gerstein Pineau, eds., *The Integration of Immigrants into American Society: Panel on the Integration of Immigrants into American Society* (Washington, DC: The National Academies Press).

8. Michael A. Clemens, Ethan G. Lewis, and Hannah M. Postel, "Immigration Restrictions as Active Labor Market Policy: Evidence from the Mexican Bracero Exclusion," *American Economic Review* 108(6), 2018: 1468–87.

9. AnnaLee Saxenian, "Silicon Valley's New Immigrant High-Growth Entrepreneurs," *Economic Development Quarterly* 16(1), 2002: 20–31.

10. Claudia Goldin and Lawrence Katz, *The Race Between Education and Technology* (Cambridge, MA: Belknap Press, 2010). See also David H. Autor, Frank Levy, and Richard J. Murnane, "The Skill Content of Recent Technological Change: An Empirical Exploration," *Quarterly Journal of Economics* 118(4), 2003: 1279–1333.

11. Interestingly, inequality in the US was quite low around the time of the American revolution as land and jobs were both plentiful, the "best poor man's country" it was commonly said. It gradually increased through the nineteenth century with the advent of industrial capitalism in the US, the robber barons,

and the emergence of the United States as an economic power. See James T. Lemon, *The Best Poor Man's Country* (Baltimore, MD: Johns Hopkins Press, 1972). Cited in Goldin and Katz, *The Race Between Education and Technology*.

12. Thomas D. Snyder, ed., "120 Years of American Education: A Statistical Portrait," US Department of Education, Tables 19, 29, and 30, 2003.

13. Anne Case and Angus Deaton, "Rising Morbidity and Mortality in Midlife Among White Non-Hispanic Americans in the 21st Century," *Proceedings of the National Academy of Sciences* 112(49), 2015: 15078–83.

14. Sherwin Rosen, "The Economics of Superstars," *The American Scholar* 52, no. 4, 1983: 449–460.

15. Kurt Badenhausen, "Stephen Curry Will Make More Than $80 Million Next Season After Signing Richest Contract in NBA History," *Forbes*, July 1, 2017.

16. "San Francisco, CA, Rental Market Trends," RentCafé.com, accessed June 11, 2018, https://www.rentcafe.com/average-rent-market-trends/us/ca/san-francisco/.

17. Thomas Piketty, *Capital in the 21st Century* (Cambridge, MA: Harvard University Press, 2014).

18. Edward N. Wolff, "Household Wealth Trends in the United States, 1962 to 2016: Has Middle Class Wealth Recovered?" NBER Working Paper no. 24085, 2017.

19. Robert Lerman and Bradford Wilcox, "For Richer, for Poorer: How Family Structures Affect Economic Outcomes in America," *Institute for Family Studies*, 2014.

20. See for example, Stephen Demuth and Susan L. Brown, "Family Structure, Family Processes, and Adolescent Delinquency: The Significance of Parental Absence Versus Parental Gender," *Journal of Research in Crime and Delinquency* 41(1), 2004: 58–81. See also R. W. Blum et al., "The Effects of Race/Ethnicity, Income, and Family Structure on Adolescent Risk Behaviors," *American Journal of Public Health* 90(12), 2000: 1879–84.

21. US Department of Commerce, Census Bureau, "College Enrollment Rates," in *The Condition of Education 2018*, National Center for Education Statistics, accessed January 23, 2019, https://nces.ed.gov/programs/coe/pdf/coe_cpb.pdf.

22. Michael Hansen and Diana Quintero, "Analyzing 'the Homework Gap' Among High School Students," *Brookings*, August 10, 2017, https://www.brookings.edu/blog/brown-center-chalkboard/2017/08/10/analyzing-the-homework-gap-among-high-school-students/#cancel. For references on test scores, see Roland G. Fryer Jr. and Steven D. Levitt, "Testing for Racial Differences in the Mental Ability of Young Children," *American Economic Review* 103(2), 2013: 981–1005.

23. David Austen-Smith and Roland G. Fryer Jr., "An Economic Analysis of "Acting White," *Quarterly Journal of Economics* 120(2), 2005: 551–583.

24. See http://files.eric.ed.gov/fulltext/ED012275.pdf for the original report.

25. Joshua Hyman, "Does Money Matter in the Long Run? Effects of School Spending on Educational Attainment," *American Economic Journal: Economic Policy* 9(4), 2017: 256–280.

26. Kirabo Jackson, Rucker Johnson, and Claudia Persico, "The Effects of School Spending on Educational and Economic Outcomes: Evidence from School Finance Reforms," *Quarterly Journal of Economics* 131(1), 1 February 2016: 157–218. See also Julien Lafortune, Jesse Rothstein, and Diane Whitmore Schanzenbach, "School Finance Reform and the Distribution of Student Achievement," *American Economic Journal: Applied Economics* 10(2), 2018: 1–26, which also finds significant impacts from school expenditure increases.

27. Dennis Epple, Richard E. Romano, and Miguel Urquiola, "School Vouchers: A Survey of the Economics Literature." *Journal of Economic Literature* 55(2), 2017: 441–92.

28. Matthew M. Chingos and Paul E. Peterson, "Experimentally Estimated Impacts of School Vouchers on College Enrollment and Degree Attainment," *Journal of Public Economics* 122, 2015: 1–12.

29. "How We Measure Success," KIPP, 2018, http://www.kipp.org/results/national /#question-1:-who-are-our-students.

30. "Focus on Character," KIPP, accessed January 23, 2018, http://www.kipp.org /approach/character/.

31. Julia Chabrier, Sarah Cohodes, and Philip Oreopoulos, "What Can We Learn from Charter School Lotteries?" *Journal of Economic Perspectives* 30(3), 2016: 57–84. Also, Will Dobbie and Roland G. Fryer Jr., "Are High-Quality Schools Enough to Increase Achievement Among the Poor? Evidence from the Harlem Children's Zone," *American Economic Journal: Applied Economics* 3(3), 2011: 158–87.

32. Christina Clark Tuttle, Brian Gill, Philip Gleason, Virginia Knechtel, Ira Nichols-Barrer, and Alexandra Resch, "KIPP Middle Schools: Impacts on Achievement and Other Outcomes" (Washington, DC: Mathematica Policy Research, 2013).

33. Chabrier, et al., "What Can We Learn from Charter School Lotteries?"

34. Atila Abdulkadiroglu, Joshua D. Angrist, Susan M. Dynarski, Thomas J. Kane, and Parag A. Pathak, "Accountability and Flexibility in Public Schools: Evidence from Boston's Charters and Pilots," *Quarterly Journal of Economics* 126(2), 2011: 669–748. Also: Atila Abdulkadiroglu, Joshua D. Angrist, Peter D. Hull, and Parag A. Pathak, "Charters Without Lotteries: Testing Takeovers in New Orleans and Boston," *American Economic Review* 106(7), 2016: 1878–1920.

35. Vilsa E. Curto and Roland G. Fryer Jr., "The Potential of Urban Boarding Schools for the Poor: Evidence from SEED," *Journal of Labor Economics* 32(1), 2014: 65–93. Also: Dobbie and Fryer, "Are High-Quality Schools Enough to Increase Achievement Among the Poor?"

36. Roland G. Fryer Jr., "The Production of Human Capital in Developed Countries: Evidence from 196 Randomized Field Experiments," in *Handbook of Field Experiments*, vol. 2 (Amsterdam: Elsevier, 2017) 95–322.
37. Chabrier, et al., "What Can We Learn from Charter School Lotteries?"
38. Joshua D. Angrist, Parag A. Pathak, and Christopher R. Walters, "Explaining Charter School Effectiveness," *American Economic Journal: Applied Economics* 5(4), 2013: 1–27.

Chapter 5: Poverty Traps

1. James Scott, *The Moral Economy of the Peasant* (New Haven: Yale University Press, 1976).
2. Joel Green, *The Gospel of Luke* (Grand Rapids: Eerdmans, 1997).
3. Matt Stevens, "Man Trapped Inside Texas A.T.M. for 3 Hours Is Rescued by Police," *New York Times*, July 13, 2017.
4. Robert M. Solow, "A Contribution to the Theory of Economic Growth," *Quarterly Journal of Economics* 70(1), February 1956: 65–94.
5. Simon Kuznets, "Economic Growth and Income Inequality," *American Economic Review* 45(1), 1955: 1–28.
6. N. Gregory Mankiw, David Romer, and David N. Weil, "A Contribution to the Empirics of Economic Growth," *The Quarterly Journal of Economics* 107(2), 1992: 407–437.
7. "GDP per Capita (Current US$)," The World Bank, accessed January 23, 2019, https://data.worldbank.org/indicator/NY.GDP.PCAP.CD?locations=KR.
8. "The Output of Educational Institutions and the Impact of Learning," OECD Publishing, 2016, http://www.keepeek.com/Digital-Asset-Management/oecd /education/education-at-a-glance-2016_eag-2016-en#page44.
9. Personal correspondence, Compassion International.
10. Available at https://www.deere.com/sub-saharan/en/planting-equipment /intergral-planters/1725-ccs-stack-fold/.
11. Ostrom's work is filled with anecdotes of indigenous institutions developed by local communities that have fostered sustainable use of the environmental commons: forests in early Japan, irrigation communities in the Philippines, fisheries in Turkey. See Elinor Ostrom, *Governing the Commons* (Cambridge: Cambridge University Press, 1990).

Chapter 6: An Impact Framework for Shrewd Samaritans

1. Because under diminishing returns to income, that the marginal utility of income diminishes as people become richer implies that it increases as people become poorer. Thus in Singer's framework, to maximize aggregate utility, the rich should continue to give their resources away until the marginal utility

of income to the poor falls and their own marginal utility of income increases until they become equal.

2. See Mark Coffey, "Ten Reasons Why I Love/Hate Peter Singer," *Philosophy Now* 59, 2007: 28–32.

3. See, for example, the perspective of the largest evangelical relief and development organization, World Vision, in Kari Costanza, "From Dependence to Dignity," *World Vision Magazine*, August 2014. Other evangelical organizations commonly appeal to the Human Dignity framework such as Food for the Hungry (https://www.fh.org/about/), Compassion International (https://www.compassion.com/newsponsor/sponsoring-a-child.htm), and Mennonite Central Committee (https://mcc.org/stories/providing-pathway-dignity-tps-recipients).

4. Mohammad Hashim Kamali, *The Dignity of Man: An Islamic Perspective* (Islamic Texts Society, 1999).

5. "Buddhism and Human Dignity," Soka Gakki International, accessed January 23, 2019, https://www.sgi.org/about-us/buddhist-concepts/buddhism-and-human-dignity.html.

6. See, "The Road to Dignity by 2030: Ending Poverty, Transforming All Lives and Protecting the Planet," United Nations, December 2014, http://www.un.org/disabilities/documents/reports/SG_Synthesis_Report_Road_to_Dignity_by_2030.pdf.

7. Eliza Villarino, "Top USAID NGO Partners: A Primer," DEVEX, September 2, 2011, https://www.devex.com/news/top-usaid-ngo-partners-a-primer-75803.

8. Paolo Carozza and Clemens Sedmak, "Introduction: Human Dignity and the Practice of Human Development," in *Human Dignity and Human Development* (Notre Dame, IN: Notre Dame University Press).

9. Genesis 1:28.

10. Thomas Aquinas, *Summa Theologiae*, Q 93, A 4.

11. Other modern scholars emphasize God's *election* of human beings to be created in his image, not based on our innate qualities but simply as those chosen by grace to bear the *Imago Dei,* much as Abraham and more fully the tribe of Israel were chosen to be vehicles for the redemption of a fallen world. See Joshua Moritz, "Chosen by God: Election, Evolution and *Imago Dei*," *BioLogos*, June 27, 2012, https://biologos.org/blogs/archive/chosen-by-god-part-3-election-evolution-and-imago-dei.

12. Donna Hicks, *Dignity: Its Essential Role in Resolving Conflict* (New Haven: Yale University Press, 2011).

13. For more on the Hebrew concept of *shalom* see Al Tizon, "Cultivating Shalom in a Violent World," Evangelicals for Social Action, 2015, https://www.evangelicalsforsocialaction.org/sanctity-of-life/life-and-peace2/. Also, Ron Sider, *Completely Pro-Life* (Eugene, OR: Wipf and Stock Publishers, 1987).

A biblical text that is often referenced for *shalom* is Leviticus 26:3–6: "If you follow my decrees and are careful to obey my commands, I will send you rain in its season, and the ground will yield its crops and the trees their fruit. Your threshing will continue until grape harvest and the grape harvest will continue until planting, and you will eat all the food you want and live in safety in your land. I will grant peace in the land, and you will lie down and no one will make you afraid. I will remove wild beasts from the land, and the sword will not pass through your country."

14. Aleksandr Solzhenitsyn, *The Gulag Archipelago 1918–1956* (London: Vintage UK, 2002).
15. Carozza and Sedmak, "Introduction: Human Dignity and the Practice of Human Development," 8.
16. Roland Bénabou and Jean Tirole, "Intrinsic and Extrinsic Motivation," *Review of Economic Studies* 70(1), 2003: 489–520.
17. Paul, as he relays the words of Jesus: "It is more blessed to give than to receive" (Acts 20:35).
18. From the parable of the sheep and the goats, Matthew 25:40.
19. Dan Heist and Ram A. Cnaan, "Faith-Based International Development Work: A Review," *Religions* 7(3), 2016. Hilary Benn, "Faith in Development," Department for International Development (DFID) in Berkley Center for International Peace and World Affairs, Georgetown University, 7.
20. "Ending Hunger and Poverty: Passing on the Gift," Heifer International, accessed January 24, 2019, https://www.heifer.org/ending-hunger/our -approach/values-based-development/passing-on-the-gift.html.
21. Medical interventions create an exception to this rule. If I have to visit the doctor, I *want* my doctor to be patronizing. She has better information about what will cure my illness than I have. I want her to tell me what I need to do. This is not a threat to my human dignity; it just makes me stubborn if I don't listen to her.
22. Adam Smith, *The Theory of Moral Sentiments* (New York: Peguin Classics, 1759).

Chapter 7: Microfinance, Enterprises, and Cash Grants

1. This includes techniques like "difference in differences," which combines comparisons between beneficiaries and nonbeneficiaries with before-and-after to generate unbiased estimates of program impacts, assuming that the trajectory of the beneficiaries would have been the same as that of the nonbeneficiaries in the absence of the program. Other good designs use statistical matching methods or natural experiments, in which being a beneficiary of a program is the product of some arbitrary rule or cutoff, around which we can compare outcomes between those who were just eligible with those who just weren't.

2. "Sluggish SME Development Hurts Jobs and the Economy, ILO Says," International Labor Organization, World Employment and Social Outlook: Sustainable Enterprises and Jobs, October 9, 2017, http://www.ilo.org/global /about-the-ilo/newsroom/news/WCMS_579872/lang—en/index.htm.

3. Mark Pitt and Shahidur Khanker, "The Impact of Group-Based Credit Programs on Poor Households in Bangladesh: Does the Gender of Participants Matter?" *Journal of Political Economy* 105(6), 1998: 956–996.

4. Brett Coleman, "The Impact of Group Lending in Northeast Thailand," *Journal of Development Economics* 60, 1999: 105–41.

5. Abhijit Banerjee, Dean Karlan, and Jonathan Zinman, "Six Randomized Evaluations of Microcredit: Introduction and Further Steps," *American Economic Journal: Applied Economics* 7(1), 2015: 1–21. For an update on the generalizability of these studies see Rachael Meager, "Understanding the Average Impact of Microcredit Expansions: A Bayesian Hierarchical Analysis of Seven Randomized Experiments," *American Economic Journal: Applied Economics*, 2018.

6. Bruce Wydick, "Microfinance on the Margin: Why Recent Impact Studies May Understate Average Treatment Effects," *Journal of Development Effectiveness* 8(2), 2016: 257–265.

7. Emily Breza and Cynthia Kinnan, "Measuring the Equilibrium Impacts of Credit: Evidence from the Indian Microfinance Crisis," NBER Working Paper no. 24329, 2018. Also see Joseph Kaboski and Robert Townsend, "The Impact of Credit on Village Economies," *American Economic Journal: Applied Economics* 4(2), 2012: 98–133, which studies the impact of a government microcredit program rolled out across villages in Thailand and found that wages increased about 7 percent in the median village of the first two years of a large government-funded microcredit program was introduced. Another recent randomized controlled trial targeted microcredit at African maize farmers during harvest, allowing them to consume out of the loan and hold their crop until prices rose after the supply on the market dwindled. The loans had substantial impacts not only on the borrowers' incomes but also on other farmers who benefited from the withheld grain on the market at harvest time. See Marshall Murke, Lauren Falcao Bergquist, and Edward Miguel, "Sell Low and Buy High: Arbitrage and Local Price Effects in Kenyan Markets," University of California Working Paper (2018).

8. World Bank, "Financial Inclusion on the Rise, but Gaps Remain, Global Findex Database Shows," press release, April 19, 2018, http://www.worldbank .org/en/news/press-release/2018/04/19/financial-inclusion-on-the-rise-but-gaps -remain-global-findex-database-shows.

9. Pascaline Dupas and Jonathan Robinson, "Savings Constraints and Microenterprise Development: Evidence from a Field Experiment in Kenya," *American Economic Journal: Applied Economics* 5(1), 2013: 163–92.

10. David McKenzie and Christopher Woodruff, "What Are We Learning from Business Training and Entrepreneurship Evaluations Around the Developing World?" *World Bank Research Observer* 29(1), 2013: 48–82.

11. David McKenzie and Susana Puerto, "Growing Markets Through Business Training for Female Entrepreneurs: A Market-Level Randomized Experiment in Kenya," World Bank Policy Research Working Paper no. 7993, 2017. Other studies that indicate significant impacts from business training are Nicholas Bloom, et al. "Does Management Matter? Evidence from India," *Quarterly Journal of Economics* 128(1): 1–51, and Stephen Anderson, Rajesh Chandy, and Bilal Zia, "The Impact of Marketing (Versus Finance) Skills on Firm Performance: Evidence from a Randomized Controlled Trial in South Africa," forthcoming in *Management Science*.

12. Francisco Campos, Michael Frese, Markus Goldstein, Leonardo Iacovone, Hillary Johnson, David McKenzie, and Mona Mensmann, "Teaching Personal Initiative Beats Traditional Training in Boosting Small Business in West Africa," *Science* 357(6357): 1287–90.

13. Wyatt Brooks, Kevin Donovan, and Terence Johnson, "Mentors or Teachers? Microenterprise Training in Kenya," *American Economic Journal: Applied Economics*, forthcoming.

14. Jeanne Lafortune, Julio Riutort, and José Tessad, "Role Models or Individual Consulting: The Impact of Personalizing Micro-Entrepreneurship Training," *American Economic Journal: Applied Economics*, forthcoming.

15. David McKenzie, "Identifying and Spurring High-Growth Entrepreneurship: Experimental Evidence from a Business Plan Competition," *American Economic Review* 107(8), 2018: 2278–2307.

16. Christopher Blattman, Nathan Fiala, and Sebastian Martinez, "Generating Skilled Self-Employment in Developing Countries: Experimental Evidence from Uganda," *Quarterly Journal of Economics* 129(2), 2013: 697–752.

17. David McKenzie, "Identifying and Spurring High-Growth Entrepreneurship: Experimental Evidence from a Business Plan Competition," *American Economic Review* 107(8), 2017: 2278–2307.

18. Suresh de Mel, David McKenzie, and Christopher Woodruff, "One-Time Transfers of Cash or Capital Have Long-Lasting Effects on Microenterprises in Sri Lanka," *Science* 335(6071), 2012: 962–966.

19. Richard Sedlmayr, Anuj Shah, and Munshi Sulaiman, "Cash-Plus: Poverty Impacts of Transfer-Based Intervention Alternatives." *Center for the Study of African Economies,* working paper, 2017, Oxford University.

20. David Price and Jae Song, "The Long-Term Effects of Cash Assistance," Stanford University Working Paper, 2016.

21. See also Robert A. Moffitt, "Welfare Programs and Labor Supply," *Handbook*

of Public Economics vol. 4, ed. Alan J. Auerbach and Martin Feldstein
(Amsterdam: North-Holland, 2002). And Hilary Williamson Hoynes and
Diane Whitmore Schanzenbach, "Work Incentives and the Food Stamp
Program," *Journal of Public Economics* 96(1), 2012: 151–62.

22. David Evans and Anna Popova, "Cash Transfers and Temptation Goods,"
    Economic Development and Cultural Change 65(2), 2017: 189–221.

23. Abhijit Banerjee, Rema Hanna, Gabriel Kreindler, and Benjamin Olken,
    "Debunking the Stereotype of the Lazy Welfare Recipient: Evidence from
    Cash Transfer Programs Worldwide," Faculty Research Working Paper Series
    RWP15–076, Harvard Kennedy School, 2015.

24. Johannes Haushofer and Jeremy Shapiro, "The Short-Term Impact of
    Unconditional Cash Transfers to the Poor: Experimental Evidence from
    Kenya," *Quarterly Journal of Economics* 131(4), 2016: 1973–2042.

25. Johannes Haushofer and Jeremy Shapiro, "The Long-Term Impact of
    Unconditional Cash Transfers: Experimental Evidence from Kenya," working
    paper, Princeton University, 2018. The waning effects of cash transfers is
    consistent with evidence from a wealth windfall granted in the Georgia's
    Cherokee Land Lottery of 1832, where virtually every adult white male had
    a chance of winning a land parcel worth close to the median level of wealth.
    Researchers found that neither the children nor grandchildren of winners
    had higher levels of education, income, or wealth than those of non-winners.
    See Hoyt Bleakley and Joseph Ferrie, "Shocking Behavior: Random Wealth
    in Antebellum Georgia and Human Capital Across Generations," *Quarterly
    Journal of Economics* 131(3), 2016: 1455–1495.

26. Craig McIntosh and Andrew Zeitlin, "Benchmarking a Child Nutrition
    Program Against Cash: Experimental Evidence from Rwanda," working paper,
    UC San Diego and Georgetown University, 2018.

27. Bruce Wydick, "The Gift of Cash," *Christianity Today*, December 2017.

Chapter 8: What Works in Education and Health?

1. Early effects of *Progresa* on health were found in Paul Gertler, "Do Conditional
   Cash Transfers Improve Child Health? Evidence from PROGRESA's
   Controlled Randomized Experiment," *American Economic Review Papers
   and Proceedings* 94(2), 2004: 336–341, and found reductions of childhood
   illness by one-quarter to one-third in recipient households. Positive impacts
   in school enrollment, attendance, and grade completion were documented in
   Paul Schultz, "School Subsidies for the Poor: Evaluating the Mexican Progresa
   Poverty Program," *Journal of Development Economics* 74, 2004: 199–250.

2. J. Hagen-Zanker, A. Mccord, R. Holmes, F. Booker, and E. Molinari,
   "Systematic Review of the Impact of Employment Guarantee Schemes and

Cash Transfers on the Poor," *ODI Systematic Review* (London: Overseas Development Institute, 2011).

3. N. Kabeer, C. Piza, and L. Taylor, "What Are the Economic Impacts of Conditional Cash Transfer Programmes? A Systematic Review of the Evidence," (technical report, EPPICentre, Social Science Research Unit, Institute of Education, University of London, 2012).

4. Schultz, "School Subsidies for the Poor."

5. Juan Esteban Saavedra and Sandra García, "Impacts of Conditional Cash Transfer Programs on Educational Outcomes in Developing Countries: A Meta-analysis," (working paper, RAND Population Research Center WR-921-1, 2012). Sarah Baird, Francisco H. G. Ferreira, Berk Özler, and Michael Woolcock, "Relative Effectiveness of Conditional and Unconditional Cash Transfers for Schooling Outcomes in Developing Countries: A Systematic Review," Campbell Systematic Reviews, 2013.

6. Bruce Wydick, Paul Glewwe, and Laine Rutledge, "Does International Child Sponsorship Work? A Six-Country Study of Impacts on Adult Life Outcomes," *Journal of Political Economy* 121(2), 2013: 393–426.

7. Bruce Wydick, Paul Glewwe, and Laine Rutledge, "Does Child Sponsorship Pay Off in Adulthood? An International Study of Impacts on Income and Wealth," *World Bank Economic Review*, 31(2), 2017: 434–458.

8. Christopher Neilson and Seth Zimmerman, "The Effect of School Construction on Test Scores, School Enrollment, and Home Prices," *Journal of Public Economics,* 120, 2014: 18–31.

9. Esther Duflo, "Schooling and Labor Market Consequences of School Construction in Indonesia: Evidence from an Unusual Policy Experiment," *American Economic Review,* 91(4), 2001: 795–813.

10. Dana Burde and Leigh Linden, "Bringing Education to Afghan Girls: A Randomized Controlled Trial of Village-Based Schools," *American Economic Journal: Applied Economics* 5(3), 2013: 27–40.

11. Lant Pritchett, "The Rebirth of Education: Schooling Ain't Learning," working paper, Center for Global Development, September 24, 2013.

12. Pritchett, "The Rebirth of Education."

13. Patrick McEwan, "Improving Learning in Primary Schools of Developing Countries: A Meta-Analysis of Randomized Experiments," *Review of Educational Research* 85(3), 2015: 353–394.

14. Another excellent reference on the effectiveness of schooling interventions in developing countries is Paul Glewwe and Karthik Muralidharan, "Improving Education Outcomes in Developing Countries: Evidence, Knowledge Gaps, and Policy Implications," *Handbook of the Economics of Education* 5, 2015.

15. Christian Wurst, Claudia Smarkola, Mary Anne Gaffney, "Ubiquitous

Laptop Usage in Higher Education: Effects on Student Achievement, Student Satisfaction, and Constructivist Measures in Honors and Traditional Classrooms," *Computers and Education* 51(4), 2008: 1766–1783.

16. Diether W. Beuermann, Julian Cristia, Santiago Cueto, Ofer Malamud, and Yyannu Cruz-Aguayo, "One Laptop per Child at Home: Short-Term Impacts from a Randomized Experiment in Peru," *American Economic Journal: Applied Economics* 7(2), 2015: 53–80.

17. Reuters, "Pupils Browse Porn on Donated Laptops," *Reuters.com,* July 20, 2007, https://www.reuters.com/article/us-nigeria-pornography/pupils-browse-porn-on -donated-laptops-idUSL1966647020070720.

18. "Africa's Water Crisis: A Quarter of a Billion Dollars Down the Drain," International Institute for Environment and Development, June 20, 2009, https://www.iied.org/africas-water-crisis-quarter-billion-dollars-down-drain.

19. "Drinking-Water: Key Facts," World Health Organization, February 7, 2018, http://www.who.int/news-room/fact-sheets/detail/drinking-water.

20. Jesse Anttila-Hughes, Paul Gertler, Lia Fernald, Patrick Krause, and Bruce Wydick, "Mortality from Nestlé's Marketing of Infant Formula in Low and Middle-Income Countries," working paper, National Bureau of Economic Research.

21. Amrita Ahuja, Michael Kremer, and Alix Peterson Zwane, "Providing Safe Water: Evidence from Randomized Evaluations," *Annual Review of Resource Economics* 2(1), 2010: 237–56.

22. S. Esrey, R. Feachem, J. Hughes, "Interventions for the Control of Diarrheal Diseases Among Young Children: Improving Water Supplies and Excreta Disposal Facilities," *Bulletin of the World Health Organization* 63(4), 1985: 757–772. Also see Vivalt (2017).

23. Marcella Alsan and Claudia Goldin, "Watersheds in Child Mortality: The Role of Effective Water and Sewerage Infrastructure, 1880 to 1920," *Journal of Political Economy,* forthcoming.

24. "Parasites: Ascariasis," Centers for Disease Control and Prevention, accessed January 24, 2019, https://www.cdc.gov/parasites/ascariasis/index.html.

25. E. Miguel and M. Kremer, "Worms: Identifying Impacts on Education and Health in the Presence of Treatment Externalities," *Econometrica* 72(1), 2004: 159.

26. Sarah Baird, Joan Hamory Hicks, Michael Kremer, and Edward Miguel, "Worms at Work: Long-Run Impacts of a Child Health Investment," *Quarterly Journal of Economics* 131(4), 2016: 1637–1680.

27. Owen Ozier, "Exploiting Externalities to Estimate the Long-Term Effects of Early Childhood Deworming," *American Economic Journal: Applied Economics* 10(3), 2018: 235–262.

28. Edward Miguel, new data presented at the UC Berkeley Development Seminar, Spring 2018.

29. For example, see David C. Taylor-Robinson, Nicola Maayan, Karla Soares-Weiser, Sarah Donegan, and Paul Garner, *Cochrane Database of Systematic Reviews*, 2015: 7. Also see Vivian Welch, et al., "Deworming and Adjuvant Interventions for Improving the Developmental Health and Well-Being of Children in Low- and Middle-Income Countries: A Systematic Review and Network Meta-Analysis," *Campbell Systematic Reviews*, 2016: 7.

30. Kevin Croke, Joan Hamory Hicks, Eric Hsu, Michael Kremer, and Edward Miguel, "Does Mass Deworming Affect Child Nutrition? Meta-Analysis, Cost-Effectiveness, and Statistical Power," working paper, NBER, 22382.

31. These include the Schistosomiasis Control Initiative, Evidence Action's Deworm the World Initiative, END Fund, and the deworming initiative of Sightsavers.

32. Michael Kremer and Edward Miguel, "The Illusion of Sustainability," *Quarterly Journal of Economics* 122(1), 2007: 1007–1065.

33. "Ten Facts on Malaria," World Health Organization, 2016, http://www.who.int/features/factfiles/malaria/en/, and C. M. Morel, "Cost Effectiveness Analysis of Strategies to Combat Malaria in Developing Countries," *BMJ* 331 (7528), 2005: 1299–1300.

34. Jessica Cohen and Pascaline Dupas, "Free Distribution or Cost-Sharing? Evidence from a Randomized Malaria Prevention Experiment," *Quarterly Journal of Economics*, 2010: 1–45.

35. Günther Fink and Felix Masiye, "Health and Agricultural Productivity: Evidence from Zambia," *Journal of Health Economics* 42(C), 2015: 151–164.

36. Kirk R. Smith, Guofeng Shen, Michael D. Hays, Craig Williams, Jerroll W. Faircloth, and James J. Jetter, "Evaluating the Performance of Household Liquefied Petroleum Gas Cookstoves," *Environmental Science and Technology* 52 (2): 904–915. Also see Joshua Bloomenthal, Kirk Smith, et al., "Implementation Science to Accelerate Clean Cooking for Public Health," *Environmental Health Perspectives* 125(1), 2017: A3–A7. See also Reginald Quansah, Sean Semple, Caroline A. Ochieng, Sanjar Juvekar, Frederick Ato Armah, Isaac Luginaah, and Jacques Emina, "Effectiveness of Interventions to Reduce Household Air Pollution and/or Improve Health in Homes Using Solid Fuel in Low-and-Middle Income Countries: A Systematic Review and Meta-Analysis," *Environment International* 103, June 2017, 73–90.

37. Rema Hanna, Esther Duflo, and Michael Greenstone, "Up in Smoke: The Influence of Household Behavior on the Long-Run Impact of Improved Cooking Stoves," *American Economic Journal: Economic Policy* 8(1), 2016: 80–114.

38. Dan Ludwinski, Kent Moriarty, and Bruce Wydick, "Environmental and Health Impacts from the Introduction of Improved Wood Stoves: Evidence from a Field Experiment in Guatemala," *Environment, Development, and Sustainability* 13(4), 2011: 657.

39. Xiaohang Wu, Erping Long, Haotian Lin, and Yizhi Liu, "Prevalence and Epidemiological Characteristics of Congenital Cataract: A Systematic Review and Meta-Analysis," *Science Reports* 6, 2016: 28564; Adnan Ansar et al., "Systematic Review and Meta-Analysis of Global Birth Prevalence of Clubfoot: a Study Protocol," *BMJ Public Health* 8(3), 2018; Brazil Bauru, "Global Registry and Database on Craniofacial Anomalies: Report of a WHO Registry Meeting on Craniofacial Anomalies," World Health Organization, 2001.

40. Daniel Scott Corlew, Blake C. Alkire, Dan Poenaru, John G. Meara, and Mark G. Shrime, "Economic Valuation of the Impact of a Large Surgical Charity Using the Value of Lost Welfare Approach," *BMJ Global Health* 1(4), 2016: e000059.

41. A. Banerjee, E. Duflo, N. Goldberg, D. Karlan, R. Osei, W. Pariente, J. Shapiro, B. Thuysbaert, and C. Udry. "A Multifaceted Program Causes Lasting Progress for the Very Poor: Evidence from Six Countries," *Science* 348(6236): 1260799–1260799.

42. McIntosh and Zeitlin, *Benchmarking a Child Nutrition Program Against Cash.*

43. Richard Monastersky, "Researchers Probe How Poverty Harms Children's Brains," *Chronicle of Higher Education* 54 no. 25, 2008: A8.

44. Sally Grantham-McGregor et al., "Developmental Potential in the First 5 Years for Children in Developing Countries," *The Lancet* 369(9555), 2007: 60–70.

45. David L. Olds, Charles R. Henderson, Jr, Robert Chamberlin, Robert Tatelbaum, "Preventing Child Abuse and Neglect: A Randomized Trial of Nurse Home Visitation," *Pediatrics* 78(1), 1986.

46. David L. Olds et al., "Long-term Effects of Nurse Home Visitation on Children's Criminal and Antisocial Behavior 15-Year Follow-up of a Randomized Controlled Trial," *Journal of the American Medical Association* 280(14), 1998: 1238–1244.

47. David L. Olds, Harriet Kitzman, Michael D. Knudtson, Elizabeth Anson, Joyce A. Smith, Robert Cole, "Effect of Home Visiting by Nurses on Maternal and Child Mortality: Results of a 2-Decade Follow-up of a Randomized Clinical Trial," *JAMA Pediatrics* 168(9), 2014.

48. Nicholas Kristof and Sheryl WuDunn, *A Path Appears: Transforming Lives, Creating Opportunity* (New York: Knopf Publishers, 2014).

49. James Heckman, Rodrigo Pinto, and Peter Savelyev, "Understanding the Mechanisms Through Which an Influential Early Childhood Program Boosted Adult Outcomes," *American Economic Review* 103(6), 2013: 2052–2086.

50. James Heckman, Seong Hyeok Moon, Rodrigo Pinto, Peter Savelyev, and Adam Yavitz, "Analyzing Social Experiments as Implemented: A Reexamination of the Evidence from the HighScope Perry Preschool Program," *Quantitative Economics* 1(1), 2010: 1–46.

51. Milagro Nores and Steven Barnett, "Benefits of Early Childhood Interventions Across the World: (Under) Investing in the Very Young," *Economics of Education Review* 29(2), 2010: 271–282.

52. To read more about Go Baby Go! Parenting Programme, visit https://www.wvi .org/maternal-newborn-and-child-health/go-baby-go.

53. Bruce Wydick, Elizabeth Katz, Flor Calvo, Felipe Gutierrez, and Brendan Janet, "Shoeing the Children: The Impact of the TOMS Shoe Donation Program in Rural El Salvador," *The World Bank Economic Review* 32(3), 2018: 727–751.

54. Garth Frazer, "Used-Clothing Donations and Apparel Production in Africa," *Economic Journal* 118, 2018: 1764–84.

55. Bruce Wydick, Elizabeth Katz, and Brendan Janet, "Do In-Kind Transfers Damage Local Markets? The Case of TOMS Shoe Donations in El Salvador," *Journal of Development Effectiveness* 6(3), 2014: 249–267.

56. Bill Gates, "Why I Would Raise Chickens," *Gates Notes*, June 7, 2016, https:// www.gatesnotes.com/Development/Why-I-Would-Raise-Chickens.

57. Rosemary Rawlins, Svetlana Pimkina, Christopher Barrett, Sarah Pedersen, and Bruce Wydick, "Got Milk? The Impact of Heifer International's Livestock Donation Programs in Rwanda on Nutritional Outcomes," *Food Policy* 44, 2014: 202–213.

58. Jonathan Argent, Britta Augsburg, and Imran Rasul, "Livestock Asset Transfers With and Without Training: Evidence from Rwanda," *Journal of Economic Behavior & Organization* 108 (December 2014): 19–39; Oriana Bandiera, et al., "Can Basic Entrepreneurship Transform the Economic Lives of the Poor?," (IZA Discussion Paper, no. 7386, Institute for the Study of Labor, 2013); A. V. Banerjee, E. Duo, R. Chattopadhyay, and J. Shapiro, "Targeting the Hardcore Poor: An Impact Assessment" (mimeo, CGAP, 2013).

59. Christopher Blattman and Paul Niehaus, "Show Them the Money: Why Giving Cash Helps Alleviate Poverty," *Foreign Affairs* (May/June 2014), https:// www.foreignaffairs.com/articles/show-them-money. The cost listed online for a heifer from Heifer International is $500. See https://www.heifer.org/gift -catalog/animals-nutrition/index.html.

60. Pierre Ferrari, "A Holistic Approach," *Foreign Affairs* (November/December 2014), https://www.foreignaffairs.com/articles/holistic-approach.

61. See FairTrade Foundation at https://www.fairtrade.org.uk/en/farmers-and -workers/coffee/about-coffee.

62. Alain de Janvry, Craig McIntosh, and Elisabeth Sadoulet, "Fair Trade and Free Entry: Can a Disequilibrium Market Serve as a Development Tool?," *Review of Economics and Statistics* 97(3), 2015: 567–573.

63. Neutral to negative impacts are found in key papers such as Barham et al., "The Economic Sustainability of Certified Coffee: Recent Evidence from Mexico and Peru," *World Development* 40(6), 2012: 1269–1279; Ruerd Ruben and Ricardo Fort, "The Impact of Fair Trade Certfication for Coffee Farmers in Peru," *World Development* 40 (3), 2012: 570–682; de Janvry et al., "Fair Trade and Free Entry." Moderately positive effects are found in Tina Beuchelt and Manfred Zeller, "Profits and Poverty: Certification's Troubled Link for Nicaragua's Organic and Fairtrade Coffee Producers," *Ecological Economics* 70 (7), 2011: 1316–1324; Jeremy Weber, "How Much More Do Growers Receive for Fair Trade-Organic Coffee?," *Food Policy* 36(5), 2011: 678–685; Raluca Dragusanu and Nathan Nunn, "The Effects of Fair Trade Certification: Evidence from Coffee Producers in Costa Rica," working paper, NBER, 2018.

Chapter 9: Common Themes Around What Works

1. Sachiko Ozawa, Samantha Clark, Allison Portnoy, Simrun Grewal, Logan Brenzel, and Damian G. Walker, "Return on Investment from Childhood Immunization in Low- and Middle-Income Countries 2011–20," *Health Affairs* 35(2), 2016: 199–207.

2. "The Heckman Curve," *Heckman: The Economics of Human Potential*, accessed January 25, 2018, https://heckmanequation.org/resource/the-heckman-curve/.

3. McIntosh and Zeitlin, *Benchmarking a Child Nutrition Program Against Cash*.

4. Robert Jensen, "The (Perceived) Returns to Education and the Demand for Schooling," *Quarterly Journal of Economics* 125(2), 2010: 515–48.

5. Ester Duflo, "Hope as Capability," Tanner Lectures, 2012. Duflo's ideas are spelled out in more detail in Abhijit Banerjee and Esther Duflo, *Poor Economics: A Radical Rethinking of the Way to Fight Global Poverty*. Public Affairs, 2012.

6. Paul Glewwe, Bruce Wydick, and Phillip Ross, "Developing Hope Among Impoverished Children: Using Child Self-Portraits to Measure Program Effects," *Journal of Human Resources* 53(2), 2018: 299–239.

7. Seema Jayachandran, "Think Positive, Climb Out of Poverty? It Just Might Work," *New York Times*, July 13, 2018, https://www.nytimes.com/2018/07/13/business/think-positive-climb-out-of-poverty-it-just-might-work.html.

8. T. Bernard, S. Dercon, K. Orkin, and A. S. Taffesse, "The Future in Mind: Aspirations and Forward-Looking Behaviour in Rural Ethiopia," Centre for the Study of African Economies-Oxford, 2014: 25; J. J. Heckman and T. Kautz, "Hard Evidence on Soft Skills," *Labour Economics* 19(4), 2012: 451–64; J. J. Heckman, R. Pinto, and P. A. Savelyev, "Understanding the Mechanisms

Through Which an Influential Early Childhood Program Boosted Adult Outcomes," National Bureau of Economic Research, 2012; Robert Jensen and Emily Oster, "The Power of TV: Cable Television and Women's Status in India," *Quarterly Journal of Economics* 124(3), 2009: 1057–1094.

9. The documentary can be viewed online at https://www.youtube.com/watch?v =gAidmWKCCD0.

10. Al Tizon, *Whole and Reconciled: Gospel, Church, and Mission in a Fractured World* (Grand Rapids: Baker Books, 2018), xviii.

11. Max Weber, *The Protestant Ethic and the Spirit of Capitalism* (New York: Scribners, 1958), 108.

12. Nathan Nunn, "Gender and Missionary Influence in Colonial Africa," in Akyeampong et al., *African Development in Historical Perspective* (Cambridge, UK: Cambridge University Press, 2014), 489–512.

13. Lullit Getachew and Tomila Lankina, "Mission or Empire, Word or Sword? The Human Capital Legacy," *Postcolonial Democratic Development* 56(2), 2012: 465–483.

14. Getachew and Lankina, "Mission or Empire, Word or Sword?," 479.

15. Kenneth A. Bollen and Pamela Paxton, "Subjective Measures of Liberal Democracy," *Comparative Political Studies* 33, 2000: 58–86.

16. Robert Woodberry, "The Missionary Roots of Liberal Democracy," *American Political Science Review* 106(2), 2012: 244–74.

17. Woodberry, "The Missionary Roots of Liberal Democracy," 254–55.

18. Y. Bai and J. Kung, "Diffusing Knowledge While Spreading God's Message: Protestantism and Economic Prosperity in China, 1840–1920," *Journal of the European Economic Association* 13(4), 2015: 669–698.

19. Felipe Valencia Caicedo, "The Mission: Human Capital Transmission, Economic Persistence and Culture in South America," *Quarterly Journal of Economics*, forthcoming.

20. Gharad Bryan, James Choi, and Dean Karlan, "Randomizing Religion: The Impact of Protestant Evangelism on Economic Outcomes" (working paper, Northwestern University, 2018).

21. While there were changes in income and spiritual measures, there were no statistically significant changes in total labor supply, assets, consumption, food security, or life satisfaction. Interestingly, those in the spiritual track also felt a significant decrease in perceived relative economic status, a phenomenon that may be consistent with higher aspirations, where some are fulfilled but some are not.

22. Bruce Wydick, *Games in Economic Development* (Cambridge, UK: Cambridge University Press, 2008).

23. Green, *The Gospel of Luke*. See also Fitzmyer, *The Gospel According to Luke*; Bekaert (1996).

Chapter 10: Giving Our Time and Money

1. David Evans and Anna Popova, "Cash Transfers and Temptation Goods," *Economic Development and Cultural Change* 65(2), 2017: 189–221.
2. Barrett A. Lee and Chad R. Farrell, "Buddy, Can You Spare a Dime? Homelessness, Panhandling, and the Public," *Urban Affairs Review* 38, 2003: 299–324.
3. Rohit Bose and Stephen Hwang, "Income and Spending Patterns Among Panhandlers," *Canadian Medical Association Journal* 167(5), 2002: 477–479.
4. Proverbs 6:10–11 in the Hebrew Scriptures.
5. Apostle Paul in 2 Thessalonians 3:10.
6. Proverbs 11:25 in the Hebrew Scriptures.
7. Jesus in Matthew 5:42.
8. In a passage that is rarely used for Sunday sermons, the book of Proverbs actually suggests in King Lemuel's directive to, "Let beer be for those who are perishing, wine for those who are in anguish! Let them drink and forget their poverty and remember their misery no more" (Prov. 31:6–7).
9. The parables of the Talents and the Sheep and the Goats in Matthew 25 sum this up well.
10. Heather Knight, "The City's Panhandlers Tell Their Own Stories," *San Francisco Chronicle,* October 27, 2013, https://www.sfgate.com/bayarea/article/The-city-s-panhandlers-tell-their-own-stories-4929388.php#page-1.
11. G. Frazer, "Used-Clothing Donations and Apparel," *Economic Journal* (118), 2008: 1764–1784.
12. William Easterly and Tobias Pfutze, "Where Does the Money Go? Best and Worst Practices in Foreign Aid," *Journal of Economic Perspectives* 22(2), 2018: 29–52.
13. Steve Corbett and Brian Fikkert, *When Helping Hurts: How to Alleviate Poverty Without Hurting the Poor—and Yourself* (Chicago, IL: Moody Publishers, 2009).

Chapter 11: The Different Roles in Addressing Global Poverty

1. See, for example, Katherine Phillips, "How Diversity Makes Us Smarter," *Scientific American,* October 2014, https://www.scientificamerican.com/article/how-diversity-makes-us-smarter/; James Surowiecki, *The Wisdom of Crowds* (New York: Doubleday, 2004).
2. Raymond S. Nickerson, "Confirmation Bias: A Ubiquitous Phenomenon in Many Guises," *Review of General Psychology* 2(2), 1998: 175–220.
3. Milton Lodge and Charles S. Taber, "The Automaticity of Affect for Political Leaders, Groups, and Issues: An Experimental Test of the Hot Cognition Hypothesis," *Political Psychology* 26(3), 2005: 455–482.
4. Joel Voss, Kara Federmeier, and Ken A. Paller, "The Potato Chip Really Does

Look Like Elvis! Neural Hallmarks of Conceptual Processing Associated with Finding Novel Shapes Subjectively Meaningful Cerebral Cortex," *Neuroscience* 22(10), 2011: 2354–2364.

5. Clair Null, "Warm Glow, Information, and Inefficient Charitable Giving," *Journal of Public Economics* 95(6), 2011: 455–465.

6. For example, a recent study published in *Forbes* indicated that nearly 40 percent of college students would actually rather part with their car than their phone. See Micheline Maynard, "Millennials in 2014: Take My Car, Not My Phone," *Forbes Magazine,* January 24, 2014, https://www.forbes.com/sites /michelinemaynard/2014/01/24/millenials-in-2014-take-my-car-not-my-phone /#2b304d42228f.

7. Ann Christiano and Annie Neimand, "The Science of What Makes People Care," *Stanford Social Innovation Review,* Fall 2018.

8. Russell Jeung, *At Home in Exile: Finding Jesus Among My Ancestors and Refugee Neighbors* (Grand Rapids, MI: Zondervan, 2016).

9. Jeung, *At Home in Exile.*

10. David Bornstein, "When Families Lead Themselves out of Poverty," *New York Times,* August 15, 2017, https://www.nytimes.com/2017/08/15/opinion/poverty -family-independence-initiative.html.

11. Family Independence Initiative National Brochure, accessed January 24, 2019, https://www.fii.org/wp-content/uploads/2017/01/FII_National-Broch_English _Nov-2017-WEB.pdf.

12. Paulina Aguinaga, Alessandra Cassar, Jennifer Graham, Lauren Skora, and Bruce Wydick, "Raising Achievement Among Microentrepreneurs: An Experimental Test of Goals, Incentives, and Support Groups in Medellin, Colombia," forthcoming, *Journal of Economic Behavior and Organization.*

13. See Barefoot College, https://www.barefootcollege.org/approach/.

14. See Terracycle, https://www.terracycle.com/en-US/.

15. 1 Corinthians 12:28.

16. 1 Corinthians 13:3.

Chapter 12: The Seventh *i*

1. Abby Ellin, "High-Tech Philanthropy in a Low-Tech Guatemalan Village," *New York Times,* June 4, 2000, https://www.nytimes.com/2000/06/04/business /personal-business-high-tech-philanthropy-in-a-low-tech-guatemalan-village.html.

2. You can see their work and order ornaments on our website at MayanPartners.org.

3. See for example Deborah Small, George Loewenstein, and Paul Slovic "Sympathy and Callousness: The Impact of Deliberative Thought on Donations to Identifiable and Statistical Victims," *Organizational Behavior and Human Decision Processes* 102(2), 2007: 143–153.

4. Another similar experiment is found in Steck et al., "Doing Poverty: Learning Outcomes Among Students Participating in the Community Action Poverty Simulation Program," *Teaching Sociology* 39(3), 2011: 259–273.

5. You can watch *Spent* at https://www.youtube.com/watch?v=e8VVvhQedTw and CAPS at https://www.youtube.com/results?search_query=Community +Action+Poverty+Simulation.

6. L. P. Browne and S. Roll, "Toward a More Just Approach to Poverty Simulations," *Journal of Experiential Education* 39(3), 2016: 254–268. See also Pedro Hernández-Ramos, Christine M. Bachen, Chad Raphael, John Ifcher, and Michael Broghammer, "Experiencing Poverty in an Online Simulation: Effects on Players' Beliefs, Attitudes and Behaviors About Poverty," working paper, Santa Clara University, 2018. And S. Y. Nickols and R. B. Nielsen, "So Many People Are Struggling: Developing Social Empathy Through a Poverty Simulation," *Journal of Poverty* 15(1), 2011: 22–42. And J. Noone, S. Sideras, P. Gubrud-Howe, H. Voss, and L. R. Mathews, "Influence of a Poverty Simulation on Nursing Student Attitudes Toward Poverty," *Journal of Nursing Education* 51(11), 2012: 617–622.

7. Peter Singer, "Excellence in Opera or Saving a Life? Your Choice," *Washington Post*, September 8, 2015, https://www.washingtonpost.com/news/in-theory /wp/2015/09/08/excellence-in-opera-or-saving-a-life-your-choice.

8. Sendhil Mullainathan and Eldar Shafir, *Scarcity* (London: Allen Lane Books, 2014).

9. Matthew 19:24.

10. To support Go-Baby-Go, go to https://www.wvi.org/maternal-newborn-and -child-health/go-baby-go.

11. To support Save the Children's Early Childhood Development program, go to https://www.savethechildren.org/us/what-we-do/global-programs/education /early-childhood-development.

12. For information on supporting KIPP charter schools, go to https://www.kipp .org/, for the Sugar Creek Charter School go to http://thesugarcreek.org/, for the Noble Network of Charter Schools go to https://nobleschools.org/, for the Alliance College-Ready Public Schools go to https://www.laalliance.org/.

13. To learn more and donate to BRAC's program, go to http://www.brac.net /program/targeting-ultra-poor/.

14. To learn more about Food for the Hungry's integrated development program, go to https://www.fh.org/our-work/our-approach/.

15. You can find out more about Village Enterprise and donate online at http:// villageenterprise.org/.

16. You can transfer cash directly into the mobile phone accounts of the poor in East Africa at http://GiveDirectly.org.

ACKNOWLEDGMENTS

I am extremely grateful for the many people who have helped me in writing *Shrewd Samaritan*. My colleagues in the Department of Economics at the University of San Francisco, particularly my frequent coauthor, Alessandra Cassar, as well as other faculty in development economics—Elizabeth Katz, Peter Lorentzen, and Jesse Anttila-Hughes—have been insightful and engaging in shaping many ideas in this book. Many colleagues at other universities have been extremely helpful in this respect, too, including colleagues at CEGA such as Ted Miguel, Paul Niehaus, Craig McIntosh, Paul Gertler, Lia Fernald, Jon Robinson, David Levine, Jesse Cunha, Marcel Fafchamps, Alain de Janvry, and Elizabeth Sadoulet.

Since 2015, my colleagues at the Kellogg Institute for International Studies at Notre Dame have shaped my thinking about the larger aspects of economic and human development as much as anyone, especially about the centrality of human dignity and human flourishing. In this regard, I owe a great debt to Paolo Carroza, Bob Dowd, Ilaria Schnyder, Clemens Sedmak, Steve Reifenberg, Sharon Schierling, Sara Sievers, Beth Simpson, and many others for extensive conversations directly and indirectly related to this book. Thank you for being my partners in so many ways, and for including me in the intellectual life of Notre Dame.

Thank you to Paul Glewwe, Chris Barrett, Jeff Bloem, Judy Dean, David McKenzie, Brian Fikkert, Chris Ahlin, Travis Lybbert, Roland Hoksbergen, and Julie Schaffner for major input on the development intervention assessments and ratings. Each of you had an important influence on the final results. This was a group exercise, and I believe if it were possible to articulate a consensus in the profession about the impacts of development interventions, we came about as close to that as possible.

Acknowledgments

I am grateful to Ron Sider for his excellent advice in setting the tone for the manuscript and for our relationship since my semester as his student, and for many fruitful conversations with my friend and former pastor Al Tizon. Thank you to my excellent tech-savvy undergraduate Austin Kerby for help with graphics, and to Sam Manning and Mustafa Zahid for outstanding research assistance.

Big thanks to my publisher, Daisy Hutton—it is always a pleasure to work with you, and I always appreciate your encouragement and creative ideas. I am indebted to Sam O'Neal for incisive edits, my agent Chris Ferebee for always being available to talk and for putting things together with HarperCollins Christian Publishing and W Publishing. Thanks also to Meaghan Porter for manuscript editing, Becky Melvin for marketing, and Emma Boyer at Smith Publicity.

So grateful for my family—for my beautiful wife, Leanne, and my daughters Allie and Kayla. Thank you for your patience with me as I wrote this book. The Lord and you three are the center of my life, and I love you more than you know.

Shrewd Samaritan is dedicated to our Mayan Partners in western Guatemala; to Max Bixcul, our faithful friend, principal, and chef; the teachers and staff at Colegio Bethel, especially Juan Gonzales; to Gloria, our village librarian; Pastor Juan and the people of Iglesia Bethel; and the Saludos Niños preschool. This book is likewise dedicated to my favorite Mayan Partners stateside—Jim, Ron, Robb, Pete, and Brooke—without whose influence both today and early in life this book could not have been written.

ABOUT THE AUTHOR

BRUCE **W**YDICK is professor of economics and international studies at the University of San Francisco and research affiliate at the Kellogg Institute for International Studies at the University of Notre Dame and the Center for Effective Global Action at the University of California at Berkeley. He has published more than three dozen academic articles in leading economics journals including the *Journal of Political Economy*, the *Economic Journal*, and the *Journal of Development Economics* and was the lead investigator of the worldwide impact study of Compassion International's child sponsorship program and the study on TOMS Shoes giving program.

His book *Games in Economic Development* was published by Cambridge University Press, and his novel, *The Taste of Many Mountains*, which is about the plight of students exploring coffee and globalization, was published by Thomas Nelson. He is also a regular writer for the *San Francisco Chronicle* and *Christianity Today*. He is a coleader of Mayan Partners, a small nonprofit working in western Guatemala, and faculty advisor to the InterVarsity Christian Fellowship group at USF.

Wydick is an active member of Berkeley Covenant Church with his wife, Leanne, and two young daughters, Allie and Kayla.

Also from Bruce Wydick

Now that you know what it means to be a Shrewd Samaritan, explore a surprising, beautifully engaging novel that illustrates the many ethical dilemmas of our increasingly globalized economy.

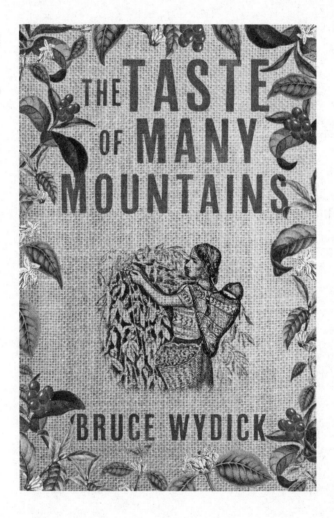

"Wydick's first novel is brewed perfectly—full of rich body with double-shots of insight."

—Santiago "Jimmy" Mellado,
PRESIDENT AND CEO OF COMPASSION INTERNATIONAL